Mania and Depression

The Johns Hopkins Series
in Contemporary Medicine and Public Health

Consulting Editors:
Martin D. Abeloff, M.D.
Samuel H. Boyer IV, M.D.
Richard T. Johnson, M.D.
Paul R. McHugh, M.D.
Edmond A. Murphy, M.D.
Edyth H. Schoenrich, M.D., M.P.H.
Jerry L. Spivak, M.D.
Barbara H. Starfield, M.D., M.P.H.

Also of Interest in This Series:

Ian R. H. Falloon, M.D., and Others, *Family Management of Schizophrenia: A Study of Clinical, Social, Family and Economic Benefits*

Paul R. McHugh, M.D., and Phillip R. Slavney, M.D., *The Perspectives of Psychiatry*

Phillip R. Slavney, M.D., *Perspectives on "Hysteria"*

Phillip R. Slavney, M.D., and Paul R. McHugh, M.D., *Psychiatric Polarities: Methodology and Practice*

Ming T. Tsuang, M.D., Ph.D., D.Sc., and Stephen V. Faraone, Ph.D., *The Genetics of Mood Disorders*

Mania and Depression
A Classification of Syndrome and Disease

George Winokur, M.D.

Paul W. Penningroth Professor
Department of Psychiatry
University of Iowa College of Medicine

The John Hopkins University Press
Baltimore and London

The Johns Hopkins University Press
701 West 40th Street
Baltimore, Maryland 21211
The Johns Hopkins Press Ltd., London

The paper used in this book meets the minimum requirements of
American National Standard for Information Sciences—Permanence of
Paper for Printed Library Materials, ANSI Z39.48-1984.

Library of Congress Cataloging-in-Publication Data

Winokur, George
    Mania and depression : a classification of syndrome and disease /
George Winokur.
        p.   cm. — (The Johns Hopkins series in contemporary medicine and
public health)
    Includes bibliographical references.
    Includes index.
    ISBN 0-8018-4187-9 (alk. paper)
    1. Affective disorders—Classification.   I. Title.   II. Series.
    [DNLM: 1. Affective Disorders, Psychotic—classification.   WM 15
W776m]
RC537.W57   1991
616.85′27′0012—dc20
DNLM/DLC
for Library of Congress   91-6345   CIP

Contents

Preface   vii

Part I. Diagnosis
1   The Depressive Syndrome   3
2   The Manic Syndrome   10

Part II. Overview and Issues of the Classification
3   Philosophical Underpinnings and Overview of the Classification   19
4   The Separation of Bipolar from Unipolar Affective Disorder   29
5   The Unipolar Depressions: Previous Classification Studies and Principles for Further Classification   43

Part III. The Classification
6   Induced Manias and Depressions (Organic Affective Syndromes)   61
7   Manic-Depressive (Bipolar) Illness   74
8   Schizoaffective Disorder   100
9   Neurotic Unipolar Depression: The Generic Syndrome and Its Components   118
10   Neurotic Unipolar Depression: Depression-Spectrum Disease   132
11   Neurotic Unipolar Depression: Secondary Depression   151
12   Reactive Unipolar Depression   167
13   The Endogenous Unipolar Depressions   178
14   An Exercise in Differential Diagnosis and Classification: Case Studies   207

References   239
Index   261

Preface

In the late 1950s the American Psychiatric Association met in San Francisco. That meeting stands out in my mind as one of the great occasions. San Francisco was beautiful. Fisherman's Wharf was exciting. I tasted strawberries in German May wine for the first time. On a professional level, I presented a paper on sexual and developmental findings in psychiatric patients. The hall, which would accommodate 1,000 people, was virtually empty. People were scattered around, looking glassy-eyed and not recognizing the immense importance of the lecture. Even my wife did not attend my presentation; she went to hear one of my friends.

I remember best an interaction that took place at that meeting. In those days, I had a catholic taste in friends and acquaintances. One of the people I had gotten to know was a writer of books in psychiatry and a purveyor of untestable hypotheses. I introduced him to my friend Eli Robins, who at that time was doing some of the best work on suicide. To Eli he directed the question, "Do people who commit suicide really want to die?" Eli's response was, "How would I know?" On occasion I am slow-witted, and I thought about that response for a long time. I think it captures the essence of what I want to present in this book.

There are a lot of classifications in psychiatry, and many studies that separate the classifications from one another. Some of the classifications cannot be validated, and I do not believe we ought to concern ourselves with these. The more usual circumstance is to subject a series of symptoms or clinical factors in a large group of patients to either a test for a bimodal distribution or a test of the break-point model. Of course, what we would like are pathognomonic symptoms that are related to autonomous illnesses, but we never get these in psychiatry. In bimodality the point of rarity never shows a zero point, and in the break-point model one never goes from a high frequency to a zero frequency. That should not surprise us. There are only a certain number of ways to show illness, and some will overlap. Though pneumonià is different from tuberculosis, both influence the lungs and they have certain overlapping symptoms. Likewise, in psychiatry the mind or brain is affected and there are only certain ways in which one can show disturbed emotions, disturbed behaviors, or intellectual deficits. The best we can hope for is a statistically reliable separation of the diseases, not a perfect one. This can be useful as long as we recognize the possibility that we will be wrong in the diagnosis of some cases. Of course, the fewer false positives, the better.

What is important is to attempt to classify in such a way that prediction, treatment, and prevention become more specific. In general, the perfect solution is to have separate etiologies that in turn could translate into specific treatments. In psychiatry, there are no proximal etiologies, that is, pathophysiologies. There are distal etiologies, largely genetic or familial. This book is heavily dependent on findings that suggest that classification can be made to a large extent by looking at the distal etiologies, namely, family background and preexisting life circumstances, including other diseases. Premorbid behavior and lifetime course of the illness are also useful in classification. If the diagnoses presented are testable, then the book is a success. If they are only a matter of opinion, they cannot be too useful. Opinions are fine, but one has a lot of trouble converting them into proof.

Sometime in the winter of 1988, I discussed this book with Bill Coryell, who is a professor in the Department of Psychiatry at the University of Iowa. The following interchange took place.

Bill: "Who is it for?"

Me: "You."

Bill: "You mean only for full professors?"

In fact, this book is for anybody who has serious interests in the affective disorders, clinical interests as well as research interests. It is written to be equally relevant for students and residents and, for that matter, people in other professions as well as professors of psychiatry.

The aim is to provide a definitive statement on the classification of affective disorders. New ideas are presented as well as an evaluation of some of the older and classical ones, and there is an attempt to buttress the new ideas with factual support. Thus two questions should be asked about the present classification: (1) does it make good sense clinically? (2) is it supported by the data?

We have achieved some reliability in diagnosis by the use of criteria that date back to 1972 and perhaps even earlier. Using the criteria does not make a diagnosis; rather, it is best to look at the criteria as being necessary but not sufficient for a diagnosis. It seems unlikely that a diagnosis of affective disorder could be made if the clinical syndrome did not conform to the criteria, but conforming to the criteria does not make a diagnosis of an illness. The present classification makes an effort to present the data in the field in terms of specific and autonomous illnesses. Probably there will be more and specific changes in the criteria. This book will be successful if it stimulates further research into psychiatric illness and also functions as a basis for clinical management.

Finally, I would like to make a comment about the writing. I know that it is no longer fashionable to use the editorial "we"; however, I find it immodest to say "I and my collaborators" or "I and others." So even though I know that the editorial "we" may not be correct, I have used it anyway. Another thing about the writing is that I have finally decided there is no need to make a presentation of ideas or data ponderous. For my model, I have used the textbook of Mayer-Gross, Slater, and Roth, which is delightfully written. Of course, having said this, I run the risk of somebody's paraphrasing Senator Bentsen in his response to Senator Quayle in the 1988 vice-presidential debate. It might run as follows: "Sir, I have read Mayer-Gross, Slater, and Roth; and Dr. Winokur, you are no Mayer-Gross, Slater, and Roth." I hope this does not happen.

I
Diagnosis

1   The Depressive Syndrome

A syndrome is a set of signs and symptoms (including emotional response and behavior) that occur concurrently and form an identifiable pattern. Diseases imply conditions that impair vital functions and are specific in terms of etiology, course, and pathophysiology. In psychiatry syndromes abound, but diseases even more so. This should not be too surprising. There are only a limited number of emotional and behavioral expressions in the repertoire of human response. On the other hand, the etiologies and combinations of the syndromes are far more frequent. Ordinarily, clinical diagnosis is made by determining the presence of a dominant syndrome. Nowhere is this more true than in the affective disorders, depressions, or manias.

There are a number of meanings of the term *depression. Webster's New Collegiate Dictionary* (1980) defines it as a state of feeling sad; a psychoneurotic or psychotic disorder marked by sadness, inactivity, thinking difficulty, decreased concentration, and feelings of dejection or a reduction in activity, amount, quality, or force; or a lowering of vitality or functional activity. The part of the definition dealing with psychoneurotic or psychotic disorder essentially concerns syndrome, and this may be found in a variety of separate illnesses.

The clinical presentation of a depression is common. In a systematic examination of 100 depressed hospital patients, some specific symptoms were seen with great frequency (Baker et al., 1971). Table 1.1 shows the symptoms that were seen in a majority of depressed patients. These patients were selected because they complained of a blue, sad, or depressed mood and had at least six symptoms (screening criteria) that were classically seen in depressed inpatients (Cassidy et al., 1957). These symptoms were scored positive only if they represented a change from the premorbid level of functioning. Depressions tend to be episodic, and it is important to determine if the

3

Table 1.1. Symptoms of Depression Seen in More Than 50% of Patients

Symptom	Total (N = 100) N and %	Male (n = 31) n	Male (n = 31) %	Female (n = 69) n	Female (n = 69) %
Reduced energy level	97	29	94	68	99
Imparied concentration	84	25	81	59	86
Anorexia	80	27	87	53	77
Initial insomnia	77	26	84	51	74
Loss of interest	77	21	68	56	81
Difficulty starting activities	76	25	81	51	74
Worry more than usual	69	21	68	48	70
Subjective agitation	67	23	74	44	64
Slowed thinking	67	20	65	47	68
Difficulty with decision-making	67	20	65	47	68
Terminal insomnia	65	21	68	51	64
Suicide ideation of plans	63	17	55	46	66
Weight loss	61	18	58	43	62

Source: Adapted from Baker M, Dorzab J, Winokur G, Cadoret R. 1971. Depressive disease: Classification and clinical characteristics. *Comprehensive Psychiatry* 12:354–365.

Note: Symptoms were scored only if they were changed from the premorbid level of function. Symptoms used as intake screening criteria are in italics. There were no significant differences in these symptoms between males and females at the .05 level.

patient says that he or she is different from his or her previous self. Between men and women, there were no differences. What comes across is a syndrome manifested by decreased energy, inability to concentrate, sleep troubles, lack of appetite, loss of interest, agitation or retardation, and a feeling of considerable pessimism.

For a more complete clinical picture of depression, we should recognize a series of symptoms that are seen less frequently but are nonetheless important. These symptoms are presented in Table 1.2. In most populations, depressed women outnumber depressed men by about 2 to 1. This was true in the study (Baker et al., 1971) from which these data derive. These symptoms also were scored positive only if they represented a change from the premorbid level of function.

There were some differences between men and women, but they were trivial. Women were more likely to complain of inability to cry and men were more likely to report multiple somatic symptoms dur-

Table 1.2. Symptoms of Depression Occurring in 10%–50% of Patients

Symptom[a]	Total (N = 100) N and %	Male (n = 31) n	%	Female (n = 69) n	%
Diurnal variation	46	15	48	31	45
Difficulty finishing activities once started	46	14	45	32	46
Prominent self-pity	45	13	42	32	46
Inability to cry	44	8	26	36	52[b]
Constipation	43	13	42	30	43
Impaired expression of emotions	42	14	45	28	41
Ruminations of worthlessness	38	13	42	25	36
Decreased libido	36	15	48	21	30
Anxiety attacks	36	9	29	27	39
Difficulty doing activities once started	35	10	32	25	36
Ruminations of guilt	32	10	32	22	32
Complains more than usual	28	10	32	18	26
Any type of delusion	27	6	19	21	30
Phobias during depression only	27	6	19	21	30
Multiple somatic symptoms during depression only	25	12	38	13	19[b]
Communication of suicidal ideas, plans, or attempts	22	9	29	13	19
Place major blame for illness on others	19	2	6	17	25
At least one depressive delusion[c]	16	5	16	11	16
Death wishes without suicidal ideation	16	6	19	10	14
Suicide attempts	15	4	13	11	16
Other delusions[d]	14	1	3	13	19
Obsessions during depression only	14	2	6	12	17

Source: Adapted from Baker M, Dorzab J, Winokur G, Cadoret R. 1971. Depressive disease: Classification and clinical characteristics. *Comprehensive Psychiatry* 12:354–365.
[a]Symptoms used as intake screening criteria are in italics.
[b]Significant difference between males and females at .05 level.
[c]Includes any delusion of guilt, sinfulness, worthlessness, or failure.
[d]Includes all delusions except of guilt, sinfulness, or failure.

ing depression only. Other differences did not approach statistical significance but seemed important nevertheless. Men were more likely to complain of decreased libido and women more likely to experience anxiety (panic) attacks during the depression. Anxiety attacks are a good example of another syndrome, neither depressive or manic, that occurred in some patients whose main reason for hospitalization was depression. Women were more likely to be delusional and to show phobias during depression only. Likewise, women were more likely to place major blame for illness on others and more likely to show delusions other than guilt, sinfulness, worthlessness, or failure.

The findings regarding mental status of these patients were notable in that agitation was seen in 30%, psychomotor retardation in 19%, and both agitation and retardation in 6%. Forty-five percent of the patients showed no evidence of agitation or retardation. About 8% of the patients showed blocking or extreme circumstantiality.

Some symptoms were seen rarely, that is, in fewer than 10% of cases. These included increased appetite, auditory hallucinations, weight gain, ideas of reference, antisocial behavior related to the depressive episode but not a life pattern, compulsions, visual hallucinations, olfactory hallucinations, tactile hallucinations, and primary delusions.

The specific diseases that show depressive syndromes are usually episodic to a greater or lesser extent, and there is some variation in symptoms with the number of episodes. Subjective agitation and tearfulness are more frequently seen in first-episode patients, but recurrent-episode patients, when evaluated in one of their later episodes, show more constipation, inability to cry, impaired expression of emotions, difficulty in getting activities accomplished, difficulty with decision making, retarded thinking, tearfulness, phobias (during depression only), and difficulty in finishing activities once they are started.

The age at the time of hospitalization exerts an influence. Older patients (i.e., over 40) complain of constipation more frequently—a report that is probably expected. Younger patients (under 40) are more likely to make plans of suicide.

The age of onset is related to more differences than is the age at hospitalization. Early-onset patients (under 40 years) manifest more guilt, ruminations, irritability, worry, tearfulness, and suicide ideas, plans, or attempts, and show less weight loss, agitation, and constipation than do late-onset patients (over 40 years).

An actuarial account of the symptoms of depression, as given above, is useful as a teaching device, but it does not capture the quality of the illness. Kraepelin (1921) described the depressive states very well; there are no better descriptions in the literature. He separated depression into a variety of types in order of severity. The least severe he called *melancholia simplex*. Patients with such a depression show an episode without psychotic symptoms such as delusions and hallucinations. Thinking is difficult. Patients cannot collect their thoughts, and feel weary and inwardly empty. Often the impressions of the world appear strange, as though from a great distance, and the voice sounds leaden. A good example of this kind of perception is a male patient whom we saw over the course of years. During his depressions, he complained of a perception of darkness and truly believed that his vision was impaired because of what he called "blackness." The mood in patients with melancholia simplex is dominated by dejection and gloominess. There is often a feeling of anxiety, and sometimes patients show restlessness. Energy is very low and often patients will say very little. We have noticed that, as an interview wears on, these patients become increasingly responsive, sometimes even approaching normality. The next day, however, they will be back to being relatively unresponsive to the interviewer. It is as if what went on the day before had not happened. Similarly, in an interview in the morning they will feel extremely depressed, and as the day wears on the depression will lighten. This is called *diurnal variation.* When these patients are seen the next day after having been nonsuicidal the preceding afternoon, they are often suicidal anew and have no insight into the fact that on the afternoon before, suicide was an unreasonable idea. Thus any insight that an individual gets during a depression is often fleeting.

A more severe type of episode described by Kraepelin is *melancholia gravis,* in which patients may see figures or corpses of relatives. Patients might hear abusive language saying "you are guilty, you are guilty." These patients have strong ideas of having sinned. A good example of this is a patient whom we saw in 1965. He had made an error on his income tax form in the late 1920s and believed that he owed the government a trivial amount, about five dollars. He believed he was the subject of an investigation by the government and that he fully deserved this, because his mistake had truly been a sin. Ideas of persecution are often seen in melancholia gravis. These persecutory ideas, however, are anchored in guilt. The patient may believe that people mock him or her. Like all types of depressive patients, the person feels very guilty and this is often the subject matter for the person's psychotic symptoms. Such psychotic symptoms that are consistent with a feeling of wrongdoing or sin are called *mood-congruent psychotic symptoms.* When the persecutory symptoms are very strong and there are many ideas of reference, such a depression may be termed a *paranoid melancholia.* A person may be quite suicidal during this kind of episode, but, in fact, suicidal thoughts are seen in all kinds of depressive states.

According to Kraepelin, depression progresses to *fantastic melancholia,* in which there is an even greater development of delusions and many hallucinations. Patients with fantastic melancholia see evil spirits, death, crowds of monsters, or other fantastic things. Satan may speak to them. A maelstrom may engulf them, and they may be sucked into a vortex of blackness, only to see special pieces of evidence of their guilt. Hypochondriacal delusions are common. Patients may feel that they have no innards (nihilistic delusions) or they may believe their liver is putrifying and creates a bad smell.

Finally, there is *delirious melancholia,* in which there is a profound clouding of consciousness and terrifying hallucinations abound. Patients may feel they are elsewhere than home. Such patients find it difficult to say a word, and they may lie in bed taking no interest in anything, showing no emotion, and acting inaccessible and mute. They may stare straight in front of them with a vacant expression on their face. Sometimes this is mistaken for catatonic schizophrenia, but a careful evaluation of the quality of the mood and the development of the episode puts it squarely in the depressive camp.

The onset of a depression can be rather rapid but usually takes weeks or months to draw attention to the patient. This perhaps is because people tend to think depression is similar to unhappiness (it is not) and to make excuses for changes in emotions and behavior.

Some other symptoms are rather typical of a depression. Often patients with depression complain of losing their mind and exhibit a fear of going insane. This symptom is a good way to differentiate normal sadness or normal grief from a depressive episode, which is not usually related to an unhappy circumstance. Patients understand a normal response; feeling blue under appropriate conditions does not lead them to worry about their sanity. Another infrequent symptom is a complaint of a burning pain someplace in the body. This strongly suggests the possibility of a depression. Delusions of poverty or sin are commonly found in depressed patients. Some data suggest that in depressive illness such mood-congruent psychotic symptoms diminish as the individual experiences subsequent episodes (Winokur, Scharfetter, and Angst, 1985b). In 59 depressed patients, 26% of the first 1 to 8 episodes were associated with psychotic symptoms but only 8% of the later 9 to 12 episodes showed this association.

Modern diagnosis is accomplished by the use of a series of criteria for a syndrome. When patients are chosen for study, the investigator often remarks that he or she has used such criteria as the Feighner criteria (Feighner et al., 1972), the third edition (*DSM-III*) or revised third edition (*DSM-III-R*) of the *Diagnostic and Statistical Manual of Mental Disorders* (American Psychiatric Association, 1980, 1987), or the Research Diagnostic Criteria (Spitzer, Endicott, and Robins, 1978). In general, the criteria are very similar. The Feighner criteria, which were the basis for all of the succeeding sets, require that the patient have a dysphoric mood characterized by feeling depressed, sad, blue, despondent, hopeless, irritable, fearful, worried, or discouraged. For a definite depression, five of the following symptoms are required (for a probable depression, four are required): poor appetite or weight loss, sleep difficulties, loss of energy (e.g., fatigability and tiredness), agitation or retardation, loss of interest in usual activities or decrease in sexual drive, feelings of self-reproach or guilt, complaints of inability to concentrate or think, and recurrent thoughts of death or suicide. Such an illness has to last at least one month in the Feighner criteria, but the time constraint differs in the other criteria.

There are a number of ways to assess severity of depression. Perhaps the most important evaluation would take into account whether the person was incapacitated for ordinary living. Thus a person who has to be put in a hospital would be considered more severely depressed than a person who could be treated as an outpatient. In some fashion, the community or the family assesses severity and puts certain persons into the hospital. As yet we do not know how the community makes this decision, but it seems that somehow nonprofessional people are often able to assess severity.

Another aspect of severity is the presence of psychotic symptoms, delusions, and hallucinations. These are easily noted as abnormalities by the family or friends. Inability to perform one's ordinary job, whether it is working as an accountant or taking care of a house, is another way to assess severity. Other possibilities that should be addressed are whether the person is seriously suicidal or has made a medically serious attempt on his or her own life and the length of the individual episode. For clinicians to obtain some value from the concept of severity, they must specify what they are looking for. In general, not being able to perform one's job, not being able to think, distorting reality, and not being able to function appropriately outside of a hospital are good measures of severity. They are probably somewhat interrelated but not necessarily so.

2   The Manic Syndrome

In general, mania is considered the mirror image of depression, and, in fact, this is not totally unreasonable. Whereas depressed patients are retarded, manic patients are hyperactive. Depressed patients are blue; manic patients are euphoric. Depressed patients think slowly; manic patients show a flight of ideas. It is certainly reasonable to think that the two states (depression and mania) are opposites. After all, the original description of manic-depressive disease dealt with patients who showed a circular or alternating psychosis—sometimes manic, sometimes depressed. The characterization of manic-depressive illness is essentially a French affair. Bonet in 1686 used the term *maniaco-melancholicus* to characterize these patients. The French clinicians Falret (1854) and Baillarger (1854) described recurring attacks of mania and melancholia. Falret used the term *circular insanity* and Baillarger the term *double-form insanity* for similar patients (Sedler, 1983). Falret had been observing depressive episodes accompanied by suicide behavior and noted that some of them turned into periods of excitement, which in turn reverted to depression. Baillarger, besides noting the two forms of the illness, observed that sometimes melancholias became stuporous states. Generally, the depressive syndromes that are seen in manic-depressive illness are similar to the ones described in Chapter 1. The syndrome of mania requires description.

In defining mania, *Webster's New Collegiate Dictionary* (1980) certainly is not at a loss for words. Mania is defined as an excitement that shows "mental and physical hyperactivity," a heightened mood, and "disorganization of behavior." That definition is not bad. It has the advantage of economy and does almost as good a job of describing mania as many new sets of diagnostic nomenclatures.

In a study of patients admitted to a psychiatric hospital who were diagnosed as having a manic episode by the clinicians, it was possible

Table 2.1. The Manic Syndrome (31 Patients)

Symptom	Patients with Symptom Recorded (N)	Patients with Symptom Recorded as Positive (%)
Hyperactivity	31	100
Euphoria	31	97
Flight of ideas	29	100
Distractibility	30	96
Circumstantiality	27	96
Push of speech	31	100
Increased sexuality	23	74
Grandiosity and/or religiosity	24	79
Decreased sleep	31	94
Delusions	26	73
Ideas of reference	26	77
Passivity	15	47
Depersonalization and/or derealization	14	43

to determine the frequency of a variety of symptoms (Clayton, Pitts, and Winokur, 1965). Table 2.1 gives this symptom picture. In more than half of the manic patients, mania was preceded by a depression. In all of the patients, the clinicians noted the presence or absence of the symptom of confusion (disorientation or memory lapses), with 58% exhibiting this symptom.

The clinical picture of mania is striking, and the triad of euphoria, overactivity, and push of speech is almost invariably seen. However, there are times when the euphoric mood is replaced by an irritable mood. The delusions of passivity and of depersonalization and/or derealization are commonly seen in another illness, schizophrenia. However, they are sometimes seen in the manic syndrome and do not necessarily signal a poor prognosis.

Delusions of passivity belong to the group of Schneiderian first-rank symptoms that are often associated with schizophrenia. Schneiderian first-rank symptoms include thought broadcasting, the experience that one's thoughts are escaping from one's head and allowed to enter into the external world; alienation, the experience that one's feelings, impulses, thoughts, or actions are not one's own but are controlled by an outside force; influence, the experience that one's body sensations, feelings, impulses, thoughts, and actions are

imposed on one by some outside external agency (delusions of passivity); and complete auditory hallucinations, namely, prolonged
voices coming from outside one's head that continually comment
about one's actions, argue about one's behavior, or repeat aloud one's
thoughts. Another symptom that is often seen in schizophrenia is
called *delusional perception* or *symbolism*. In this a perception has a special meaning to the patient and may lead to an elaborate secondary
delusional system. A delusional perception is similar to what has been
called a *primary delusion* (Kadrmas, Winokur, and Crowe, 1979). About
28% of manic female patients have such first-rank symptoms.

We may cite an example of a 21-year-old postpartum woman who
was admitted in the early 1930s. It was noted in the chart that she had
been preoccupied with television and with the idea that her thoughts
and words were being collected by radio, sorted out, and then transmitted through the state. This patient also had a delusional perception that spectacles (eyeglasses) were television. She believed that her
thoughts were being recorded. Another example is a 20-year-old
woman with a mania who talked about a message from her dead
father telling her to make the right hand do as much as the left. A
third example is a 26-year-old woman admitted in the middle 1930s.
She felt that her local medical doctor had hypnotized her and exerted
a power over her so that he could impose strange things on her. As an
example, he made her skin itch and made her desirous of sexual
relations with him. These patients all had ordinary diagnoses of mania. Such cases are discussed further in Chapter 7 because they meet
reasonable criteria for schizoaffective disorder. In the above patients,
the prognosis was as good as in the manic patients who did not have
schizophrenic-type symptoms accompanying the mania.

Like the depressive patients referred to in Chapter 1, bipolar patients seem to lose their psychotic symptoms as they have more and
more episodes. Thus in those patients who had 1 to 8 episodes, 21% of
the episodes were accompanied by psychotic features, and in patients
with 9 to 16 episodes, 23% of the episodes were accompanied by
psychotic features; however, in patients who had even more episodes
(17 to 24), only 12% of the episodes were accompanied by psychotic
symptoms (Winokur, Scharfetter, and Angst, 1985b). Considering
that never-psychotic bipolar patients have about the same number of
episodes as psychotic bipolar patients, these data suggest that psychotic states are more common in the earlier episodes.

As already noted, manic episodes may succeed a depressive episode; in fact, when a manic episodes abates, it is often followed by
another and longer depression (Winokur, Clayton, and Reich, 1969).

The onset of the manic syndrome may be extremely acute, and

Table 2.2. Length of Illness before Index Admission
(94 Manic Patients)

Length	Males	Females
N	36	58
2 weeks–1 month	69%	62%
3 months	11%	12%
6 months	11%	10%
1 year or more	6%	15%

Table 2.3. Factors Precipitating Hospital Admission

Symptom	Percentage of Episodes in Males ($N = 37$)	Percentage of Episodes in Females ($N = 63$)
Extravagance	30	17
Assaultive or destructive behavior	8	17
Alcohol abuse	32	8
Sexual problems	3	8
Sleeplessness	11	37
Overtalkativeness and overactivity	22	25
Delusions, hallucinations	11	25
Work disability	27	13

sometimes patients are able to make statements such as "I became manic at 11 o'clock last Saturday." The abruptness of onset is far more frequent in the manic syndrome than in the depressive syndrome. Sixteen percent of manic patients have an onset that necessitates hospitalization within two weeks of onset; only 3% of depressive patients have an onset of less than one month (Morrison et al., 1972). Table 2.2 presents data on the acuteness of onset for those manic patients who had at least two weeks of illness; as can be seen, men and women do not differ significantly on this variable. Abrupt onsets in mania are more likely associated with the presence of delusions and extreme motor activity than are more gradual onsets.

Hospitalization is precipitated by a variety of factors, and these are presented in Table 2.3 (Winokur, Clayton, and Reich, 1969). Manic episodes are associated with sleep changes in most cases. There is a large number (one-third) with initial insomnia, one-quarter with terminal insomnia, and another quarter with both terminal and initial

Table 2.4. Drinking Behavior

Behavior	Males n (%)	Females n (%)	Total (N = 100)
	Episodes in		
Admissions in teetotalers	5 (14)	6 (10)	11
Increased consumption	20 (54)	22 (35)	42
Decreased consumption	0 (0)	0 (0)	0
No change in consumption	12 (32)	35 (56)	47

insomnia. Patients with mania show heightened sexuality and are generally considered uninhibited. In some patients, increased sexuality is in thoughts and statements only, but in one-third, increased sexual activity of a socially approved sort occurs. In only 11% of episodes is the patient's sexuality shown in a socially disapproved fashion. Promiscuity is more frequent in younger patients.

Commonly, consumption of alcohol changes in individuals when they experience mania. Table 2.4 presents some of the changes. Neither men nor women decrease the amount of drinking, but men are proportionately more likely to show an increased intake of alcohol.

Thinking in mania has always been described as rapid, and the patient describes the experience of racing thoughts. Classically, there is a flight of ideas, which means that ideas rapidly follow each other but are only tenuously connected. Andreasen (1979; Andreasen and Powers, 1974) studied thought disorder in manic patients and found that it could be characterized as being overinclusive. Manic patients were particularly likely (as opposed to schizophrenic and depressive patients) to show pressure of speech, distractible speech, and circumstantiality. Also, manic patients sometimes were tangential and had derailment and incoherence. They were often illogical. These symptoms were equally prominent in mania as in schizophrenia. The difference between the manic and schizophrenic patients was on an entirely different variable. Schizophrenic patients more likely had poverty of speech and poverty of content.

Catatonic symptoms during mania have been reported by Abrams and Taylor (1976).

Kraepelin (1921) described acute mania very well. He pointed out that the beginning of the illness was fairly sudden. Patients became restless and their speech was disconnected. They were sensible and sometimes approximately oriented. They were, however, extraordinarily distractible in their perception and in their train of thought.

They might be delusional. Their mood was unrestrained, merry, ex-
ultant, and occasionally pompous. However, this quickly changed to
irritability and irrascibility. As a rule, they were free and easy and
unmannerly, and often would run after the physician. They constantly interrupted others. If the illness became more severe, they
became delusional and hallucinated and ultimately became delirious.
As clouding of consciousness occurred, the patients became disori-
ented regarding time and place. During this time, such catatonic
symptoms as waxy flexibility, echolalia, and echopraxia were often
observed.

Hypomania is the term used when the illness is mild. In hypomania
the mood is high, and there is an intrusiveness into the business of
others. Patients often feel exalted and show sexual excitability. Such
people are lively and talk a lot. In a sense, the hallmark of hypomania
and mania is excessiveness in mood, talk, thinking, eating, sleeplessness, activity, spending, self-concept, and sexual behavior.

The mood, though generally euphoric, high, "tops," or "on top of
the world," is sometimes irritable. Of 94 manic patients, 30% were
only elated, 62% elated and irritable, and 8% only irritable. In the
minority who have only the irritable mood, such symptoms as financial extravagance and grandiosity (sometimes delusional) are less often seen than in the elated manic patients. Thus a cluster of symptoms
is often seen: euphoria, increased spending, and a high opinion of
oneself (Winokur and Tsuang, 1975). The irritable mood is often
reactive. When crossed, the patient may go from euphoric to irritable
rather rapidly.

One of the most common findings in mania is the lability of the
mood. An individual might be talking constantly, enormously euphoric, and suddenly fall into a depression for a short period of time. This
can be considered a microepisode of depression (Winokur, Clayton,
and Reich, 1969). Sometimes these short depressive episodes can be
brought on by asking the patient about a sad occurrence such as a
failure or the death of a parent. In 68% of patients who were clinically
observed, the depressed mood was seen during the manic episode
and this was usually a fleeting tearfulness or sadness, lasting a very
short period of time. In a few cases, such lability manifested itself for a
day or a couple of days, but generally the microepisode was minutes or
hours and often only a matter of seconds. During microepisodes of
depression, the patient might have been apprehensive and agitated or
withdrawn, and psychomotor retardation and latency of response
could be seen. The onset of the melancholic episode was usually
abrupt and the disappearance was equally as rapid. Such short depressive episodes were more frequently seen in female manic patients

(almost 80%) than in male manic patients (less than 50%).

The length of the episode is variable: about 73 days in men and about 42 days in women. Of course, often the manic episode and the euthymia are followed shortly thereafter by a longer lasting depressive episode.

In patients who show unequivocal mania at some point during their lives, a "mixed" manic-depressive episode sometimes is noted (Winokur, Clayton, and Reich, 1969). Such patients have clear pressure of speech and grandiose ideas and at the same time are suicidal and severely depressed. In others there is psychomotor retardation with euphoric statements. More women than men with a mixed episode were observed. As noted, microepisodes of depression were also more frequent in women than men, and perhaps mixed episodes and microepisodes of depression have something in common. Microepisodes of depression, however, are different from mixed episodes. The later show both manic and depressive symptoms at the same time; the former show an alternation of mania with short bursts of depression, with no mixture.

Mania is not commonly misdiagnosed, but there are times when garrulousness and the bizarre, chronic, grandiose delusions that are seen in chronic schizophrenic patients may be mistaken for mania (Fish, 1962). However, the lability and the episodic nature of the mania help differentiate it from the more chronic presence of manic-type symptoms in schizophrenia.

Like the diagnosis of depression, the diagnosis of the manic syndrome is made by the use of criteria. Most of the sets of criteria are similar to each other. The Feighner criteria, which were the first, demand the presence of euphoria or irritability and the presence of three of the following symptom groups: hyperactivity, including motor, social, and sexual activity; push of speech or pressure to keep on talking; flight of ideas or racing thoughts; grandiosity, which may or may not be delusional; sleep decrease; and distractibility. Such a syndrome should last at least two weeks. As noted, however, other sets of criteria have different time constraints.

II
Overview and Issues
of the Classification

3 Philosophical Underpinnings and Overview of the Classification

Previous Classifications

What has transpired so far in this book is nothing more than a description of two syndromes, mania and depression. As noted, these are not autonomous illnesses. Medicine is rife with syndromes that have several different etiologies. For example, the parkinsonian syndrome may be seen as an accompaniment of acute or chronic use of neuroleptic drugs. The syndrome may also be idiopathic. It may be found as a sequela to encephalitis: after the 1918 epidemic, many cases of postencephalitic Parkinson's syndrome were described. Epileptic-type convulsions may be seen in high fevers in infants, as an idiopathic illness, or as a symptom of various kinds of brain lesions and tumors. In no sense can the convulsion be considered a disease. It is simply a sign. The British geneticist Penrose put this very well in 1938 (Harris, 1973) when he discussed mental deficiency: "It has never seemed at all probable that a single cause could account for all mental deficiency in the same way that the *Spirochaeta pallida* accounts for all syphilis. The etiology of mental defect is multiple, and a facile classification of patients into primary or secondary, endogenous or exogenous, cases would have only led to a factitious simplification of the real problems inherent in the data" (p. 526). This statement is as true for depression as it is for mental deficiency. We have had classifications in the past, and they have included primary and secondary depression, neurotic and endogenous depression, reactive and psychotic depression, delusional and nondelusional depression, as well as a host of other classifications based mainly on clinical picture. Usually such classifications have been dichotomous, and consequently we have not been able to classify appropriately the entire range of the depressive and manic phenomena. It is not that each of these classifications does not have some truth in it. However, they do not provide a complete picture and do not account for a good part of the occurrence of the syndromes.

More modern classifications, such as the *Diagnostic and Statistical Manual of Mental Disorders (Third Edition-Revised) (DSM-III-R;* American Psychiatric Association, 1987), have focused on the clinical differences during the period of illness. The *DSM-III-R* is a later development of the St. Louis or Feighner criteria (Feighner et al., 1972). In the Feighner criteria, the classification separated mania from depression on the basis of symptomatology. Likewise, the Feighner criteria separated primary from secondary affective disorders, secondary being defined in the same way as primary (at least as regard symptoms) but occurring after either a preexisting nonaffective psychiatric illness that might or might not still present or a life-threatening or incapacitating medical illness that preceded or paralleled the symptoms of depression. It should be noted that in the Feighner criteria there is a mixture between the use of clinical criteria in diagnosis and the use of preexisting circumstances (possibly etiologic) criteria. Nevertheless, in the Feighner criteria the concept of secondary is simply temporal, not etiologic. It means that a depression occurs after a preexisting medical or psychiatric illness, not necessarily that it is caused by the preexisting illnesses. However, considering that secondary depression is a common sequela of a primary psychiatric or medical illness, one might entertain the possibility that some etiologic meaning is contained in the definition.

The *DSM-III-R* goes much further than the Feighner criteria in the use of classification by varying clinical description. The *DSM-III-R* classification includes levels of severity and the presence of mood-congruent or -incongruent psychotic features. Likewise, the quality of remission is noted. Thus a patient can have a variety of diagnoses, depending on the interplay of these particular features. The generic diagnosis, that of a major depression, is likewise classified by levels of severity and by the presence of psychotic features, mood congruent or incongruent. The quality of remission again may be used for classification. Special criteria are offered for a melancholic type of depression as well as for a depression that follows a seasonal pattern. If the individual has both manias and depressions, there are special ways to separate out the various kinds of bipolar disorders. Other aspects of the clinical description include separation on the basis of whether the depression is seen as a single episode or has been recurrent. A mild but relatively chronic depression, called *dysthymia,* is considered a primary type of depression defined as a "mood disturbance" not related to a preexisting nonaffective psychiatric illness. Specification of the primary or secondary type is part of the definition of dysthymia. Finally, there is an organic mood syndrome that encompasses a mania or depression in which a specific organic etiology is judged to be present.

The *DSM-III-R* criteria, like the Feighner criteria, straddle the question of classification by etiology. Etiology is integrated into the concept of an organic mood disturbance, but in some of the other categories, there is no way of knowing whether they deserve separate consideration. For example, whether a single- or multiple-episode course is indicative of a different illness cannot be clearly answered at this time. The levels of severity could very well be meaningless. Chronicity may or may not be relevant to autonomy in diagnosis, and the presence of psychotic symptoms, whether mood congruent or incongruent, may not be in any way related to the definition of a specific disease.

Coryell and Zimmerman (1987) compared three different diagnostic classifications that appeared sequentially at four-year intervals. The appearance of these new systems implies that there was progress toward greater validity in classification. Whether this was true was tested on 98 consecutively admitted patients with nonmanic psychoses. The validity of all three of the systems was strongly supported by family history and six-month follow-up material, but the difference between the systems was trivial. There was no reason to believe that one was clearly superior to the other.

The use of clinical descriptive material was well discussed by Kendall (1982). As he pointed out, we are really trying to "identify a subgroup of patients" that show "either a relatively homogeneous treatment response or a relatively homogeneous long-term outcome" (Kendall, 1982, p. 1335). Likewise, "we are probably trying to identify a group of patients whose symptoms have a common etiology or pathogenesis or who share an as yet unidentified biological predisposition" (p. 1335). We may then subject a group of clinical symptoms to a discriminant function analysis and attempt to notice whether the distribution of scores is unimodal or bimodal (a point of rarity). Using the clinical symptomatology, this has shown only partial success between two such diverse illnesses as schizophrenia and affective psychosis. One may also employ a break-point model that shows a nonlinear relationship between symptomatology and some other independent variable. In a test that was truly different between two illnesses, there would be a difference in the percentages of positive testers versus negative testers in different syndromes, and this could be demonstrated by comparing the percentage of positive testers at a series of points along a linear axis showing a gradation in symptomatology. There would be a sharp drop at the point at which one illness became rare and the other common.

Using the break-point model, Cadoret, Woolson, and Winokur (1977) showed a clear relationship between the age of onset in unipolar affective disorder and the risk of alcoholism in parents of female depressive patients. Parental alcoholism rates showed a break point (a decrease) with the onset of depression over the age of 40 in female depressive patients, suggesting two types of depression within the large group of depressed women. Interestingly, the success of this method depended not specifically on the phenomenology but rather on the age of onset.

The Medical Model

Barring clear evidence of an etiologic factor in separating diseases, we are left with the possibilities described above and the medical model. In discussing the medical model, Guze (1977) pointed out that it is not based on any specific definition of disease. He noted that although one may argue the definition of disease, there is a lot more agreement when one deals with specific medical disorders, such as tuberculosis, diabetes, or mania. Essentially, the medical model in psychiatric disorders means that we will employ the same kind of thinking and actions as physicians use in general medicine. We would assume multiple illnesses and assume that such illnesses are different from each other in a variety of ways. The specific operation in the medical model consists of finding people with similar syndromes and then looking at this group of patients to determine a variety of clinical and biologic factors that might define specific illnesses.

Table 3.1 presents the kinds of data that might be used to establish the validity of a specific affective illness when the etiology is unknown. The items owe a great deal to the criteria for establishing diagnostic validity in psychiatric illness that have been described by Robins and Guze (1970), but they are expanded and altered somewhat. Any kind of classification must, in fact, be relevant to the establishment of valid and autonomous psychiatric illnesses and, in this book, affective illnesses.

A number of items may be used to establish diagnostic validity. The first of these is the clinical description of the illness. This would include such things as the symptoms of the illness as well as the behavior. It would include the symptom characteristics of manias and depressions. Robins and Guze (1970) discussed the delimitation (differential diagnosis) from other disorders and pointed out that it is necessary to specify exclusion criteria so that patients with other illnesses are not

Table 3.1. Aspects of Illness Useful for the Establishment of Diagnostic Validity

Clinical description
Epidemiology
Premorbid personality
Course, including age of onset
Family history of psychiatric illness
Laboratory findings
Response to treatment

included in the group to be studied. This is what we have always called differential diagnosis, and part of the work on the clinical description should include the relative frequency of certain kinds of affective symptoms in certain kinds of affective illnesses. As an example, one might cite the fact that many patients have only depressions, either a single episode or multiple episodes, and other patients also have manias. Patients who have manias usually also have depressive episodes, although not invariably. Does the absence of manic episode give one the right to consider a purely depressive illness as separate from the combination of mania and depression? This would then be part of the differential diagnosis.

The clinical description should also include such factors as the presence of individual symptoms or clusters of symptoms.

The second item used to establish diagnostic validity is epidemiology, and this should include such things as race, sex, and socioeconomic status. As an example of the use of epidemiology, we might cite something like pellagra in which people living in a particular socioeconomic group and in a particular part of the country had a dietary deficiency that ultimately led to symptoms of psychiatric illness. The epidemiology not only might help in defining a disease but also might contribute something toward knowledge of the etiology. In the 1800s it was noted that whereas British Catholic nuns rarely had general paresis, this illness was common in British sailors. At that point, it was considered that the sea air might have something to do with general paresis. Nevertheless, it could have been a clue to understanding the extremely important illness syphilis and how it was spread. Epidemiologic data sometimes tell us about the cause of the illness. In discussing "mongolism" (now called Down's syndrome), Jenkins (1933) noted that when the syndrome occurred in a pair of twins of separate sex only one was affected; but when it occurred in monozygotic twins, both were affected. This suggested to him that there was a genetic explanation for "mongolism." He noted also that the syndrome occurred rarely in more than one member of the same family and that the incidence of "mongolism" varied widely as a function of the age of the mother. "Mongolism" was progressively more likely to occur with increasing age of the mother. He concluded as early as 1933 that "the hypothesis that mongolism is due to a diminished viability of the ovum, makes it possible to assume that this diminished viability of a small number of ova occurs with increasing maternal age" (Jenkins, 1933). He dismissed paternal age as simply being a reflection of the correlation between ages of parents. It was not until many years later that Down's syndrome was mainly accounted for by an abnormal nondysjunction of chromosome 21, that is, a change in the germ cell.

The next set of data useful in establishing diagnostic validity concerns the course of the illness. This includes the age of onset, the presence of factors that precede or precipitate the illness, and what happens over the course of time in the illness. Acuteness of onset is a factor in the course. Of major importance in the course is whether or not the illness changes over time into something else. We might cite an individual who appears in the hospital for a depression, is discharged as essentially well, and then a few months later develops unequivocal symptoms of chronic schizophrenia, which persist for 12 years. This is a change in the character of the illness: schizophrenia has taken the place of depression. If the symptoms of schizophrenia lasted several years, certainly one would clearly change the diagnosis from depression to schizophrenia. The actual structure of the course is also important. Is the illness episodic or chronic? Does the individual have periods of illness and then periods of complete wellness, or is the individual chronically suffering from some form of the illness even though severity differs at various times? Certainly the questions of episodicity, how long each episode lasts, how many years a person has episodes, and when the person settles into a chronic presentation are very important in describing the course of the illness. This set of data, which takes into account the onset as well as the course after identification, is perhaps one of the most important factors in establishing validity.

The premorbid personality poses a special problem. Certain depression may be related to the presence of certain kinds of life-styles and personal difficulties. A stormy life-style with multiple marital and sexual problems may be associated with certain kinds of depression. Whether the premorbid personality should be considered a *forme fruste* of the illness or an affective episode is the result of the premorbid personality problems remains to be determined; we will take up these matters as we progress further. Suffice to say that the presence of premorbid personality differences is a matter of some significance.

The family history of psychiatric illness is extremely important in establishing diagnostic validity. Just as certain medical patients show similar kinds of illness in their family members, far to the excess of what would be normally expected, patients with certain kinds of affective illnesses may have nonaffective psychiatric illnesses in their family. Using a family history of a nonaffective illness to classify a subtype of depression is a new and unusual methodology. This may be very useful in separating autonomous affective diseases. The family history give information about the etiology (genetic or environmental). However, it rarely tells us much about the mechanism, the pathophysiology of the affective disorder.

Finally, the response to treatment should be taken into account. There are different types of treatment for affective episodes, both psychologic as well as somatic. Some of these are, in fact, prophylactic; some of them are used to simply treat the acute episode. In any event, it is important to note that certain kinds of treatment may be relevant to only certain kinds of affective illness.

Overview of the Classification

Now that some of the philosophical underpinnings of the classification have been discussed, the classification itself can be presented. This is illustrated in Figure 3.1. All of the illnesses in this classification manifest themselves by either a depressive or a manic syndrome or both. Sometimes these syndromes are accompanied by psychotic symptomatology, sometimes not. One other thing is important to note about the classification. In general, though not invariably, these syndromes are episodic. This does not mean that the individuals necessarily are well all of the time. It is quite possible that a syndrome that is secondary in a temporal fashion to another nonaffective illness will show an episodic nature for the affective episodes but a nonepisodic nature for the other and primary illness.

This classification is not a simple dichotomy. There are multiple groups of depressed and manic patients. The classification depends on three things: (1) when possible, there is a clear presentation in terms of etiology; (2) when a clear etiologic presentation is not possible, there is a presentation in terms of what would appear to constitute autonomous or independent illnesses; and (3) there is an effort to classify on the basis of more than one criterion that has been presented as useful in validation (see Table 3.1).

The organic affective syndromes are manias and depressions that

Affective Disorders

Organic affective syndrome (Induced)	Bipolar disorders	Unipolar disorders	Schizoaffective disorder
Structural Physiological Withdrawal	Bipolar I Bipolar II		

Reactive depression	Endogenous-psychotic depression	Neurotic
Bereavement	FPDD	DSD
Depression secondary to medical illness	SDD	Secondary Depression, to neurosis, personality disorders, alcoholism & drug abuse disorders

FPDD, familial pure depressive disorder
SDD, sporadic depressive disorder
DSD, depressive spectrum disorder

Figure 3.1. A Classification of the Affective Disorders

are induced by some space-occupying lesion, medication or other substance, infection, or metabolic abnormality. In these cases the affective syndromes are induced. Though they are secondary to some other medical entity, this does not truly present the appropriate quality. They are, in fact, caused by some aspect of a preexisting illness or state. "Secondary" in this case is related directly to etiology.

Bipolar disorders manifest themselves by the presence of manias but are not clearly and unequivocally induced by some other known organic state. These disorders are defined not only by their clinical picture but also by a very specific family background. They are divided into mild (cyclothymia and bipolar II) or severe. The presence of mania defines a bipolar disorder. In general, most bipolar disorders show both manias and depression, but some show only manias.

Schizoaffective disorders are defined by the concomitant presence of affective syndromes, either mania or depression, and schizophrenic symptoms. There is a big question as to whether these cases are mainly schizophrenic or mainly affective or whether, in fact, they constitute a third and separate type of psychosis. By virtue of their characteristics, we may be able to arrive at a reasonable answer to this question.

The unipolar disorders are characterized by one or more depressions in the course of a lifetime. Some of these are responses to life events, and these may be called reactive depressions. There are few models for this kind of depression, but we believe that bereavement and a reaction to the adversity imposed by a medical illness might be reasonable models. A depression secondary to a medical illness does not imply an organic affective syndrome or an induction by some physical factor. Instead, it suggests the idea that the individual's medical illness is severe, incapacitating, or life threatening and the individual's response is a depression. We are not postulating any reactive manias.

Endogenous unipolar depressions tend to be severe, are often familial, and show evidence of disturbed ability to test reality. Patients may have delusions and hallucinations. These are mainly congruent with the mood. One type is a familial depression, in which the individual has a family history of depression but no mania, alcoholism, or antisocial personality. These illnesses are primary in that they do not occur after the onset of another nonaffective illness. There is possibly a second type of endogenous depression, a sporadic depressive illness. This would occur in an individual with no family history. The question of whether such an illness truly occurs is not possible to answer, but we will discuss it to some extent.

Finally, there are neurotic depressions. There are two types of illness. The first is ordinary depressions in which there is a family history of alcoholism or antisocial personality (depression-spectrum disease). The depressions are primary, but they occur in the context of a stormy life-style and many personality problems. Nevertheless, they do not meet criteria for another diagnosis. The second type of neurotic depression is secondary to neurosis, personality disorders, or substance abuse disorders. A secondary depression is a depression that occurs after the onset of another, nonaffective psychiatric illness. The diagnosis of a secondary depression is based simply on the temporal relationship of the depression and the nonaffective illness. Such a depression may occur after the onset of alcoholism, drug abuse, anxiety disorder, schizophrenia, antisocial personality, or organic brain disorder.

Essentially the definition of a neurotic depression is a depression occurring in the course of a life that is studded with many personal problems and unstable characteristics. Both secondary depression and depression-spectrum disease fulfill this characterization.

Some affective illnesses are hard to classify in this fashion. They may fit in one as well as another type, and their appropriate place in the classification is not known. An example of these kinds of illness might be a depression secondary to schizophrenia or a postpartum mania. It is quite possible, however, that as we learn more about affective illnesses we will be able to put these kinds of syndromes into their appropriate slot in the classification.

One of the limitations of previous classifications of affective disorder is that they have often depended on such things as precipitating factors, consequences of the illness, or minor clinical differences. However, such things as epidemiology, family history of psychiatric illness, and premorbid personality and function are independent of the illness and the circumstances surrounding it and may be more valid discriminators. The affective episode itself is likely to result from things that occurred years before the illness occurred.

4 The Separation of Bipolar from Unipolar Affective Disorder

Through a fortuitous confluence of the planets or something like that, 1966 was a very good year for the study of affective disorders. The linchpin for the diagnosis and classification of depressions and manias was created at that time. Studies performed in widely disparate places by independent investigators suggested that within the broad rubric of the affective disorders were two types of illness, bipolar illness (manic-depressive disease) and unipolar depressive illness (only depressive episodes). In Sweden, Perris (1966) demonstrated that the heredity for manic-depressive psychosis was greater in bipolar than in unipolar probands. More specifically, the presence of bipolar illness (manias plus depression in the same patient) was more frequent in the family members of the bipolar patients than in the family members of the unipolar patients. Perris had compared 148 patients who had bipolar (manic-depressive) psychosis with 150 unipolar depressive psychotic patients. He evaluated 2,396 relatives. In Zurich, Angst (1966) evaluated 46 patients with bipolar illness, 105 with an "endogenous" depressive psychosis, 103 with involutional melancholia, and 73 with a mixed affective schizophrenic psychosis. Angst evaluated 2,599 family members. He too found an increase in affective illness in the bipolar patients as well an increase in mania in their family members compared with the unipolar depressive probands and their family members. Angst and Perris (1978) published a joint paper showing the similarity of their findings. In St. Louis, Winokur and Clayton (1967) independently arrived at a similar conclusion: the family background for manic-depressive patients differed from that of patients who showed only depression. Their material was presented at the annual convention and scientific program of the Society of Biological Psychiatry in Washington, D.C., in June 1966. They studied 426 probands who were diagnosed as having

29

int loss, bereavement?

primary affective disorder. A primary affective disorder is a depression or a mania that occurs in the absence of any other type of preceding psychiatric or medical illness. They noted a marked difference in the frequency of mania in the proband at the time of admission if the patients were separated according to whether they had a positive family history for affective disorder (two generations affected) or a totally negative family history. Whereas probands with a totally negative family history were unlikely to be manic (3.1%), those with a two-generation family history were manic in a much higher proportion of cases (14.3%). Thus, the familial or "genetic" findings in all three studies seem to indicate the existence of two types of affective disorder.

These findings set the stage for a classification that separated bipolar affective illness from unipolar affective illness. Note, however, that the separation of unipolar from bipolar illness may have been rattling around in the recesses of psychiatric thinking for a much longer period of time. In 1895 in Denmark, Karl Lang suggested a separation. This was discussed by Schou (1927). Later Schou and his coauthors (Pederson, Poort, and Schou, 1947) noted that a "periodical depression" had no manic phases. It differed from manic-depressive psychoses in heredity and prognosis. Their data suggested that manic-depressive patients were more likely to have chronic illness and were more disabled than periodic depressive patients, who were more likely to recover and be discharged. Leonhard (1957) suggested that bipolar and unipolar forms of affective illness might be different or separate or autonomous illnesses. Leonhard noted that the incidence of endogenous psychosis in first-degree relatives was higher in bipolar than in unipolar probands. Leonhard's contribution was known to both Angst and Perris, and both gave him credit for his contribution.

A valid separation of bipolar from unipolar illness might be accomplished by using the variables noted in Chapter 3 to describe the medical model. We would expect the two forms of affective disorder to differ with regard to clinical description, epidemiology, premorbid personality, course, family history of psychiatric or other medical illness, and response to treatment (see Table 3.1).

Of course, there is a marked clinical difference between bipolar patients and unipolar depressive patients. By definition, the description of the two illnesses depends on the fact that bipolar patients have mania and unipolar patients do not. Bipolar patients often have a preceding depression to their mania and equally often have a depression that follows the manic episode. Thus they are biphasic or sometimes even sometimes triphasic in their presentation (Winokur, Clayton, and Reich, 1969). Are they different in any other way? The depressions that occur in bipolar illness have been compared with unipolar depressions. Bipolar depressive patients have been noted to be more hypersomniac and to show more diurnal variation and less pacing behavior, anger, and somatic complaints than unipolar depressive patients (Beigel and Murphy, 1971; Detre et al., 1972). Himmelhoch et al. (1972), and Himmelhoch, Fuchs, and Symons (1982) noted that there is a depressive symptom cluster of anergia, motor retardation, inhibition of volition, and usually hypersomnia. These patients rarely show anxiety, irritability, and agitation. Like Kraepelin, Himmelhoch and his co-workers suggested that such a depression was very likely found in bipolar depressive patients. Winokur and Wesner (1987) evaluated 22 bipolar patients who at time of admission to the hospital showed only depression. These were compared with 203 unipolar patients who never became bipolar. For an undetermined reason, the unipolar patients who became bipolar were significantly more likely to be male. Also, they manifested more marked self-reproach and guilt. Interestingly, in a large multicenter study of affective disorders, the depression in bipolar relatives of bipolar probands showed marked guilt in 95% of cases, compared with only 65% of cases of depressed relatives of unipolar depressive probands (T. Reich, personal communication, 1988). Black and Nasrallah (1989) evaluated hallucinations and delusions in 1,715 patients with unipolar and bipolar affective disorders. Bipolar manic patients were more likely to have such psychotic symptoms as auditory and visual hallucinations as well as mood-congruent and -incongruent delusions. For any kind of delusion or hallucination, 48% of the manic patients showed such symptoms, as opposed to 19% of the unipolar depressive patients. However, when the unipolar depressive patients were compared with the bipolar depressive patients (the depressive episode in the bipolar patient), there was no significant difference (19% vs. 17%). Thus the major differences in psychotic symptoms between bipolar and unipolar patients occur during the manic episodes rather than during the depressive episodes. Most of the clinical differences, except the findings on delusions and hallucinations, have been reported on only a few occasions. These differences sorely need replication.

Of course, the major differentiation between bipolar illness and unipolar illness occurred on the basis of the family history. Table 4.1 shows some of the differences in the original studies of Perris, Angst, and Winokur and Clayton. It is apparent that affective disorder is more frequently seen in the family members of bipolar patients than in the family members of unipolar patients, and, specifically, mania is more frequently seen in the bipolar family members. Bertelsen, Harvald, and Hauge (1977) published the only modern twin study in the

Table 4.1. Familial Differences between Bipolar and Unipolar
Affective Disorders

Familial Findings	Percentage in Patients with Bipolar (Manic Depressive) Disorder	Percentage in Patients with Unipolar (Only Depressive) Disorder
Affective disorder in parent	52	26
Two-generation families	54	32
Affective disorder in primary relatives or extended family	63	36
Mania in first-degree relatives	3.7–10.8	0.29–0.35
Pairwise concordance in monozygotic twins	74	43

Note: All differences are statistically reliable.

affective disorders. The data were clear. The bipolar patients were far
more likely to show concordance in monozygotic twin pairs than were
the unipolar patients (concordance in monozygotic bipolar pairs =
74%, in monozygotic unipolar pairs = 43%). In the dizygotic pairs,
however, there was no difference in pairwise concordance. Unipolar
patients showed 19% concordance, as opposed to the 17% concordance in bipolar patients. One would have expected the dizygotic
concordances to reflect the differences in the monozygotic concordances. The reason for this discrepancy is unknown. The differences
in concordance among the monozygotic twins have been ascribed to
the unipolar patients' being "less genetic" than the bipolar patients.
An equally plausible explanation for the difference is that the unipolar group is composed of a heterogeneous group of depressive patients, some of whom are familial and some of whom are not.

   Not every study has shown the same findings. Table 4.2 presents a
family history study of bipolar and unipolar affective disorder that
was done in Iowa (Winokur, 1985a). The patients were selected from
those hospitalized at a tertiary care center between 1935 and 1940. In
those years only the sickest patients were hospitalized and often had
to travel over hundreds of miles of bad roads. Severity was a factor
leading to hospitalization between 1935 and 1940, and this could
conceivably play a role in decreasing the differences between the
bipolar and unipolar patients regarding the amount of affective disorder in families. Evidence that these patients are somewhat unusual

Table 4.2. Family History of Affective Disorder

Number of Family Members[c]	Parents[a] and Siblings[b]	
	Bipolar	Unipolar
At risk[d]	402	799
Ill (morbid risk %)	50 (12.4)	121 (15.1)

[a]Includes bipolar disorder, depression, remitting illness, and undiagnosed psychosis.
[b]Affective disorder and remitting illness.
[c]Individual comparisons of bipolar versus unipolar illness: fathers, 15% versus 15%; mothers, 12% versus 13%; brothers, 12% versus 15%; sisters, 11% versus 15%.
[d]Ages of risk: 15–60.

is the fact that 64% of the bipolar patients were psychotic (had delusions and/or hallucinations), as were 56% of the unipolar patients. Though the differences in amount of family history of affective disorder did not differentiate the two groups, these patients were later evaluated on the basis of a long follow-up and all available first-degree relatives were personally interviewed (Winokur, Tsuang, and Crowe, 1982). The morbidity risk for affective disorder in the family study for bipolar families was 12.8% and for the unipolar patients was 11.2%. These percentages refer to the morbid risk for illnesses in the relatives (parents and siblings), and morbid risk is defined as the percentage of relatives who have or will have the illness if they live through the age of risk (15 to 59 years) for affective disorder. Likewise, among the interviewed relatives there was no significant increase in the number of bipolar patients among the relatives of the bipolar probands (1.5% for bipolar probands, 1% for unipolar probands, and 0.3% for controls). However, deceased first-degree relatives were also investigated by evaluating clinical material that had been accumulated during a variety of hospitalizations. Bipolar probands were more likely than unipolar or control probands to have had bipolar relatives who had been hospitalized. Among the bipolar patients 47% of the deceased first-degree relatives who had had an affective disorder had had a mania, whereas among the unipolar patients 20% of the deceased first-degree relatives who had had an affective disorder had had a mania. Within the deceased relatives, there was also a suggestion that there was more hospitalized psychiatric illness for affective disorder in the bipolar group (71% vs. 63%).

Other research has also shown a difference between bipolar and unipolar probands as regards the risk of affective disorder in the family. A Polish study (Trzebiatowska-Trzeciak, 1977) showed a 11.42% morbidity risk for affective disorder (certain diagnoses) among first-degree relatives of bipolar patients, as opposed to a 7.41% morbidity risk for affectively disordered relatives of unipolar patients. Among second-degree relatives, the morbidity risk for affective psychoses was lower for unipolar than for bipolar probands (3.4% vs. 5.3%). A Chinese investigation also supported the familial difference between bipolar and unipolar illness (Zhenyi, Mingdao, and Heqin, 1980). In this study, 46% of 320 bipolar patients and 38% of 384 unipolar patients showed a positive family history for mental diseases ($p < .05$). In a comparison of more serious types of illness (i.e., psychosis) in first-degree relatives of the unipolar and bipolar index cases, the authors found more serious illness in the latter group than in the former group (23.6% vs. 31.2%, $p < .01$). Further, bipolarity was far more frequent proportionately in the affectively ill first-degree relatives of the bipolar patients than in the affectively ill family members of the unipolar patients.

The risk of bipolar affective disorders is always higher in the first-degree relatives of bipolar index patients than in the first-degree relatives of unipolar index patients. Although the difference in the amount of affective illness between bipolar and unipolar patients varies with studies, and may relate to diagnosis or other methodologic differences, the finding of an increased amount of bipolarity in family members of bipolar patients has been almost invariable. Finding more mania in the family members of bipolar patients is the hallmark of the bipolar/unipolar separation. It is again seen in another study (Winokur, 1985a); the data are presented in Table 4.3. In this study, the data on bipolar and unipolar probands were collected as an Iowa University contribution to a large national collaborative study (five different study centers) on the affective disorders. All of the first-degree relatives were personally interviewed. As can be seen in Table 4.3, the proportions of relatives with a major affective disorder in these Iowa bipolar and unipolar probands were approximately equal. However, of 281 relatives of bipolar probands, 14 suffered a mania (4.9%). Of 327 relatives of unipolar probands, only 4 suffered a mania (1.2%). All of these probands were evaluated at the University of Iowa Hospital in the 1970s.

In another family study of bipolar and unipolar, and control probands, all patients had been admitted to the medical institutes of the National Institutes of Health. Those with affective disorders had been admitted to the National Institute of Mental Health, but the controls had been hospitalized at other medical institutes (Gershon et al., 1982). The amount of serious bipolar disorder was three times as

Table 4.3. Interviewed Parents and Siblings of Bipolar and Unipolar Probands

Family Members	N	Mean Age	Major Affective Disorder (N)	Manic Disorder (N)	Major Affective Disorder (N)
		Bipolar			
Mothers	56	60	11	1	20
Fathers	56	58	11	4	20
Sisters (17 or older)	82	37	16	3	20
Brothers (17 or older)	87	34	14	6	16
		Unipolar			
Mothers	61	61	19	0	31
Fathers	61	60	6	1	10
Sisters (17 or older)	108	38	34	1	31
Brothers (17 or older)	97	42	20	2	21

frequent in the relatives of the bipolar probands as in the relatives of the unipolar probands (4.5% vs. 1.5%). For all affective illnesses, there was a prevalence of 25.3% in the relatives of bipolar probands, as opposed to 19.6% in the relatives of unipolar depressive probands. Thus, this study showed both of the general findings that separate bipolar from unipolar illness—more familial affective illness and more manic relatives among bipolar patients.

Epidemiologic research has also indicated a difference in the frequency of occurrence of mania and depression in both control and general populations. Tsuang, Winokur, and Crowe (1984) found a morbid risk for bipolar disorder of 0.3% to 0.9% in relatives of a surgical patient (appendectomy or herniorrhaphy) population who were screened to remove psychiatric illness. The morbid risk for depression in the same relatives varied between 7.3% and 8.1%. In this case, depression was unipolar depression and did not include depressed patients who had ever had a history of mania. If the relative ever had a mania, he or she was diagnosed as having bipolar depression.

A very large scale epidemiologic study (Robins et al., 1984) was accomplished using three sites (New Haven, Baltimore, and St. Louis). The lifetime prevalence of a major depressive episode varied between 3.7% and 6.7%. The lifetime prevalence for a manic episode varied between .6% and 1.1%. This study did not separate the patients into those having bipolar illness and those having unipolar illness, but it supports the fact that there is a difference in the frequency of major depression and mania in the general population, with depression being about six times more frequent.

Finally, in a group of 265 relatives of normal controls, Gershon et al. (1982) found no bipolar illness but observed a prevalence of 5.8% for unipolar depression. Though it is clear that the frequency of bipolar illness and unipolar depression differs in the population, no obvious epidemiologic variables explain this difference.

Personality traits have long been thought to separate bipolar and unipolar illness. As an example, Rowe and Daggett (1954) studied prepsychotic personality traits in 50 affectively disordered patients. Twenty-four of these had only depressions, 15 had depressions and manias, and 11 had only manias. Patients who suffered depressions only were described as being shy, conscientious, sensitive, and possessed of good judgment. They were not insecure, unstable, "intelligent," egocentric, or promiscuous. Patients who suffered from depressions and elations were described as being "intelligent," shy, active, and possessed of good judgment. They were not insecure, ambitious, thrifty, or promiscuous. Finally, the patients who suffered from manias only were active, egocentric, "intelligent," rigid, self-reliant, and reliable. They were not conscientious, dependent, or thrifty. If one separated the depressive patients from the two groups who had elations, depressive patients were frequently conscientious, usually not particularly active, and rarely considered "intelligent" or egocentric. Hirschfeld et al. (1986) compared personality traits of 45 bipolar patients with those of 78 unipolar patients, all of whom were fully recovered. The findings suggested great similarity of personality between the recovered bipolar and unipolar patients. Both bipolar and unipolar patients differed substantially from a control group on measures of emotional strength. Bipolar men had normal levels of extraversion, whereas bipolar women and unipolar women were introverted. Unipolar men tended to be significantly lower in extraversion and sociability than the bipolar men, a finding not totally unexpected if bipolar patients show a more cyclothymic or hypomanic personality than unipolar patients.

Aside from the specific differences in family history between bipolar and unipolar patients, the other major differentiating factor is the course of the illness. Most studies suggest that bipolar patients become ill earlier in life than do unipolar patients. In a study of a large number of bipolar patients, there was a highly significant difference in the age of onset between the two forms of affective disorder (Winokur, 1985a). Table 4.4 shows the differences. What is noteworthy is the fact that between the ages of 10 and 19, 27% of the bipolar patients fall ill for the first time, as opposed to only 5% of the unipolar

Table 4.4. The Age of Onset of First Illness

Age	Bipolar[a] N (%)		Unipolar N (%)	
10–29	33	(27)	10	(5)
20–29	37	(30)	54	(27)
30–39	19	(16)	48	(24)
40–49	15	(12)	46	(23)
50–59	16	(13)	37	(18)
60–69	1	(1)	7	(3)
Total	121	(99)	202	(100)

[a]Bipolar patients become ill earlier than unipolar patients ($p < .0001$).

patients. For ages 40 to 69, the proportion of first episodes for unipolar patients is 44% and for bipolar patients only 26%.

Table 4.5 presents other aspects of the differences in the course (Winokur, 1985a). Episodes in bipolar illness are far more acute in their onset. Thus 70% of bipolar patients had been ill for three months or less at the time they entered the hospital. Probably the most striking difference between bipolar and unipolar patients in the course of the illness is that the former are far more likely to have had episodes in follow-up. Table 4.5 shows that the bipolar and unipolar patients are similar in having had one or more previous episodes of illness, but in follow-up the bipolar patients are more likely to have had episodes of illness as well as hospitalizations. Thus bipolar illness typically shows more episodes of illness than does unipolar illness. This finding has been reported by a recent Japanese study (Fukuda et al., 1983). Angst et al. (1973) studied 604 unipolar depressive psychoses and 393 bipolar manic-depressive psychoses in an attempt to evaluate the course of each illness. In general, the analysis was based on case histories and hospitalizations. Both unipolar and bipolar forms of the affective disorders showed a periodic course, but the bipolar patients had a mean number of episodes of eight to nine, as opposed to the unipolar patients, who had only five to six episodes. In bipolar illness, the length of the episodes was about 20% shorter than the length of the episodes in unipolar disease. As noted above, the mean age at first episode was lower (around 30 years) for the bipolar psychoses than for the unipolar depressions (around 43 years). The differences in follow-up between bipolar and unipolar patients were already noted 20 years ago by Bratfos and Haug (1968) in Norway. Of 42 manic patients, 15 were discharged from the hospital as totally free of symptoms, but in a follow-up of six years, only 3 of the 42 had

Table 4.5. Course of Illness in Bipolar Versus
Unipolar Patients

Course Variable	Bipolar (N = 122)		Unipolar (N = 203)		p
	n	(%)	n	(%)	
Poor premorbid adjustment or work history	4	(4)	7	(3)	N.S.
One or more previous episodes of illness	62	(51)	89	(44)	N.S.
One or more previous hospitalizations	46	(38)	30	(15)	<.0005
Ill 3 months or less at index episode	86	(70)	90	(44)	<.0005
One or more postindex Iowa psychiatric hospitalizations	22	(18)	18	(9)	<.025
One or more episodes in follow-up	52	(43)	56	(28)	<.01
Two or more hospitalizations in follow-up	32	(25)	29	(14)	<.025

remained well for the entire period of time. A higher proportion of unipolar patients in this study remained well over the same follow-up period.

The major difference between the bipolar and unipolar forms of the affective disorders lies in the earlier age of onset and the marked episodicity that are seen in the former. If one evaluates the two types of affective disorders over a 30 to 40-year field follow-up, they do not turn out to be different in final outcome in any significant fashion (Tsuang, Woolson, and Fleming, 1979). Patients who were originally admitted for bipolar illness were compared with those patients who were originally admitted for unipolar depression by Tsuang, Woolson, and Fleming (1979). Such outcome variables as marital status, occupational status, residential status, and psychiatric status were compared between the bipolar and unipolar groups, and there were no significant differences in the mean ratings. Twenty-four percent of the bipolar patients were found to be incapacitated for work as a result of mental illness, as opposed to 17% of the unipolar patients.

As regards outcome for psychiatric symptomatology, a good outcome was defined as having no psychiatric symptoms. Fifty percent of the manic patients in the follow-up showed a good outcome, as opposed to 61% of the depressive patients. This was not a significant difference, but it suggests that the depressive patients may have had a somewhat better outcome. Of course, this may also be interpreted as due to the possibility that if the manic patients had more episodes it is more likely that they would have been picked up in the middle of an episode, thus accounting for the nonsignificant difference in outcome for psychiatric disability between manic and depressive patients. Likewise, there was a nonsignificant difference for the worst outcome. This was for the presence of psychiatric symptoms that were incapacitating. Twenty-nine percent of the manic patients showed this at last follow-up as opposed to 22% of the unipolar depressive patients.

Another way to evaluate the differences in follow-up is to determine whether there are any changes in diagnosis over time. In a study by Tsuang et al. (1981), of patients who were diagnosed as bipolar originally and were rediagnosed in follow-up, 8% were considered to have shown a "schizophrenic-type" picture in follow-up. This could be compared with 5.7% of the unipolar group who showed a schizophrenic-type picture on subsequent follow-up interview. Data based on records are more strikingly different. Of 46 bipolar patients, 6 (13%) were given a final diagnosis of schizophrenia, whereas of 108 unipolar patients, 5 (4.6%) were given such a diagnosis. These data suggest that the stability of diagnosis is somewhat better in the unipolar group, but one should note that the illness of the unipolar group was extremely severe and these patients were originally admitted to the hospital 30 to 40 years before the follow-up assessment. This does not necessarily mean that the patients had become schizophrenic over time; rather, it suggests that a few schizophrenic symptoms appeared and caused the diagnosticians to change their assessment.

One of the major problems in the differentiation between bipolar and unipolar illnesses is the fact that often bipolar patients are seen for a depression early in their illness. In the course of time, they change their character and show manias. In a systematic follow-up of 225 patients who had unipolar depression, 22 (9.7%) became bipolar some time during a 40-year follow-up (Winokur, Tsuang, and Crowe, 1982). Generally such patients become manic within 5 years of their index admission for depression, but sometimes a longer period elapsed before the mania presents itself. In any event, in a group of unipolar depressive patients it would appear that in around 10% there would be a change from unipolar illness to bipolar illness over a long period of time (i.e., 40 years).

Winokur and Wesner (1987) studied 29 patients whose illness changed from unipolar depression to bipolar illness over time. The potential bipolar patients had more episodes before the onset of their mania and more hospital admissions than did stable unipolar patients. During their index admission, they were more likely to have remained hospitalized for a longer period of time. In the follow-up period, the unipolar patients who became bipolar had more hospitalizations than the stable unipolar patients, which, of course, is expected in bipolar illness. These data suggest that one way to identify potential bipolar patients from a unipolar population is to evaluate the number of previous episodes and admissions; if these are relatively high, the chances of bipolarity occurring might be significant.

Another validating factor in the differentiation of bipolar from unipolar affective disorder would be observation of a differential response to specific treatments. Noyes et al. (1974) investigated such a response to lithium carbonate in 22 patients hospitalized for endogenous depression. There was a statistically significant difference in response between the bipolar and unipolar patients. Of 6 patients with a prior history of mania, all responded to the drug; however, only 7 (44%) of those 16 without such a history responded well to the treatment. There are other data relevant to a differential effect of treatment. Prien et al. (1984) conducted a double-blind long-term follow-up study of 117 bipolar patients and 150 unipolar patients. The goal of their study was to determine which drugs might prevent subsequent episodes in these patients. The patients received lithium carbonate, imipramine, lithium carbonate with imipramine, or placebo. They noted that in the bipolar patients lithium carbonate with or without imipramine was superior in preventing manic recurrences. They also noted that lithium was as effective as imipramine in preventing depressive episodes in bipolar patients. This was different from the unipolar patients for whom imipramine or imipramine with lithium was more effective than lithium alone in preventing recurrences of depression. In both cases, the combinations provided no increase in effectiveness. The active drug in preventing bipolar episodes was lithium, and the active drug in preventing depressive episodes in unipolar patients was imipramine.

There may be differential effects of some antidepressant drugs on bipolar versus unipolar depressions. Himmelhoch et al. (1972) evaluated the efficacy of tranylcypromine as opposed to placebo in bipolar patients. These were patients who had an anergic major depression, which he noted occurred typically in bipolar patients. There was a significantly greater improvement for the tranylcypromine-treated patients on all measures of symptomatology when compared with placebo-treated patients. In this study, 24 of the 29 bipolar patients had previously failed to respond to tricyclic antidepressants for their depression, and he suggested that it would be useful to compare tranylcypromine with imipramine to determine the antidepressant of choice for manic-depressive illness. In a subsequent study, Himmelhoch et al. (1986) compared imipramine, a tricyclic antidepressant, with tranylcypromine, a monoamine oxidase inhibitor. Tranylcypromine was significantly more effective than imipramine in the treatment of anergic bipolar depression. The findings suggested imipramine might be relatively ineffective for this kind of depressive illness. A direct evaluation of the two drugs in bipolar versus unipolar depression would be useful. In general, clinicians use imipramine as a treatment of choice for patients with unipolar depressive illness; one might find that there is, in fact, a differential effect of imipramine and tranyclypromine on the two forms of affective illness, bipolar depression and unipolar depression. However, this study still needs to be done.

Should bipolar affective disorder and unipolar depression be considered as separate illnesses? The alternative is to consider them as part of the same illness, each representing a threshold on the continuum of underlying multifactorial vulnerability. Such a vulnerability would contain multiple genes as well as possible environmental factors, both psychosocial and otherwise. Gershon et al. (1982) espoused this viewpoint. They studied patients and their relatives. The patients had schizoaffective disorder (mainly manic), bipolar I disorder (clear manic episodes), bipolar II disorder (minor manic episodes but clear depressive episodes), and unipolar depression. In addition, there was a group of normal controls. The lifetime prevalences for the family members for major affective disorder in these groups, respectively, were 37%, 24%, 25%, 20%, and 7%. The bipolar patients would be considered more severely ill than the unipolar patients. Gershon et al. analyzed these familial data to determine whether they suggested a multifactorial inheritance. The data were such that a multifactorial model could not be rejected.

One possible criticism of this theory is that not all data sets support that kind of systematic decrease in familial affective disorder between unipolar and bipolar patients. For example, the data published by Winokur, Tsuang, and Crowe (1982) do not support a significant difference in the family background of bipolar and unipolar probands. This study dealt with very severe patients admitted in the 1930s who were followed up after 40 years and the first-degree relatives of whom were personally interviewed. The risk of morbidity in the bipolar patients' families was 14.3% and in the unipolar patients' families was 12.2%.

However, using the same data base, Tsuang, Faraone, and Fleming (1985) evaluated a two-threshold multifactorial polygenic model to determine whether bipolar and unipolar disorders were manifestations of the same underlying factors or were different illnesses. This is similar to Gershon et al.'s idea that the two disorder might share a common pool of etiologic factors but might differ in the quantity of these factors needed to make the disorder manifest. Bipolar disorder would be considered to require more of these causal factors than unipolar disorder. In performing these multifactorial analyses, Tsuang, Faraone, and Fleming found that the common etiology model could not be rejected, which was consistent with their previous finding that relatives of bipolar probands are not significantly different from these of unipolar probands with regard to risk for affective disorders. In that particular study, there was a difference among the deceased relatives as regards bipolar illness, with the bipolar patients having twice as many bipolar relatives as the unipolar patients, but in the part of the study that depended heavily on personal examination of live family members there was no more mania in the interviewed family members of bipolar patients than in those of unipolar patients. The finding was in only the ill family members who were deceased and admitted to hospitals (Winokur, Tsuang, and Crowe, 1982). Also, there may be other problems with the multifactorial model. There may be some question as to whether it is appropriate if one of the other two diseases is highly heterogeneous. Each study uses a somewhat different methodology, and until there are several replications in favor of either a separate disease model or a multifactorial model, we will not be able to obtain a final answer about the autonomy of the types. There is considerable reason to believe that the unipolar group comprises two or more separate types, which may be separated on the basis of their specific family history. To evaluate unipolar depression as if it were one disease may not be appropriate. Likewise, bipolar illness may contain some heterogeneity.

In contrast, if one uses the concept of the medical model, the bipolar patients separate themselves from the unipolar patients rather well. There are clear differences in family background, clinical picture, and course; differences in epidemiology; and possible differences in premorbid personality and response to treatment. Again, because the unipolar patients may be heterogeneous, the separation may be meaningful only in terms of having defined a clear autonomous illness, that is, bipolar illness. There is considerable reason to believe that bipolar illness should be separated from unipolar illness on a clinical basis because the separation may have value in predicting course as well as specifying treatment. Thus on a pragmatic level the separation is meaningful. In addition, the fact remains that the separation may truly differentiate an autonomous illness, bipolar disorder, from the mass of affective disorders.

5 The Unipolar Depressions: Previous Classification Studies and Principles for Further Classification

The bipolar-unipolar dichotomy is the organizing principle from which a discussion of the classification of unipolar depression should depart. Depressive episodes that include major depressions as well as dysthmyias outnumber manic episodes in the population by a factor of 9 to 1 (Robins et al., 1984). This marked preponderance of depressions over manias does not even take into account depression that may be caused by such circumstances as bereavement, depression in response to a major medical illness, or depression that occurs in the course of other psychiatric illnesses, such as anxiety disorders, somatization disorders, and personality disorders. If one included these depressions, the ratio would be far greater than 9 to 1.

The separation of bipolar from unipolar depression became a significant matter in 1966 as a result of research in Sweden, Switzerland, and St. Louis. Before 1966 the classifications of depression did not take into account the possibility that there were two illnesses that demanded separation. Because the depressions seen in people who also suffer from mania are quite similar to those seen in people who have only depressions, it seemed reasonable to include the bipolar depressions in any classification of depressive syndromes. By 1966, however, the finding that there were differences in age of onset, course, family background, premorbid personality, and, to some extent, response to treatment made it sensible to look at the unipolar depressions as a separate entity. Still, the research on the classification of depression prior to 1966 is of interest and may still be quite relevant to a more modern view. Starting from Kraepelin and ending with modern times, Ban (1989) collected 25 sets of diagnostic criteria and classifications of depressive disorders. Kendall (1976) presented several classifications that were divided into simple typologies, tiered typologies, and dimensional systems. Although there is certainly a surfeit of classifications, it is quite possible that recent investigations have put us in an advantageous position for at least another one.

Older Classification Studies

Before the distinction between manic-depressive (bipolar) illness and depressive (unipolar) illness, the classifications essentially dealt with dichotomous evaluations of depressions. Sometimes the dichotomy was referred to as endogenous versus exogenous; at other times, as psychotic versus neurotic or endogenous versus reactive. Exogenous, neurotic, and reactive were usually considered to be highly related. However, in Chapters 9 through 12 we will see some evidence that suggests separating reactive from neurotic although both are "nonendogenous." Not only is there overlap between some of the terms, there is considerable communality between a variety of the classifications. If we were to compare one classification with another one using Ban's compilation of the different diagnostic groups, we would be able to make 300 different comparisons. The formula for the number of comparisons is as follows:

$$\frac{N(N-1)}{2} = \frac{25 \times 24}{2} = 300.0$$

A young psychiatrist could make a career comparing one classification with the other, albeit a fairly boring career.

One can pick up the argument about classification in the middle to late 1930s when Aubrey Lewis (1934) published an influential paper surveying clinical aspects of depressive states. He reached the conclusion that precipitating events were not useful in separating out different kinds of affective illnesses. He also suggested that dichotomous classifications did nothing more than separate acute and chronic and mild and severe. Manic depression was acute and severe, whereas another kind of depression was chronic and mild (Lewis, 1938). To this he added that there were probably real differences between cases of hereditary causation and those in which environmental causes predominated. However, he did not think the clinical differences were useful in separating these groups. Nevertheless, this is a forerunner of a classification based on familial differences, which is discussed later with regard to familial pure depressive disease, depression-spectrum disease, and sporadic depressive disease.

The question of whether there were two types of depressive illnesses, endogenous and reactive, was a very vigorous controversy with many proponents on either side. Hamilton and White (1959) separated depressive patients into two groups, one reactive and the other endogenous, on the basis of precipitating factors or life events. Those who had such life events were considered to have a reactive depression. Patients with endogenous depression differed from those with reactive depression in that they had more severe and more numerous symptoms of a retarded depression. These symptoms included a depressed mood, guilt, suicide, insomnia, and retardation. There were no mutually exclusive criteria for the two diagnoses. However, Hamilton and White concluded that one could differentiate the reactive depressions from the endogenous or psychotic depressions by both precipitating factors and the presence of certain symptoms. Of 64 patients who were evaluated, however, only 11 (17%) were considered to have endogenous depression and 26 (41%) were considered to have reactive depression. This left 42% whose type of depression was considered uncertain. The high percentage of uncertain cases presents a problem. A definition of a "reactive" depression seemed difficult.

Rose (1963) used the same rating scale as Hamilton and White and diagnosed 50 depressed patients as having either a reactive or endogenous depression. He reported that the endogenous group, who were diagnosed on the absence of precipitating factors, responded more favorably to electroconvulsive therapy (ECT) but there was no difference in the severity of the clinical picture. There is a problem of differentiating solely on the basis of response to treatment. This is particularly true when the treatment is symptomatic rather than etiologic. As an example, anticonvulsive medication might be used for the central nervous system symptoms of lupus erythematosis, which include convulsions, but it would have no value in treating the cardiac or renal symptoms. A diagnosis of reactive depression might well be made in relation to a poorly adjusted person with a lot of premorbid personality difficulties. This would produce a poor response to ECT because of the chronicity of the illness in the patient or even the possible presence of another psychiatric disorder, such as somatization disorder or alcoholism. In these cases, the depression would be secondary to the primary diagnoses of anxiety disorder, alcoholism, or substance abuse disorder.

Winokur and Pitts (1964) compared 75 patients who had primary reactive depressions with 212 patients who had endogenous affective disorders (mainly unipolar but some bipolar depressions). It was assumed that patients with endogenous depression would have a different kind of family history than those with reactive depression. There were no clear differences in numbers of suicides in first-degree family members or in the presence of affective illness. However, there was a significant increase in alcoholism in the siblings of the patients with reactive depression. Thus although there was a familial difference, it occurred from a most unexpected quarter—alcoholism rather than depression. Of particular note is that reactive depression in this study was a diagnosis made by clinicians, and these patients would have fit under the rubric of either reactive or neurotic depression. In 12 of the 75 patients, there was agreement that reactive depression was a reasonable diagnosis. These were unusual in that 5 patients were under 20 years of age. Distressing medical illnesses were seen in 2, and other psychiatric diagnoses, such as alcoholism and anxiety neurosis, might have been reasonably entertained in the remainder. The findings led to the conclusion that no reliable criteria existed for clearly diagnosing depressions as reactive in the absence of long-standing medical and psychiatric illness. Interestingly, the only positive finding in this study—that patients diagnosed as having reactive depression by clinicians had a larger family history of alcoholism—was not noted when the study was published, mainly because the authors did not think it was very important. Their mind-set was such that they were not looking for this kind of familial background. As we shall see later in this book, a familial background of alcoholism can be used as a defining factor for some of the diagnoses in the classification of affective disorders.

In the early 1960s, again before the separation of bipolar from unipolar affective disorder, Kiloh and Garside (1963) published an influential paper on the separation of endogenous from neurotic depression. With the factor analytic method, these investigators evaluated 35 clinical features obtained from 31 patients with a "reasonably certain" clinical diagnosis of endogenous depression and 61 patients with a "reasonably certain" diagnosis of neurotic depression. These diagnoses are clinical diagnoses, and Kiloh and Garside made the point that they were "the best of an imperfect range available. They have the advantage of being understood even by those who profess not to accept them" (1963). Among the clinical features that were obtained were personal details, personality traits, history of previous attacks of depression, and symptoms of the present illness. With the factor analytic methodology, the authors concluded that the data could not be produced by a single depressive condition but had to be produced by two separate conditions. Though these conditions had some clinical features in common, they isolated a factor that was very similar to the correlations with diagnosis. Table 5.1 shows the differences between the clinically diagnosed neurotic depressive patients and the endogenous depressive patients. Of course, there may be something circular in this: such diagnoses might have been made simply by virtue of the fact that such differences in symptoms were

Table 5.1. Some Clinical Features That Correlate (in
Decreasing Size of Correlation) with Diagnosis of Neurotic
Versus Endogenous Depression

Neurotic depression	Endogenous depression
Reactivity of depression to life circumstances	Early awakening
	Diurnal variation
Precipitation	Retardation
Self-pity	Concentration difficulties
Hysterical features	Significant weight loss
Immaturity	Previous episodes
Inadequacy	
Irritability	
Hypochondriasis	

Source: Kiloh L, Garside R: The independence of neurotic depression and endogenous depression. *British Journal of Psychiatry* 109:451–463, 1963.

part of the mind-set of the clinicians and thus led to alternative diagnoses.

In keeping with this finding, Kay et al. (1969a, 1969b) followed 104 cases divided into endogenous and neurotic depression. Their findings are presented in Table 5.2. What is noteworthy is that the endogenous patients were significantly more likely to have recovered on leaving the hospital and more likely to have a readmission in a five- to seven-year follow-up. Likewise, though this finding did not reach significance, the endogenous depression patients were more likely to exhibit prolonged ill health or "chronicity."

Using a discriminant function analysis, Kendell (1968) investigated the possibility of two separate types of depression in 1,080 patients admitted to Maudsley Hospital between 1949 and 1963. Kendell found no clear bimodality in the Maudsley patients. He argued that depressive illness was best regarded as a single continuum extending from the traditional neurotic and psychotic stereotypes. Likewise, he suggested that the results of studies such as of Kiloh and Garside's (1963) were due to the "biasing of their ratings by uncontrolled halo effects" (Kendall, 1968). For the clinical diagnoses of the Maudsley group, outcome was found to be better for psychotic depression and involutional melancholia than for neurotic depression. Though there was no clear bimodality, the clinically diagnosed neurotic depressive patients were less likely to have a parental history of affective illness and more likely to have a parental history of neurotic illness. Neurotic depressive patients were more likely to show childhood neurotic traits

Table 5.2. Follow-up in Patients with "Endogenous" Syndrome
Versus Follow-up in Those with "Neurotic" Syndrome

Follow-up Variable	Endogenous Syndrome	Neurotic Syndrome
N	31	39
Recovered on leaving hospital	22 (71%)	12 (31%)
Readmission in follow-up	15 (48%)	9 (23%)
Prolonged ill health	7 (23%)	16 (41%)

Source: Kay D, Garside R, Roy J, Beamish P: "Endogenous" and "neurotic" syndromes of depression: A 5–7 year follow-up of 104 cases. *British Journal of Psychiatry* 115:389–399, 1969.

and previous hysteria and tension symptomatology. Precipitating factors were more likely found in the neurotic depressive patients, whereas retardation and agitation were more frequent in the psychotic depressive patients. Thus there are some similarities between Kendell's findings and those of Kiloh and Garside.

Mendels (1968) evaluated a group of 100 depressed patients and noted that the presence of such reactive symptoms as neurotic traits in childhood and adulthood precipitating factors, inadequate personality, and emotional lability separated patients into two groups better than such endogenous items as family history of depression, feelings of self-reproach, diurnal variation, delusions, and early-morning awakening. He also found a poor response to ECT if the patient showed neurotic traits in childhood. A good response to ECT was found if psychomotor retardation was present.

In yet another attempt to separate types of depressed patients, Paykel (1971) used a cluster analysis methodology. He studied a total of 165 patients who came from an outpatient setting, a day hospital, an emergency admission unit, and an inpatient mental health center. In a two-group partition, the patients were divided into those who were old and had severe illness versus those who were young and had mild illness. Another analysis produced four approximate groups. Group A was called "psychotic" and was characterized by considerable severity, sometimes with delusions, on a background of good premorbid adjustment. These patients' illness corresponded to psychotic depression described previously in the literature. Group B was called "anxious." These patients were moderately depressed with considerable anxiety, a high incidence of previous illnesses, and high neuroticism scores. Group C was said to have "hostile" depression and showed provocative, demanding, and hostile behavior. Finally, Group D was placed under the rubric of "young depressive with personality disorder." These patients had relatively mild illnesses. How separate Groups B, C, and D were may be questioned. Cluster analysis picks up symptoms that hang together in separate patients but does not necessarily define separate diseases.

Up to this point, we essentially have dealt with the differences between endogenous and neurotic possibilities for depression. There is one other problem that needs to be discussed in terms of the classification, and that is involutional melancholia. This may be synonymous with the concept of late-onset affective disorder of a unipolar type. Stenstedt (1959) found a low incidence of family history of affective disorder in patients with involutional melancholia. He thought that these "sporadic" depressions were heterogeneous and were composed of patients with manic-depressive illness, reactive depression, and organic affective disorders. Winokur and Ruangtrakool (1966) were unable to show any clinical differences between patients who had a family history of affective disorder and those who did not. The most interesting study on late-life depression was reported by Hopkinson and Ley (1969). They divided 182 affectively ill probands into ages of onset in decades. Using a break-point methodology, they showed that the amount of affective illness in relatives sharply dropped when the onset of the depression was at 40 years of age or older. This departure from linearity (i.e., a gradual drop in risk for affective disorder in relatives) was not due to chance. The fact that the sharp break in relationship occurred between family history and age of onset in probands suggested to Hopkinson and Ley that there were two nosologically distinct groups, one an early-onset affective disorder and the other a late-onset illness. This break-point methodology, using familial alcoholism rather than familial depression, was also used by Cadoret, Woolson, and Winokur (1977) to separate familial subtypes of depression. In the Hopkinson and Ley data, which strongly suggest the presence of a late-onset or involutional illness, there is a methodologic problem, however. Their original group included bipolar patients, who classically have a very young age of onset and may account for the sharp change from linearity. The appropriate place in the classification for a late-onset depression is discussed later in this book, but suffice to say it is not an issue that has been resolved.

Modern Classification Studies

The modern studies of the separation between endogenous and neu-rotic depression involve an elimination of bipolar patients, a change in definition, and the use of laboratory tests to provide more resolving power. The current fashion in classifying the unipolar affective disor-ders is to attempt to separate endogenous depression as a first step. This is based on the implicit assumption that endogenous depression is more distinct and more specific than other kinds of depression. This may be so. However, there is one more assumption that exists— that the criteria for endogenous are both reliable and valid in making such a separation. Essentially the criteria for endogenous are similar to those in Table 5.1. This is true even though those criteria were founded on studies that did not segregate unipolar from bipolar patients. Using this sequence in classification, one ends up with an endogenous group and a nonendogenous group, the latter being essentially a group that exists by exclusion. However, as we shall see later, it is possible that the criteria for neurotic or "nonendogenous" depression may be more reliable than the criteria for endogenous depression. The criteria for the neurotic group essentially are based on a stormy life-style and personality problems that have existed for long periods of time. The criteria for the endogenous group are based on symptoms that may be evanescent.

In fact, there are several sets of criteria for endogenous depression. The Research Diagnostic Criteria (Spitzer, Endicott, and Robins, 1978) require (a) the depressed mood be perceived as distinctly dif-ferent from the kind of feeling a patient would have following the death of someone close, (b) there is a lack of reactivity to environmen-tal changes, (c) the mood is worse in the morning than in the evening, or (d) there is a pervasive loss of interest or pleasure. Other symptoms that are not so discriminating are feelings of self-reproach, early-morning awakening, psychomotor retardation or agitation, poor ap-petite, weight loss, and decreased sexual drive or some loss of interest in sex.

The criteria in the third edition and revised third edition of the *Diagnostic and Statistical Manual of Mental Disorders* (*DSM-III and DSM-III-R;* American Psychiatric Association, 1980, 1987) are rather simi-lar. The *DSM-III* requires a loss of pleasure in all or almost all activities and a lack of reactivity as well as series of other symptoms. The *DSM-III-R* does not give special status to any of the symptoms, as do the two previous sets of criteria. The *DSM-III-R* requires at least five of the following: loss of interest or pleasure in all or almost all activities, lack of reactivity, depression worse in the morning, early-morning awakening, psychomotor retardation or agitation, significant anorexia or weight loss, no significant personality disturbance before the first major depressive episode, one or more previous major depressive episodes followed by complete or nearly complete recovery, and previous good response to specific antidepressant therapy.

One should note that, for the first time, one of the criteria is of a different quality—the requirement that no significant personality disturbance existed before the first major depressive episode. In this sense the *DSM-III-R* is somewhat similar to the Newcastle Endogenous Depression Diagnostic Index, which attempts to divide depressive illness into endogenous and neurotic types. This scale allows one to make the endogenous-neurotic differentiation and gives weights to various symptoms. Such findings as no precipitating factors, a distinct quality of mood, weight loss, presence of a previous episode, abnormal psychomotor activity, nihilistic delusions, and guilt weigh in on the side of endogenous depression; other findings, such as inadequate personality, anxiety, and blaming others, suggest a neurotic depression. Davidson et al. (1984) tested the validity and reliability of the Newcastle Endogenous Depression Diagnostic Index. A scale similar to the Newcastle scale has been published by Feinberg and Carroll (1982). In addition to the positive symptom weights for endogenous depression, there is one negative weight, the lack of precipitating factors. The presence of precipitating factors weighs for the nonendogenous and against the endogenous diagnosis.

Thus there are a variety of possibilities for dichotomizing depressions into endogenous versus nonendogenous or neurotic types. Numerous studies have been accomplished and numerous findings reported on how efficient these sets of diagnostic criteria are in making the separation. Such efficiency depends not only on a variety of clinical variables but also on some laboratory findings. The two biologic variables that have been most associated with classification in the affective disorders are the dexamethasone suppression test (DST) and a series of findings that occur during sleep. These sleep variables include rapid eye movement (REM) latency.

In the overnight DST, patients receive 1 mg of dexamethasone at 11:30 P.M. Blood samples for plasma cortisol determination are obtained at 8:00 A.M., 4:00 P.M., and 11:00 P.M. the following day. Often the test is performed in such a way that only the 4:00 P.M. blood drawing is used. A plasma cortisol value of 5 μg/dl or higher the next day is the cutting point for abnormal nonsuppression (Carroll et al., 1981). Normal controls with no psychiatric diagnosis usually show postdexamethasone plasma cortisol concentrations below 5 μg/dl. Of 70 controls, this was found to be true in 67 (96%). An abnormal nonsuppression was found in 2% of patients diagnosed as definitely nonmelancholic, in 21% of patients meeting the Research Diagnostic Criteria for probable melancholia, and in 50% of patients who met the criteria for definite melancholia. Within the nonmelancholic group, there were 100 patients with nonendogenous depression and 53 with miscellaneous other psychiatric disorders, such as schizophrenia, personality disorders, and neuroses. Thus, in Carroll et al.'s hands the DST performed very well and identified a group of patients with endogenous depression. Zimmerman et al. (1985) explored a series of definitions for endogenous depression and found that patients with endogenous depression defined according to *DSM-III* and the Newcastle scale had a significantly higher rate of nonsuppression than nonendogenous depressive patients, but this was not true if one used the Research Diagnostic Criteria and Feinberg-Carroll criteria. Using the Research Diagnostic Criteria in particular, 33% of the non-endogenous depressive patients were nonsuppressors, 32% of the patients with probable endogenous depression were nonsuppressors, and 36% of patients with definite endogenous depression were nonsuppressors. One of the things that should be considered is the fact that the same criteria used by different groups of investigators may not always identify the same patients.

In an extensive review, Arana, Baldesarini, and Ornsteen (1985) assessed the DST for diagnosis and prognosis in psychiatry. Though the emphasis of their study was on the practical use of the DST for patient care, their data are quite relevant to the use of the DST in diagnosis and classification. The overall sensitivity (true positive rate or nonsuppression among those with index diagnosis) was 44.1% in a total of 5,111 cases with major depressive illness. The DST distinguished between major and minor (dysthymic disorder) depression quite significantly. The sensitivity for dysthymic disorder (which bears a marked relationship to the concept of neurotic depression) was 22.9%, approximately half that for major depressive disorder. These data suggest that the sensitivity is quite different for the two types of depression, and one may be confident of the test in separating subgroups for research purposes. The specificity of the test (defined as a true-negative rate, or suppression among those lacking the index diagnosis, or false-positive rate minus 100%) was also encouraging. The specificity or normal suppression among dysthymic disorders was 77%. Interestingly, the specificity of the DST was high in distinguishing patients with major depression from normal persons with bereavement (Das and Berrios, 1984). One may assume from the evaluation of the data that the DST is a usable test in diagnosis and classification. This finding suggests that bereavement, which is often accompanied by a full panoply of symptoms of depression, is rarely associated with an abnormal test. Carroll (1982) reported that for inpatients with melancholia, sensitivity was 67% (two-thirds of the patients diagnosed as having endogenous depression gave a positive DST). Specificity was 96%. Rush et al. (1980) showed a sensitivity (proportion abnormal) of 38% and a specificity (proportion of nonendogenous depressive patients who tested normal) of 94%. In another presentation of their data, Giles and Rush (1982) evaluated 55 patients with endogenous depression and found that 44% were nonsuppressors. Of 95 patients with nonendogenous depression, only 4% were nonsuppressors. One may conclude that although not all studies agree with the separation of endogenous and neurotic depression by the use of the DST, most do, and it is a useful and important addition to our efforts in classification.

The other major laboratory test that has been used to evaluate different kinds of depression involves electroencephalographic sleep variables. Kupfer et al. have pioneered research in this area (1985). Such sleep abnormalities as decreased slow-wave sleep activity (Stages 3 and 4), reduced REM latency (minutes of sleep until the onset of the first REM), and altered REM sleep activity have been reported by these investigators. There is a highly significant difference between depressive and normal subjects on the basis of these variables. In particular, REM latency in minutes was 45.8 minutes for a group of depressive subjects as opposed to 73.4 minutes for a group of normal subjects. The separation of subtypes of depression by the use of sleep variables has been investigated by Giles et al. (1987b). Patients with endogenous depression were separated from those with nonendogenous depression using the Research Diagnostic Criteria. Reduced REM latency was clearly higher in those with endogenous depression. Interestingly enough, the DST was also used in this study, and it too separated endogenous from nonendogenous depression. In general, the two tests tend to vary together. In REM latency, the patients with definite endogenous depression measured 55.5 minutes and those with nonendogenous depression measured 79.6 minutes. Patients with definite endogenous depression had a DST response of 5.0 µg/dl and those with nonendogenous depression, 1.9 µg/dl. The REM latency had better resolving power on a statistical basis in this particular study than did the DST for the differentiation of definite endogenous from nonendogenous depression.

In keeping with the above findings, Thase, Kupfer, and Ulrich (1986) evaluated 27 psychotic and 79 nonpsychotic major depressive patients. Psychotic depressive patients were more likely to have extremely short sleep-onset REM latencies, and sleep in psychotic de-

pressive patients was characterized by increased wakefulness and decreased REM activity. Psychotic depression has often been used as a
synonym for endogenous depression, though not invariably. In any
event, psychotic depression and endogenous depression appear similar in terms of the sleep variables and quite different from the variables in nonendogenous or nonpsychotic depression.

This review of classifications has focused mainly on separation into
dichotomous groups. It would appear there was much that was valid
in the early studies, even though they were not perfect and may have
had considerable diagnostic impurities. However, from modern research, it is clear that we have a series of clinical differences as well as
some useful laboratory tests.

Some Principles in the Further Classification
of Unipolar Disorders

In Chapters 9 through 13, an effort is made to classify appropriately
the different types of unipolar depressions. A few precepts should be
kept in mind when reading those chapters. First, even though some of
the older contributions were based on erroneous circumstances (lack
of separation of bipolar and unipolar disorders), it is quite possible
that they contributed a great deal to the evolution of our current
thinking. It is not as if our current knowledge of the affective disorders in psychiatry arose like the phoenix from the ashes of poor
methodology and poor knowledge and flowered to its full plumage in
the last few years. Instead, there has been a slow accretion of knowledge and findings, and what we know today was partially known
before. The researchers of the past must be credited with having
made significant contributions and setting the stage for our current
understanding.

Another point that should be made concerns the use of language in
psychiatry. Currently there seems to be some feeling that if we change
the words we will have changed the subject for the better. By tinkering
with terminology, we have gone from neurotic or reactive depression
to dysthymia. In fact, most psychiatrists knew neurotic depression for
what it was, a depression that occurred in the context of considerable
personal instability. This concept and this term existed long before
the advent of defense mechanisms or the idea that anxiety was prevented or partially prevented by the symptoms of depression. Changing the word has not changed the problem; nor has it solved the
problem. Perhaps less effort to deal with words and more effort to
deal with data would be useful, particularly in classification.

One concept that might be important in the classification of the unipolar disorders is the idea of a generic classification versus a specific entity. Nowhere is this better noted than in the studies on "neurotic depression" (see Figure 3.1). It is possible that a definition of neurotic depression will fit a number of different kinds of illnesses but that these illnesses may be quite separate. Thus, one may note that one illness under neurotic depression is depression-spectrum disease, an illness that is defined by a familial background. The other is a depression secondary to a variety of psychiatric disorders (antisocial personality, anxiety disorders, somatization disorders, or substance abuse disorders). Secondary depression is defined not by a family background but rather by the timing of which came first, the depression or the primary psychiatric illness that is not depressive in nature. The simple fact that both meet the generic criterion may not be so important as the fact that each is different from the other and thus may deserve different status as regards classification and treatment.

In the present classification considerable credence is given to the concept of a familial classification of unipolar disorders. Such a classification depends on the idea that different kinds of depression have different kinds of family backgrounds. In our classification, depressions are divisible into three familial subtypes. The first is depression-spectrum disease, which is an ordinary depression seen in an individual who has a family history of alcoholism and/or antisocial personality. Such an individual may also have a family history of depression but does not have a family history of mania. The second type is familial pure depressive disease. This would include persons with an ordinary depression who have a family history of depression only. Such individuals have no family history of alcoholism, antisocial personality, or mania. The third type is sporadic depressive disease. An individual with sporadic depression has typical depression but has no family history of depression, mania, alcoholism, or antisocial personality. Considerable effort is made to define these familial subtypes in the present classification.

Equally important is the concept of secondary depression. A secondary depression is a depression that occurs sometime after the onset of another medical or psychiatric disorder. Thus a secondary depression might occur after the onset of an anxiety disorder, alcoholism, schizophrenia, or anything else, for that matter. It is to be differentiated from a primary depression, for which an individual cannot meet criteria for any other diagnosis except an affective diagnosis in the past. Thus, a person with a primary depression may have a series of depressive illnesses but never show a preexisting anxiety disorder or somatization disorder. A person with secondary depression, however, may show a preexisting somatization disorder or anxiety disorder and develop a depression in the course of this. The distinction between primary and secondary depression, like the familial classification, is crucial to the present classification.

Probably for the first time in the history of psychiatry we have come to the point where we may be able to use some laboratory tests in helping us resolve issues of classification. This seems appropriate because some of the laboratory tests, as noted earlier in this chapter, do separate out subgroups of depressive illness. No doubt over time there will be more tests, but the current tests provide us with a reasonable starting point. The presence of abnormal biologic findings suggests that some or all affectively disordered patients may have some kind of biologic background. This is strengthened by the findings in the genetic realm. In a sense, then, it is possible that all disorders are "organic," but certainly not in the sense that there is cerebral pathology in all cases. It is this point that generally differentiates the organic affective syndromes from the other syndromes that have similar clinical pictures at times. Of course, the demonstration of a cerebral pathology may depend on a method of detection we have not yet discovered. The unequivocal finding of abnormally large lateral ventricles in schizophrenia occurred after the development of new brain-imaging techniques. The ventricular abnormality had been noted years before by the use of pneumoencephalography but had been poorly accepted.

Finally, we need to recognize that the moment of truth in classification comes when we have some etiologic variables to put into the equation. The present classification depends heavily on family background and possible genetic factors. These, of course, exist long before the onset of the illness and therefore, by definition, must be considered to be related to etiologic factors. Further, in some cases there are diagnoses that are dependent on preexisting personal behavior and personality. These also exist prior to the onset of the depressive episode and therefore also must be considered as having at least some relationship to etiology. In the same way, life stresses, precipitating factors, life events may also account for producing some kinds of affective syndromes. All of these things—the family or genetic background, the premorbid personal behavior, and the presence of overwhelming precipitating factors—give us an opportunity to classify according to etiology rather than clinical picture. Syphilis of the central nervous system or general paresis manifests itself by a certain set of symptoms, and these symptoms are different from those of syphilitic aortitis. Nevertheless, the etiology is the same though the anatomical location is different. If we classified on the basis of specific syndromes, syphilitic aortitis and general paresis would be separate diseases. If we classify on the basis of a known etiologic factor, they are simply different manifestations of the same disease. This illustrates the need for classification by etiology, if possible.

III
The Classification

6   Induced Manias and Depressions
(Organic Affective Syndromes)

Manias and depressions may occur as secondary to either brain disorders or general medical diseases that affect brain function. These affective syndromes are secondary to the medical or neurologic illness, but they are not secondary simply in timing: they must have been caused by the preexisting medical condition in some biologic fashion. We call these *induced affective states*. These states might be caused by a number of medical and cerebral diseases, such as malnutrition, infection, tumor, or abnormal metabolism; injury to the brain; drugs (both as a toxic response as well as a response to drug or alcohol withdrawal); cerebrovascular insult; or possible environmental changes.

The diagnosis of such syndrome is classified in the *Diagnostic and Statistical Manual of Mental Disorders (Third Edition-Revised (DSM-III-R)* as "organic affective syndrome" (American Psychiatric Association, 1987). The criteria include a prominent and persistent depressed or elevated or expansive mood and evidence from the medical workup (history, physical examination, and laboratory tests) that leads to the judgment that a specific organic illness may be etiologically related to the affective change.

The subject of induced affective syndromes is quite broad, and an excellent and exhaustive review of cerebral disturbances leading to psychiatric syndromes and symptoms, both affective and otherwise, has been provided by Lishman (1983); this book is a major contribution, an encyclopedic account of organic brain syndromes of all sorts. Because our interest is mainly in classification, it behooves us to prove that organic brain syndromes can lead to depression and/or mania and to discuss the differentiation of induced affective states from other kinds of affective states. Often there will be overlap, and one will not be able to make a clear decision as to whether the mania or depression is the result of a medical or cerebral illness or occurs independently. Most of the time, however, this is not a major problem.

Induced Depression

Most studies of depression associated with cerebral disease or the influence on brain function of a systemic disease do not give the clinical symptomatology in much detail. Ordinarily, patients are noted to be "depressed" with a scattering of some of the symptoms that are generally associated with an ordinary autonomous depression. Some studies use rating scales that have been used to characterize depression, for example, the Hamilton Depression Rating Scale (Hamilton, 1967); these scales assess the severity of the depression in terms of a specific numerical quantity.

Huber, Paulson, and Shuttleworth (1988) studied a group of 60 patients with Parkinson's disease. All were taking levodopa-carbidopa therapy for their clinical symptomatology. Nineteen patients were considered to have a significant depression and 41 a mild depression. The rating of severity was on the basis of the Hamilton Depression Rating Scale. The severity of the depressive symptoms was not related to any of the parkinsonism characteristics. However, those 19 patients who had a significant depression, that is, met systematic criteria (*DSM-III*; American Psychiatric Association, 1980), had more severe bradykinesia and greater rigidity. Those patients who had mild depression, that is, did not meet the criteria for the diagnosis, were significantly more likely to have tremor. Those patients with a significant depression were also more likely to be taking levodopa-carbidopa for a longer period of time and in higher dosage. This study shows the complex relationships in affective disorder related to a cerebral disease. Although some studies found that the severity of the depression increased with the severity of Parkinson's disease, this study found a relationship to specific subgroups, those with rigidity or bradykinesia. Furthermore, whereas other studies have indicated that there is no relationship, this study showed a relationship between treatment and depression.

There is always the possibility that the disability of Parkinson's disease creates a reactive depression, but there is an equal possibility that the actual pathophysiology of the disease manifests itself by a depressive syndrome.

Mayeux (1988) studied 56 consecutive patients with Parkinson's disease and found that 40% had a major depression or a milder dysthymic disorder. These patients showed sleep disturbance, fatigue, psychomotor retardation, loss of self-esteem, and guilt more prominently than did the nondepressed Parkinson's patients. He found that cerebral spinal fluid 5-hydroxyindole acetic acid (5-HIAA) was lower in depressed than in the nondepressed parkinsonism patients and that those with major depression had the greatest reduction. The reduced 5-HIAA correlated with psychomotor retardation and loss of self-esteem. These metabolic findings led Mayeux to give the serotonin precursor 5-hydroxy-tryptophane in an open trial. It reduced the severity of the depression and produced no adverse effects of the Parkinson's disease.

Cushing's syndrome is the result of increased production of cortisol by the adrenal gland. Of 29 patients with Cushing's syndrome Cohen (1980) reported that 25 (86%) were significantly depressed. Seven of these were mildly depressed with a lowering of mood but no other symptoms. Thirteen were moderately depressed with symptoms that included tearfulness, irritability, hypochondriasis, sleeplessness, and occasionally depersonalization. Five patients were severely depressed. One of these had attempted suicide and one had depressive delusions. There was no consistent relationship between the severity of depression and the level of circulating cortisol. Of 15 depressed patients with adrenal hyperplasia causing hypercortisolism, 12 had a bilateral adrenalectomy. In 11 of these, the depression remitted, sometimes within a few days, usually within a few weeks; occasionally as long as a year elapsed before there was complete clearing. Cohen pointed out that because the depressive symptoms were ameliorated by the removal of the adrenals, a substance produced by them must be responsible for the depression. Nevertheless, because the depressive symptoms were not related to the plasma cortisol, it seemed unlikely that the cortisol itself was the responsible agent.

Kelly, Checkley, and Bender (1980) compared 15 patients with active Cushing's syndrome with 15 other patients who had been successfully treated for Cushing's syndrome and 13 patients with other pituitary tumors. Those with active Cushing's syndrome were significantly more depressed on the Hamilton Depression Rating Scale than were other patients.

Hudson et al. (1987) evaluated 16 patients with Cushing's disease, all of whom had pituitary adenoma documented by computerized tomography or histology. They compared these patients with a control group who had rheumatoid arthritis ($n = 14$). The patients with Cushing's disease had a lifetime prevalence rate of 81% for a major affective disorder, which was significantly greater than the rate of 14% among the patients with rheumatoid arthritis. The diagnoses were made by using *DSM-III* criteria for a major depression or bipolar disorder. Five of the 16 patients had bipolar disorder and 9 had major depression. The risk of morbidity for major affective disorder among the first-degree relatives of the patients with Cushing's disease was 9.7% and for the first-degree relatives of the patients with arthristis, 4.8%. This was not a significant difference. First degree relatives of patients with major depression showed a far higher risk of morbidity, 23.9%. The difference in risk of morbidity between first-degree relatives of Cushing's disease patients and first-degree relatives of the patients with major depression was significant.

One may conclude that an induced affective disorder, usually depression but sometimes mania, occurs in patients with Cushing's syndrome or Cushing's disease.

An unusual etiology for depression in the United States is famine. Basta (1988) made some clinical observations in the Sudan during the 1984–1986 famine. He noted that as the famine worsened, several women fell into what could only be described as a serious clinical depression. Some of these Nomadic women refused to feed or care for their children, and their personal habits broke down. It would be difficult to determine the actual cause of the depression in this circumstance because these women were displaced, were starving, and had endocrine changes. Nevertheless, this may well be a case of an induced depression.

Neurosyphilis manifests itself by depressive symptoms relatively frequently (Dewhurst, 1969; Lishman, 1983). Depression was a major aspect in 27% of patients with general paresis. Only an organic brain syndrome was more frequent than depression in patients with paresis. Such depressed patients who have neurosyphilis are usually retarded, are sometimes suicidal, and may manifest melancholia as well as nihilistic delusions and agitative symptoms (Dewhurst, 1969; Lishman, 1983).

Depressive symptomatology is common in brain tumors. Chambers (1955) reported on eight noninstitutionalized cases that he saw as a neurosurgeon. These patients had a wide range of symptomatology, including depressive symptoms. He pointed out that brain tumors can present as agitated depression and involutional psychosis. In fact, Larson (1940) reported that in a survey of 2,000 autopsies of one mental hospital there was a 3.45 incidence of brain tumors. Larson also cited a smaller series with a 13.5 incidence of intracranial tumor; of these, meningioma accounted for 20% to 30% of the group. Such autopsy studies are not specific for a diagnosis of depressive syndrome, but it is clear from the case reports that such syndromes do occur in conjunction with space-occupying lesions.

Research has shown that major depression is common after a stroke. Lipsey et al. (1986) compared 43 patients who had a poststroke major depression with 43 patients who had a major depression without a known medical cause. The groups looked quite similar in such items as general anxiety, affective flattening, agitation, ideas of reference, lack of energy, worrying, and irritability. However, the poststroke patients were different on some variables. Poststroke depressive patients had more slowness and underactivity, slow speech, muteness, and restriction of quantity of speech than the non-poststroke depressions (69% vs. 30%). Also, lack of interest and concentration was less frequent in the poststroke group (70% vs. 98%). Generally, the two types of depression were quite similar.

Subsequent research by the same group (Starkstein, Robinson, and Price, 1988) compared stroke patients who had major depression with those who did not become depressed, controlling for the size and location of the lesion. The depressed patients had greater cognitive impairment. Also, subcortical atrophy, which likely preceded the stroke lesion, might have produced a vulnerability for depression after the stroke. It is possible that the location of the lesion may play some role in mood changes in stroke patients. Depression and vegetative symptoms were found in 15 of 28 patients with left-sided stroke injury compared with 2 of 20 with right-sided injury; those with right-sided injury were more likely to have inappropriate cheerfulness, (7 of 20 vs. 0 of 28). Also, left-sided anterior lesions were more likely to have associated depressive symptoms than were left-sided posterior lesions. Twenty-five percent of left-sided patients with major depression had met *DSM-III* criteria and 60% of those who had their left lesions in the anterior region had a depression that met the criteria (Robinson et al., 1983).

Not all studies have supported the lesion location in depression. Sinyor et al. (1986) attempted a replication of the lesion location in poststroke depression but was unable to do this. They did, however, find a negative linear relationship between the severity of the depression and the distances of the lesion from the frontal pole in left-hemisphere patients, although this association was only a trend.

A most specific kind of depressive response occurs when an individual is detoxified from alcohol. In any common disease, such as alcoholism, there will be a chance association with another common disease, for example, primary affective disorder, an affective disorder that stands by itself and has no psychiatric or medical disease preceding it. Winokur, Rimmer, and Reich (1971) presented data suggesting that about 12% of alcoholic patients admitted to a psychiatric hospital also had a diagnosis of primary affective disorder. This finding suggests that two diseases may coexist but does not tell us anything about what happens when a person is detoxified. Keeler, Taylor, and Miller

(1979) studied 35 male alcoholic patients. They used a variety of rating scales (the Hamilton Depression Rating Scale, the Zung Self-Rating Scale, and the Minnesota Multiphasic Personality Inventory) as well as clinical diagnosis. Depression varied according to what instrument was used to evaluate the detoxifying patients. Thus for clinical diagnosis, 8.6% showed a depression; for the Hamilton Depression Rating Scale, 28%; for the Minnesota Multiphasic Personality Inventory, 43%; and for the Zung Self-Rating Scale, 66%. The scales do not make diagnoses, but rather itemize symptoms. It seems clear that depressive symptomatology occurs very frequently after the individual is brought into the hospital and detoxified from alcohol. The highest percentages of those suffering from depression are those who rate themselves as depressed.

Another study on the depression accompanying the alcohol withdrawal syndrome was conducted by Borg and Weinholdt (1982). They too used a rating scale for such symptoms as anxiety, depression, restlessness, and tremor. As part of their evaluation of depressive symptomatology, they assessed sleep, retardation/agitation, death wishes, and lack of interest. They studied 60 severely alcoholic patients using this kind of symptom checklist. What is interesting is that they also treated 28 of the patients with bromocriptine, a dopamine agonist, and found the treated patients did better than 24 patients who received a placebo. The most profound effect was on the depressive symptomatology and the anxiety. In the placebo group, there was a striking decrease in symptomatology in about 10 days. However, the treated group had a more significant decrease in symptomatology, and the decrease occurred more quickly. Thus in the Borg and Weinholdt (1982) study we have a syndrome that was studied using the characteristics mentioned in Table 3.1. There are data on symptoms, on follow-up and time required to improve, and on treatment. To this one may add the fact that there was a significant increase in serum prolactin in the placebo-treated patients. Thus there were some laboratory tests that might be used to define the alcohol withdrawal syndrome. Brown and Schuckit (1988) studied 191 alcoholic patients who were brought into the hospital for treatment of their alcoholism. Using the Hamilton Depression Rating Scale to evaluate depressive symptomatology, they found that 42% of the patients had significant levels of depression at intake but only 6% remained clinically depressed at Week 4. Interestingly, the largest reduction in symptoms occurred at Week 2, in general agreement with Borg and Weinholdt's findings. Though there are only a few studies on depression and withdrawal, they conform very well to the medical model and suggest a rather specific depressive syndrome.

If an induced affective disorder or depression bears some relationship to a spontaneously occurring depression, the consequences should be rather similar. This is, of course, an argument by analogy, implying that if two kinds of depression have similar consequences, they must, in fact, bear some relationship to each other. The data on suicide are relevant to this particular argument. Considerable data support the idea that suicide is a common sequela or consequence of a depressive illness (Murphy, 1986). In a review of six studies, Murphy noted that the syndrome of depression was relevant in 49% of the cases. He remarked that an episode of depression is a significant precursor of suicide, and with or without the existence of another illness such a depression shows a "lethal potential."

A number of medical and cerebral illnesses show an association with suicide. Henriksen, Juul-Jensen, and Lund (1970) evaluated a group of epileptic patients and the cause of death as ascertained from death certificates. These investigators found that among 2,763 patients the suicide rate was 2.5 to 3 times the expected number. They excluded patients with other diseases that might have reduced life expectancy and found that 20% of the deaths were due to suicide, 3 times the expected rate. Achté and Anttinen (1963) showed that after head injury the expectancy of suicide increased a great deal. The head-injured patients studied by these investigators had considerable interpersonal problems and abused alcohol, and this boded poorly for the future. In Achté, Hillbom, and Aalberg's (1967) study, 41% of patients with war injuries affecting the brain who had committed suicide had done so during a depressive psychosis. Achté and Anttinen (1963) noted that more than half of the patients who committed suicide had been psychotic in the past and that a change of character had occurred in more than 40%. The same circumstance applies to patients with Huntington's chorea. Bickford and Ellison (1953) collected data on 21 patients, 5 of whom showed depression. Three of the 5 showed a depression before the chorea. The authors remarked that suicide might occur before the development of the dementia or the chorea.

The association of a known brain disorder with depression is well described by Folstein et al. (1983) in their study of the association of affective disorder and Huntington's disease. Of 88 patients with Huntington's disease, 36 had a major affective illness. Of the 36, 8 were bipolar and 28 were unipolar. The lifetime prevalence rate for affective disorder among the patients was 41%. What is most interesting is that the affective symptoms preceded the chorea and dementia in 23 out of 34 cases, and this precedence was noted to occur by an average of 5.1 years. In 6 cases, there was concurrent affective illness and chorea; in 5 cases the affective illness followed the chorea. The reason the timing is so important is that it would be easy to ascribe the depression as a response to a debilitating and potentially fatal illness, but this seems unlikely in the Folstein et al. study because the affective symptoms occurred so much earlier than the chorea and dementia symptoms. Of the 36 patients who had a major affective illness, 20 had suicidal thoughts or attempts. The authors evaluated the patients' family histories and noted that Huntington's disease and affective illness bred true. In other words, those patients who had Huntington's disease and affective disorder had family members who showed a similar association, whereas families who had only Huntington's disease were less likely to show the association with affective disorder. These findings suggested to the authors that there was either a close link between affective disorder and Huntington's disease or possibly genetic heterogeneity, with some kind of Huntington's disorder showing affective disorder as well. The importance of this study cannot be overestimated. It shows a clear and unequivocal association between depression and an illness of the brain that cannot easily be ascribed to a simple psychologic response to a severe illness.

Any discussion of induced depression runs the risk of inducing boredom. This is because such a discussion is ordinarily little more than a stodgy list of references and findings compiled in a vain attempt to be complete. Within a year, new findings will almost certainly make for obsolescence. To write a complete review of induced affective disorder would no doubt take hundreds of pages, and, in fact, the best part of this work has been done already by Lishman (1983). To prevent the encroachment of stodginess and boredom in our present attempt, we propose making use of the vast amount of information that is available by a comparative study of induced depressions. Some of the depressions are induced by systemic diseases, others by specifically located tumors and injuries, others by withdrawal, and others by brain lesions that are related to specific loci or areas. It would appear that a useful next step might be to compare the various kinds of syndromes, taking into account their particular qualities. Table 6.1 presents a model for the comparative study of induced affective disorders. No doubt such data as have been noted above on alcoholism withdrawal and on Huntington's disease might lend themselves to comparative evaluations. However, by using the localizing information or the particular systemic abnormality, we may be able to shed some light on the pathophysiology of depression. Whether this would have some relevance to a spontaneously occurring depression is difficult to say, but only after such comparative study would we be able to make that kind of assessment.

Table 6.1. A Model for the Comparative Study of Induced Depressions

Symptom	Systemic (Cushing's Syndrome)	Tumor (Specific Location)	Stroke (Specific Location)	Withdrawal (Alcoholism)	Cerebral Lesion (Parkinson's Syndrome)
Depressed affect					
Decreased sleep					
Anorexia					
Fatigue					
Guilt					
Retardation					
Agitation					
Delusional guilt					
Other delusions					
Suicidal					
Decreased con- centration					
Acute onset					
Chronic or re- mitting course					
Family history of depression					
Impaired senso- rium					

Induced Mania

Many of the same points made above about induced depression might also be made about mania, but the problem is simple. Mania is less common than depression. There are no data that strongly support the idea of a reactive mania (Winokur, Clayton, and Reich, 1969). Thus the idea of a psychologic response to a difficult life situation (e.g., a major crisis) that would result in a manic episode seems implausible.

Winokur, Clayton, and Reich (1969) evaluated the idea of an induced mania. They noted that a common clinical picture in general paresis or syphilis of the brain included euphoria, expansiveness, and grandiosity. These rather typical manic symptoms, however, occurred in the presence of an organic brain syndrome with memory difficulties, disturbances of consciousness, and deteriorating judgment. It was estimated that about 40% of the patients with general paresis showed an accompanying euphoria or expansiveness together with a dementia. Here then is a clear and unequivocal organic illness that shows a mania, is caused by the *Treponema pallidum,* manifests itself by atrophy in the frontal, temporal, and parietal regions of the brain. The brain destruction is so extensive that it would be difficult to specify areas that might be involved in the production of manic symptomatology.

Winokur, Clayton, and Reich (1969) went on to evaluate other kinds of induction of manic states. Oppler (1950) presented the case of a young man with a parasagittal meningioma demonstrating clear manic behavior. This patient improved after an operation. At the time of admission, he was admitted to a veterans hospital with hypomanic behavior and occasional confusion. Stern and Dancey (1942) reported a patient with a glioma of the diencephalon who manifested a prolonged attack of mania. In a review of the literature, Stern and Dancey also suggested that manic attacks are seen in tumors near the base of the brain, rather than in tumors affecting the hemispheres. Oppler, reviewing previous literature, pointed out that any mechanical stimulation of the anterior section of the hypothalamus might produce a manic picture. Starkstein, Boston, and Robinson (1988) described 12 patients who developed mania after vascular, traumatic, or neoplastic brain lesion. Five were female and 7 were male. All patients showed elation, 9 of 12 showed hyperactivity, and 8 of 12 showed pressure of speech that appeared in temporal conjunction with the brain insult. Six patients had a positive psychiatric family history. Some patients showed only mania, whereas others cycled between depression and mania. Five of 6 patients on lithium showed a response. The lesions were located primarily in the right hemisphere in the orbitofrontal and basotemporal cortex, head of caudate, and thalamus, which locations are in limbic or limbic-related areas that are connected to the frontal lobes. Upon reviewing the literature, these researchers pointed out that the previous reports also favored an association between right hemisphere pathology of limbic- or lubric-connected areas and induced mania. All of these statements were made on the basis of very few cases and cannot be taken as the final word, but they are certainly interesting and could be true.

Hunter, Blackwood, and Bull (1968) described three patients with meningiomas at different frontal sites. Apathy, incontinence, dementia, and fits were seen in association with middle and superior frontal lesions. The authors said the symptoms might be mistaken for those of either depression or presenile cerebral atrophy. Alternatively, excitement and hallucinosis were seen in association with a basal frontal lesion. This lesion might mimic psychotic symptoms such as hypomania. The authors thought this might be particularly significant if the tumor encroached on the third ventricle and the adjacent structures.

Krauthammer and Klerman (1978) discussed manic syndromes associated with antecedent physical illness or drugs. Though they called this kind of syndrome a "secondary mania," the quality of their cases specifically suggests an induced mania. Thus the studies reviewed by Krauthammer and Klerman mainly concerned cases in which drugs, metabolic disturbances, or infection might have influenced the brain or in which brain lesions were involved (e.g., neoplasm of the brain or epilepsy). In this extremely useful article the authors described manias that occurred in conjunction with steroids, monoamine oxidase inhibitors, levodopa, hemodialysis, influenza, acute fever, and encephalitis. As regards the more localized lesions, mania was associated with right temporal lobe epilepsy and with a variety of neoplasms. The authors evaluated what family history was available in the various reports and noted that in the cases of "secondary mania" (what we prefer to call "induced mania"), there was a lack of association with a positive family history of affective disorder. This suggests that mania that is induced is qualitatively different from mania that occurs spontaneously and is associated with a positive family history for both mania and depression (Winokur, Clayton, and Reich, 1969).

Cook and his collaborators (Cook, Shukla, and Hoff, 1986; Cook et al., 1987) have studied the question of mania with associated organic factors in some depth. They matched 39 patients with bipolar illness who had had a preceding organic insult with 39 nonorganic or spontaneously bipolar controls. The match was for age and sex. All patients were systematically interviewed with a structure interview. Table 6.2 shows the differences between the groups. The group that was considered to have organic bipolar disorder had prior evidence of neurologic abnormalities, abnormal electroencephalographs, head injuries, developmental delays, neuropsychologic defects, birth traumas, and medical problems such as encephalitis, brain tumors, or seizure disorders that might affect the central nervous system. As can be seen in Table 6.2, there was a notable lack of family history for affective disorder among the patients with organic affective syndromes and there was a striking lack of psychotic features during mania among the patients with organic bipolar disorder. Furthermore, personality changes occurred at the time of index admission in this group. In another study by the same group, the results suggested that the patients with organic bipolar disorder (neurologic mania) were more dysfunctional in intellect than the patients with primary or spontaneous bipolar disorder (Hoff et al., 1988). In this matched

Table 6.2. Difference between Organic Bipolar and
Spontaneous Bipolar Illness

Variable	Percentage of Patients with Organic Bipolar Illness (N = 39)	Percentage of Patients with Spontaneous Bipolar Illness (N = 39)	$p <$
Positive for family history of affective disorder	18	77	.005
First episode was mania	69	74	N.S.
Assaultive when manic	41	10	.005
Mainly irritable when manic	82	10	.005
First-rank symptoms when manic	26	54	.01
Organic personality disorder at index	54	0	.005

group of 14 patients with neurologic mania and 14 patients with
primary mania, the former were more likely to relapse (50%) than the
latter (14%). Relapse was defined as rehospitalization for an affective
episode during a four-year follow-up.

Thus an induced mania, like an induced depression, does occur
and shows certain kinds of differences from spontaneous manias. It
would be possible to construct a table similar to Table 6.1 in which we
might compare a variety of induced manias to determine whether any
specific pathophysiologies could be associated with specific clinical
aspects of the syndrome.

Up to this point, we have presented data on depressions and manias in which there is an association with a fairly clear-cut disease—
metabolic, systemic, or cerebral. However, most depressions and manias that are seen by psychiatrists do not show these kinds of associations. In fact, most of them show no clear evidence of any etiology
unless it be familial and possibly genetic or possibly reactive to a major
life stress. Thus in our classification we are dealing with psychiatric
illnesses that show a distal (e.g., familial or genetic) but not a proximal
(i.e., pathophysiologic) etiology. For appropriate studies on proximal
etiology as well as specific treatment, it is necessary to have a reasonable classification and to follow it for the investigations. In the case of
the induced depressions, it is not unreasonable to assume that oblit-
eration of the underlying systemic or cerebral disease should alleviate
the affective syndrome. In most of the diseases or illnesses that are

discussed in the following chapters, the underlying pathology or im-mediate cause is unknown. However, it is necessary to address the problem of heterogeneity in the affective disorders in order to gain knowledge of pathology or cause, and the following chapters make an effort to do so.

7   Manic-Depressive (Bipolar) Illness

Of all the mental afflictions that beset people, bipolar illness best deserves consideration as a specific and autonomous entity. We have already noted that there are some organic etiologies for the manic syndrome, and we may also note that there may be some heterogeneity in manic-depressive patients for whom no organic etiology is obvious. However, in general, most of the patients who manifest the bipolar syndrome appear to be manifesting a specific disease. Because of this, it is the one major psychiatric illness in psychiatry that lends itself very well to a classification based on the medical model. Thus, the following description addresses itself to the clinical picture, epidemiology, premorbid personality, family history, course of the illness, and response to treatment.

The Clinical Picture

Clinically, patients with manic-depressive (bipolar) illness show marked mood swings into either a manic syndrome or a depressive syndrome. The episodes may start with either a mania or a depression and be succeeded by the alternate state. Sometimes the patients will show a short depression, a somewhat longer mania, and a much longer depression. The symptom pictures of the depressive and manic syndromes are shown in Tables 1.1, 1.2, 2.1, and 2.2. The clinical picture has been fully described by Winokur, Clayton, and Reich (1969). Suffice to say that during the manic episode the patient may show extreme motor activity, flight of ideas, distractibility, and incessant talking to the extent of garrulousness. The patient may show delusions and, less frequently, hallucinations during the manic episode. These psychotic symptoms usually are congruent with a high or euphoric mood, but sometimes the delusions and hallucinations may be incongruent as regards their relationship to the mood. Patients may be extravagant, be assaultive, or abuse alcohol. Patients may be in constant motion and may believe themselves to have an extremely high capacity for almost any endeavor. The themes of the manic episodes are often religion, politics, business, or sex, and the delusions may be about the same kinds of subjects. Most manic patients have problems with initial insomnia as well as terminal insomnia. The duration of the manic episode from the onset of mania through admission to euthymia is around two months with modern treatment.

The depressive phase of the illness, which may precede or follow the mania or, in fact, occur independently at times (i.e., without any relation to a mania), is usually present about 3 months before hospitalization. Patients are admitted often because of delusions and hallucinations, insomnia, or alcohol abuse, but the major reasons are suicidal behavior and inability to function. Interestingly, insight is usually present at the time of admission in the depressive phase of bipolar illness. The symptoms are the usual ones that have been described before: melancholia, tearfulness, irritability, trouble concentrating, trouble thinking, psychomotor retardation, and some memory complaints. Such things as delusions and hallucinations are usually mood congruent but occasionally are mood incongruent. Most studies suggest that psychotic symptoms are less frequent during the depressive phase than during the manic phase (Black and Nasrallah, 1989; Winokur, Clayton, and Reich, 1969). Patients complain of initial insomnia and often terminal insomnia. They show marked diurnal variation, being worse in the morning. Unlike male patients in the manic phase, who drink to excess, male patients in the depressive phase have no change of any note in alcohol intake.

Epidemiology

A number of studies on the frequency of bipolar illness in the population have been conducted. In general, they tend to be modern studies, because the separation of bipolar illness from unipolar illness did not occur until 1966. However, one early study is informative. Helgason (1961, 1964) studied the frequency of psychiatric illness in Iceland. He evaluated all of the inhabitants of that country who were alive on December 1, 1910 and who had been born in Iceland during the years 1895 to 1897. There were 5,395 persons in all. These patients, of course, lived in a small country where there was a superb ability to obtain information on their medical and psychiatric status. Of the group of people at risk, there were 320 probands in the population whose diagnosis included the term "depressive." Thirty-one of these

probands had had a mania in the course of their lives (9.7%). For men
and women combined, the morbid risk for the depressive psychoses
in Iceland was 6.71%. Assuming that the age of risk for the bipolar
patients parallels that for the unipolar patients, a simple proportion
may be done and one can calculate a morbid risk for bipolar illness of
0.65%. Interestingly, these calculations come up with about the same
amount of bipolarity as is reported in the Epidemiologic Catchment
Area study accomplished in Baltimore, St. Louis, and New Haven
(Robins et al., 1984). There are some other good studies in Scan-
dinavia, but most of them do not separate the bipolar from the unipolar types of affective disorder. A study of mental illness in Samso
(Nielsen and Nielsen, 1977) used census data. The researchers were
able to get information on all but 20% of the population of that
Danish island. Eight percent of all persons in the population had what
were called "manic depressive psychoses." Unfortunately, it is not
possible to determine how many of those were unipolar depressive or
bipolar patients.

Boyd and Weissman (1981) evaluated the literature on the lifetime
risk per hundred people for bipolar disorder in a variety of places and
countries, including New Haven, New Zealand, England, Iceland,
and Denmark. The risks were 0.6%, 0.24%, 0.88%, 0.79%, and
0.61%, respectively. It should be noted that, except for the 0.24% in
New Zealand, the risks are quite comparable.

As regards the annual incidence rates for mania, Leff, Fischer, and
Bertelsen (1976) conducted a cross-national epidemiologic study of
mania. The study was carried out in London and in Aarhus, Denmark. Interestingly, the annual incidence of mania was found to be
the same in both Denmark and London (2.6 per 100,000 population).
This was somewhat surprising, because the London sample contained
a large percentage of immigrants and the Danish sample had only a
negligible number of immigrants. In London, male West Indians in
particular were overrepresented. The authors also evaluated the role
of life events in the onset of mania. They attempted to evaluate events
that were either clearly or probably independent, that is, outside the
control of the subject. About 28% to 29% of the samples experienced
an independent event in the month before the onset of mania and 5%
to 12% experienced a "possible" independent event in the same
period. These events were either pleasant or unpleasant. Thus they
were not necessarily the kinds of stresses we usually consider to be
precipitants. About 14% of the normal population experienced an
independent event three weeks before the interview. These data were
not collected systematically, but the fact that the events were outside
the control of the subject (i.e., independent) makes them of interest.

Of course, it is possible that the patient's mental state may have some influence in the amount of reporting of these events and the quality of them.

In the clinical lore surrounding bipolar illness, there has always been a view that bipolar patients have episodes in the spring and fall rather regularly. If this were true, it might have within it the seeds of some contribution to etiology or pathophysiology. Therefore, it is worthy of study. Frangos et al. (1980) studied affective episodes in Greece and found a significant seasonal variation, with peaks in the spring for both depressive and manic episodes. Parker and Walter (1982) examined the month of admission data from 1971 to 1976 in psychiatric facilities in New South Wales, Australia. They observed 1,876 manic-depressive patients in the manic phase and found a striking seasonality for mania in the spring (September to November in New South Wales). Carney, Fitzgerald, and Monaghan (1988) examined the monthly rates of admission of manic patients in Galway, Ireland, for a five-year period. They found that the admission rates for mania were higher in the sunnier months and in the months with greater average length of day. This suggests an abnormal response to light in bipolar patients. The overall seasonal pattern, as in the previous study, showed a striking peak in spring and summer with some decline in autumn and rises in winter. Thus, in both Northern and Southern Hemispheres, there appears to be an increased admission rate for mania in the spring to summer months.

Manic-depressive illness or bipolar illness may be related to high socioeconomic status (Winokur, Clayton, and Reich, 1969). Helgason (1961) studied affective disorders including both bipolar and unipolar disorders in Iceland. He found some evidence for a relationship between a higher social class and such broadly defined "manic depressive patients." Social Class I included professionals, technical workers, teachers, employers, administrative personnel, ship officers on large vessels, and some farmers. This was the highest of the three classes and also reflected education background. Broadly defined manic-depressive patients resided in this class more often than was expected.

With the separation of bipolar and unipolar illnesses, it became possible to compare social achievement between the two groups. Woodruff et al. (1971) compared the educational and occupational levels of bipolar and unipolar patients. Bipolar subjects achieved strikingly higher educational levels than unipolar subjects; similar, but less striking, results were found for the occupational data. However, the probands and their brothers appeared to be similar in occupational and educational levels, suggesting that in the bipolar families some sort of familial factor might influence both the ill probands and their well siblings to achieve higher socioeconomic status. The patients in this study came from a private hospital sample. These findings were investigated further by Monnelly, Woodruff, and Robins (1974). They found that a social advantage among bipolar patients was supported in a public hospital sample, but only if the sample had had a previous history of private hospitalization. This is an unusual finding and suggests some sort of threshold effect that is supported by the fact that some patients functioned well and then, after falling on hard times, had to go to a public hospital. Monnelly, Woodruff, and Robins concluded by offering additional evidence that social advantage was associated with bipolar illness compared with unipolar illness in private hospital populations. Obviously, there may be interaction between social factors and illness factors (e.g., a specific diagnosis). Rather than a comparison between bipolar and unipolar patients, we need a comparison among bipolar probands, their families, and the normal population. It is possible that bipolar illness does confer some kind of socioeconomic advantage, but a final decision about that is not possible at this point.

Premorbid Personality

The personality studies lack a clear indication of any differences from the normal population. What we have are comparisons between unipolar and bipolar illnesses in recent years. Winokur, Clayton, and Reich (1969) evaluated personality among 78 bipolar patients and found that 80% were considered cyclothymic or hypomanic. This seems high, but it is not possible to compare it with a group of controls. Von Zerssen (1977), in an exhaustive review of premorbid personality and affective psychoses, examined comparisons between bipolar patients and controls. He reported that, regarding melancholic-type personality characteristics (dependent, conventional, meticulous, and cautious), the bipolar group showed no significant deviation from control groups. Most interesting, however, was the fact that the bipolar patients showed no deviation from the controls in the cyclothymic kinds of personality characteristic (independent, unconventional, broadminded, imaginative, and daring).

Hirschfeld et al. (1986) compared bipolar patients, unipolar patients, and normal controls. Compared with the normal controls, the bipolar patients showed some differences on a variety of personality scales. The bipolar patients were more neurotic and less emotionally stable than the controls. This was true for both men and women. Bipolar patients showed more emotional reliance on others and lacked self-confidence more frequently than controls. However, this latter characteristic was true only for women. Bipolar women showed less extroversion than normal controls, and both male and female bipolar patients showed less ego control than controls. On a temperament scale, bipolar men showed less general activity than controls, but bipolar women were exactly the opposite, showing more general activity. Finally, in another personality inventory, bipolar women showed more "hysterical" patterns.

As can be seen, there are marked differences between men and women with the same diagnosis. One wonders whether better tests might be devised in the future to pick up personality differences. Perhaps differences in personality might be better defined in more operational terms, that is, in terms of events rather than general attitudes about oneself. Considerably more work needs to be done on personality characteristics of all kinds of affectively disordered patients, including bipolar patients.

Family History

In illness for which the etiology is unknown, a variety of findings suggest a genetic etiology or the importance of genetic factors. These include a greater frequency of the same illness in relatives of patients compared with relatives of the general population. Also, there is greater concordance in monozygotic than dizygotic twins. To this may be added the finding of an increased occurrence of the illness in adopted children of ill parents or an increase of the illness in biologic parents of adopted probands with the illness.

A number of family studies and family history studies have looked at the occurrence of affective disorder and mania in the relatives of bipolar probands. Most studies show some methodologic differences from one another. Some studies involved simply a family history obtained from a sick proband or an accompanying relative. Other studies involved a family study method, whereby all available relatives were interviewed. The family history method suffers from an excess of false negatives according to Winokur, Clayton, and Reich, (1969). Essentially it was found that by obtaining a family history, a lot of people who were considered ill by interview were considered well by family members. There was almost no false-positive error. Thompson et al. (1982) assessed the accuracy of family history data in ascertaining psychiatric disorders in relatives. They compared diagnoses based on family history with those based on direct interview. They found high specificity for the family history method, but sensitivity was generally low. This is the same as the large number of false-negative family histories found by Winokur, Clayton, and Reich. Accuracy was

Table 7.1. Familial Affective Disorder in Bipolar Probands and Controls

	Bipolar Probands			Controls		
Reference	N	Relatives with Affective Disorder (%)	Proportion of Mania in Affected Relatives (%)	N	Relatives with Affective Disorder (%)	Proportion of Mania in Affected Relatives (%)
Winokur, 1970[a]	89	27	32	—	—	—
Winokur, Tsuang, and Crowe, 1982[b]	122	14.3	11	160	7.6	3
Winokur, Tsuang, and Crowe, 1982[c]	122	3.8	66	160	0.3	0
Angst et al, 1980[d]	95	13	24	—	—	—
Gershon et al, 1982[e]	96	26.4	17	82	7.6	0

[a]Morbid risk for parents and siblings; Weinberg abridged method; risk period, 15–60 years.
[b]Morbid risk for first-degree relatives; all relatives personally interviewed; risk period, 15–59 years.
[c]Proportion of deceased relatives with a mental hospital chart.
[d]Morbid risk for parents and siblings; Stromgren method, some interviews, and some records.
[e]Lifetime risk in percentage of relatives 18 or older; interviews, records, and family history.

better for the affective disorders and alcoholism than for the less severe disorders. The high specificity of the family history method suggests that if one uses it to compare family members of probands with a control population, the results should be valid. One would expect an underestimate of the number of ill people in both groups, but because this underestimate probably is true in both cases, the two groups should be comparable. Thus one should look for patterns rather than specific amounts of illness. If, using the same methodology, a group of probands and their relatives and a group of controls and their relatives were compared, any difference might be valid in that both groups would be subject to the same kinds of error. It seems clear that, depending on the method, the absolute number of ill relatives in any group might be different but the patterns of differences might be the same as long as either the family history or the family study method was used. Of course, there may be a problem of differential reporting between patients and controls. In fact, there are always enough methodologic questions that one may never arrive at a "correct" proportion of ill family members. The best one might be able to do is to arrive at a comparison that would achieve validity.

A number of family studies of bipolar illness have been reported. Table 7.1 presents some of these and some of the methodologic differences between the studies. The numbers of affectively ill relatives of bipolar patients varies depending on the study, but the fact is that whenever it is compared with the number of affectively ill relatives of controls there is a clear difference. Thus, the patterns remain the same even though the absolute numbers change. This is also true in the proportion of mania in affected relatives. The percentage is always higher in the affectively ill relatives of bipolar probands than in the affected relatives of controls. It seems clear that there is a familial aggregation in bipolar illness and that this aggregation is true for depression as well as for mania. One of the items of note in Table 7.1 is the fact that most of the affectively ill relatives of the bipolar probands had a unipolar depression only. In all of the studies save one, mania varied between 11% and 32%. The 66% figure for mania was relevant to only hospitalized relatives who were deceased. Therefore, severity becomes a factor and probably accounts for the higher percentage of mania in the affected relatives. The modal illness in the families of bipolar probands is a depression, not a mania, but a mania is more frequent in the relatives of bipolar probands than in the relatives of any other kinds of probands in psychiatry.

Occasionally one sees patients who show only manias (unipolar manias). These are relatively uncommon. In Perris's (1966) study, 11% of probands who showed mania showed only unipolar mania.

The family history for the unipolar manic patients was essentially the same as that for the bipolar patients. This has also been found by Pfohl, Vasquez, and Nasrallah (1981, 1982). These authors found few clinically meaningful differences between patients with unipolar mania and patients with bipolar disorder on demographic, symptomatic, or familial variables. They also developed a mathematical model to predict the frequency of admission for an apparent unipolar mania, given that such patients might have the same illness as the bipolar patients. They suggested that most studies of unipolar mania were heavily contaminated by patients with unipolar manic illness because they had not yet developed a depressive episode. They concluded that unipolar mania and bipolar mania were essentially the same disorder. Certainly, in two studies (the Pfohl and Perris studies), the family history of the unipolar manic patients was essentially the same as that for bipolar manic patients.

There is an unusual sex polarity effect in bipolar illness (Winokur and Crowe, 1983). Of 14 studies that were reviewed, 13 showed more unipolar depression than mania in women; likewise, there was more unipolar depression in women than in men. If one assesses the sex and polarity of all the affectively ill relatives of bipolar patients in these studies, the following is found: manic men, 17%; depressive men, 23%; manic women, 18%; and depressive women, 42%. Essentially what we are talking about is the entire universe of the affectively ill relatives in the 14 studies. Thus, the preceding percentages add up to 100%. Why depressed women should make up the dominant proportion of the affectively ill relatives (42%) is difficult to explain. One possibility is that the studies on bipolar illness contain a contaminant, that is, a very common depressive illness seen mainly in women and only occasionally in men. This would be consistent with the general population data, in which ill female unipolar patients outnumber ill male unipolar patients by an enormous amount (Winokur, Tsuang, and Crowe, 1982). Another possible explanation is related to the idea that bipolar illness and unipolar illness are related. If bipolar illness were a more severe manifestation of affective disorder and if there were X chromosome linkage involved in bipolar illness, then the affected men might be more likely to be bipolar because they do not have a normal gene on the other X chromosome to compensate for the defective one, as women do. Thus, women would be affected more frequently and would more often have unipolar depression than would men.

In the most complete twin study that has been done in recent times, Bertelsen, Harvald, and Hauge (1977), using a Danish nationwide twin register and central psychiatric register, evaluated concordance in 27 monozygotic and 36 dizygotic bipolar twin pairs. Pairwise concordance for the monozygotic pairs varied between 74% and 96%, depending on the diagnoses of the probands. For the dizygotic twin pairs, the concordance varied between 17% and 36%. In seven cases, there was one twin member who was bipolar or manic and the other unipolar. Thus in the monozygotic twins the bipolar illness manifested itself occasionally by unipolar depression only.

Price (1968) reported on an evaluation of twin cases that he obtained from published series. Two sets of twins were monozygotic and reared apart because of early separation. In both sets, there was concordance for affective disorder. In one set there was specific concordance for bipolarity, and in the other set one member was bipolar and the other unipolar.

Like the family history, family study method, and twin studies, there is an adoption study that supports genetic transmission in manic-depressive illness. Mendlewicz and Rainer (1977) evaluated 29 bipolar adoptees, 31 bipolar nonadoptees, 22 normal adoptees, and 20 patients who had poliomyelitis. They found clear evidence of a greater degree of psychopathology and, in particular, affective illness in the biologic parents of manic-depressive adoptees than in the parents who raised those individuals: For the bipolar adoptees, 12% of the adoptive parents had an affective illness, but 31% of the biologic parents had an affective illness. The biologic parents of the bipolar nonadoptees appeared similar to the biologic parents of the bipolar adoptees, and the adoptive and biologic parents of the normal adoptees and poliomyelitic controls were similar to the adoptive parents of the bipolar adoptees. Thus there was substantial evidence of genetic transmission in this study.

One other adoption study has been published (Wender et al., 1986). The investigators studied 10 bipolar adoptees as part of a larger study of the affective disorders. Of 71 biologic relatives, 13 received a psychiatric diagnosis (18%). These diagnoses varied among a hard affective spectrum disorder, suicide, or other psychiatric diagnoses. Of 346 relatives of controls, 11% had a psychiatric diagnosis. Ten percent of the biologic relatives of the bipolar patients had a diagnosis of affective disorder. This was true for only 2.5% of the biologic relatives of controls. To put it another way, 7 (of 71) relatives of the bipolar patients had one or more diagnoses of affective disorder or suicide. This was true of only 9 (of 346) of the control relatives.

One may conclude from the family studies, the family history studies, the twin studies, and the adoption studies that there is strong evidence in favor of a genetic factor in bipolar illness. This constitutes one class of data that suggests that bipolar illness exists as a specific disease.

In recent years there have been other ways of assessing a genetic contribution to bipolar illness. The first and simpler method is by assessing association. This occurs when two genetically separate traits have a nonrandom occurrence in a population. This is probably most likely explained by a pleiotropic affect of a single gene. Peptic ulcer has long been demonstrated to be associated with type O blood, and in fact the ABO blood groups have been reported in some studies to show an association with the affective disorders. Rinieris et al. (1979) showed a positive association between bipolar affective disorder and type O blood, and a corresponding negative association between bipolar disorder and blood type A. This study was evaluated using population controls from Greece. Type O blood was seen in 56% of bipolar patients and type A blood in 26% of bipolar patients. This can be contrasted to the 31% of the type O blood in the Greek population versus the 40% of type A blood in that population. There is some question as to whether a population control is appropriate for a study of association, because by chance a subpopulation may show a different frequency of any particular kind of blood type.

Tanna and Winokur (1968) also evaluated association and the ABO blood system. They used a group of first-degree relatives as a control. Unfortunately, the probands were not separated into bipolar and unipolar groups, but the investigators did look at a group that contained affective disorder in the families as a specific subgroup. Type B blood occurred with greater frequency in the group with a family history of affective disorder than in the controls. Thus, there was a suggestion in this study that type B blood might be related to depression or manic-depressive illness or bipolar illness. However, these authors also looked at pairs of siblings with a positive family history of mania in a first-degree relative. A positive finding of concordance for illness in like blood types or discordance for illness in unlike blood types would be in favor of either linkage or association. There was no evidence for either in the group.

Finally, James, Carroll, and Haines (1977) found no evidence of any relation between bipolar affective disorder and ABO blood types. A series of human lymphocyte antigen assiciations with bipolar illness has been reported (Shapiro et al., 1976), but a subsequent study (Johnson, 1978) showed no significant differences in human lymphocyte antigens between control and experimental groups. The concept of association remains an attractive one, however. It implies that an association with another known genetic trait is really relevant to the disease being investigated. The implication is that the other genetic trait makes some contribution toward the pathophysiology of the disease. With the development of molecular genetics and the concept of the candidate gene, there may be a renewed interest in association. A positive finding would at least give some direction to the search for etiology.

Linkage is another methodology that has come to the fore in the study of bipolar illness. Linkage of two gene loci occurs when two genes, each responsible for a genetic trait, are close enough on the chromosome that they sort in a dependent fashion. Within the general population there may be no association between two specific traits, but within a family, if the gene loci are close enough, the traits will hang together. In the population the specific traits will no longer be associated because of considerable crossing over during time. A finding of positive linkage proves a genetic etiology; it tells where and on which chromosome a locus for bipolar illness might reside, offers some option for predicting who within a family might become ill, and provides clear evidence for the homogeneity of a particular type of illness.

Linkage studies started with the proposal and presentation of data in support of a possible role of an X-linked dominant factor in manic-depressive disease (Winokur and Tanna, 1969). Linkage, and more particularly X linkage to a specific marker on the X chromosome (the color blindness locus), was pursued by Reich, Clayton, and Winokur (1969). In a study of 59 bipolar probands and their families, almost twice as many female as male probands were found. There was a deficit of ill father/ill son pairs, but ill mothers had several ill sons. Two families that contained color blindness (protan and deutan) were also informative for bipolar illness. The possibility of linkage to color blindness in these two families did not seem due to chance. In these families, for each affectively ill person there was a 50 : 50 chance that person would also entertain the color blindness allele. In 11 possibilities the color blindness allele and the affective disorder were associated. Later, another ill person was added to one of the families and there became 12 concordances between the color blindness allele and the affective disorder. In this study, there were no exceptions: the specific allele was associated with the illness (Winokur, Clayton, and Reich, 1969). In a continuation of the X linkage story and specifically the X linkage with the color blindness loci, Gershon et al. (1979) were unable to replicate the earlier findings with color blindness. Such a negative finding could mean one of two things: either there is no linkage between the color blindness loci and bipolar illness or bipolar illness is genetically heterogeneous, sometimes transmitted in an

X-linked fashion and sometimes not. Risch and Baron (1982) evaluated the pooled data in the literature and showed them to be consistent with a model of genetic heterogeneity. In other words, a subgroup of pedigrees had close linkage with markers on the X chromosome and another subgroup was not linked to X chromosome markers.

Del Zompo et al. (1984) evaluated X chromosome markers in bipolar illness in Sardinia. They found two informative pedigrees and noted that the results were consistent with the hypothesis of X linkage in these families. Specifically, they looked at the protan-deutan glucose 6 phosphate dehydrogenase (G6PD) region of the X chromosome. X linkage to the G6PD locus on the X chromosome was investigated by Mendlewicz, Linkowski, and Willmotte (1980). In a multigenerational family, they found clear linkage between G6PD and bipolar illness. Further support for X linkage comes from a study of X chromosome markers in an Israeli population (Baron et al., 1987). In this study, there was highly significant evidence that color blindness and G6PD deficiency were linked to bipolar affective illness. This study was done by clinically assessing for color vision and G6PD activity in erythrocytes as determined by a spectrophotometric method. These findings support not only X linkage but also the idea that there is heterogeneity in the transmission of bipolar illness. Families where male-to-male transmission occurs could not have an X-linked type of bipolar illness. Such families have been found. At this point, the preponderance of evidence is in favor of X linkage, though some researchers still question whether it has been proven beyond the shadow of a doubt.

The focus of linkage studies has shifted from blood groups and plasma proteins to the area of molecular genetics. The molecular genetic methods, however, have attempted to analyze the segregation of restriction fragment length polymorphisms on a specific chromosome. The first positive finding with this method was in favor of a dominant gene that conferred a predisposition to manic-depressive disease, this gene being located near the end of the short arm of chromosome 11 (Egeland et al., 1987). The marker gene was that of Harvey ras-1. The study was done on a very large kindred in the Amish.

Attempts to replicate that finding have not been successful. Detera-Wadleigh et al. (1987) studied three families in North America. Their results indicated an absence of linkage between affective disorder and the insulin gene-Harvey ras-1 region in those pedigrees. Hodgkinson et al. (1987) studied three Icelandic families in which it appeared that a single autosomal dominant disease allele was segregating. They found no evidence for linkage between the insulin gene-Harvey ras-1 region and affective disorder. A third attempt to replicate was reported by Gill, McKeon, and Humphries in Ireland (1988). They too showed no evidence of linkage between the Harvey *ras*-1 insulin loci and manic depression (bipolar). Thus three attempts to replicate the original finding among the Amish have so far failed, but this may simply indicate more evidence of heterogeneity in genetic transmission in bipolar illness. It may also be possible that there is more than one autosomal locus; certainly, some of the negative findings for Harvey *ras*-1 could not have been due to X linkage because of male-to-male transmission. The major setback to the Harvey *ras*-1 finding, however, has come from the original investigators. After reanalyzing the Amish pedigree, Kelsoe et al. (1989) included new persons and recorded "two changes in clinical status." This produced a reduction in the linkage probability between the Harvey *ras*-1 oncogene and insulin loci and bipolar affective disorder on chromosome 11. There was a lateral extension of the original pedigree that was also evaluated; in this extension linkage could be excluded. One may conclude that linkage on chromosome 11 between bipolar illness and the aforementioned markers is improbable. Finally, Mendlewicz et al. (1987) reported linkage between manic-depressive illness and coagulation factor 9 at the XQ27 region of the X chromosome. This area may not be in close proximity to the color blindness and G6PD loci, and thus the finding could be relevant to the possibility of more than one X-linked locus for bipolar illness. No doubt with subsequent studies the transmission of bipolar illness will be clarified and the problem of heterogeneity will be solved.

The Course of the Illness

As already noted (Table 4.4) the age of onset in bipolar illness is rather young. In a sample of 89 manic probands, 25% became ill before the age of 19 and 53% became ill before the age of 29. Only 3% of the entire group became ill after the age of 60 (Winokur, 1970). There was a tendency in this sample for men to become ill earlier (57% before age 30) than women (50% before age 30). However, this finding is anything but invariable. In a group of 251 bipolar probands, 75% of the women became ill before the age of 30, as opposed to 61% of the men (Winokur, Crowe, and Kadrmas, 1981). This turned out to be significant, with the men being significantly older at onset. Early onset is likely whether the patient is male or female, and it seems unlikely that there are any reliable data that clearly separate the sexes in terms of the age of onset.

The immediate course is, as noted above, biphasic or triphasic.

Table 7.2. A Characterization of the Course of Illness over Two Years
in 28 Bipolar Patients

Patients	Chronically Ill (%)	Partial Remission with Episodes (%)	Partial Remission with No Episodes (%)	Well with Episodes (%)	Well in Every Way (%)
Men ($n = 10$)	0	10	30	30	30
Women ($n = 18$)	17	22	0	56	6
Total ($n = 28$)	11	18	11	46	14

Mania is often (51%) preceded by a depression of relatively short duration and is often (58%) succeeded by a much longer depression. Sometimes individuals show a triphasic course of depression, mania, depression (Winokur, Clayton, and Reich, 1969). During a hospitalized manic episode, some admixture of depressive symptoms is often (68%) seen. The duration of the episode has changed over time. As noted above, it is a matter of relatively few months in the modern sample, but in the past it was reported to be somewhat longer. Wertham (1928) noted that among 2,000 cases the modal duration was four months, but the average duration was close to six months for the manic episode. Wertham also reported on six cases of prolonged manic excitement. In these cases the episode lasted from 5 to 11 years. The majority of the patients (four) had previous or subsequent manic attacks. Generally, the onset of the prolonged attack occurred in mature age, two in the 30s and four in the 50s.

There is no easy formula to describe the course and outcome of bipolar illness. Suffice to say that the hallmark of the course is multiple episodes and considerable interepisode morbidity. Table 7.2 shows an evaluation of a bipolar course over a short time (Winokur, Clayton, and Reich, 1969). Of the total group of patients over a two-year period of time, only 14% remained well in every way. Sixty-four percent had episodes in that short follow-up, and 29% had only a partial remission. Among those who experienced partial remission, insomnia, depressive mood, difficulty in concentrating, irritability, push of speech, overactivity, apathy, extravagance, and euphoria were seen in 45% or more. Though those in partial remission usually worked during the follow-up (64%), they had marital problems, were dependent, and were considered disabled.

The question of the number and length of episodes was studied in considerable depth by Angst et al. (1973). These authors evaluated

393 patients with manic-depressive (bipolar) psychoses. Their analysis was heavily based on case histories and verbal information. Their sample contained only hospitalized cases, and thus the majority of the episodes that were observed were hospital admissions. A minority of episodes had been treated on an outpatient basis, and a few had not been treated at all. The time of observation varied between 5 and 55 years, but only 53 were followed for only 5 years (13%). Only 2 patients out of the 393 had a single-episode course. Sixty-four percent of the bipolar patients were followed for 10 years and 49% for at least 15 years. The median number of episodes was 7 to 9 for the bipolar psychoses. The mean number of episodes for patients who had been under observation for 40 years was not higher than that of patients who had been under observation for only 15 years, and this suggests that there may exist a self-limited number of episodes in a patient. The length of the cycle (the time from the beginning of one episode to the beginning of the next) shortened from episode to episode and approached a threshold value. The majority of episodes were short and did not exceed three months, but with aging the cycle length, and thus the length of the intervals between the episodes, became shorter.

Some findings suggest that episodes occur in bursts that are followed by quiescent periods. Thus, the number of prior episodes may not predict relapse with any consistency (Saran, 1969; Winokur, 1975).

The markedly episodic nature of bipolar illness that Angst et al. reported is not supported by all other studies. Pollock (1931) evaluated patients who were admitted to the New York State Department of Mental Hygiene between October 1, 1909, and June 30, 1920. About 55% of manic patients had only one recorded episode. Thus, Pollock's data and Angst et al.'s data are markedly different. Less than 1% of the patients in Angst et al.'s study had a single attack, but more than half of the patients reported by Pollock had only one attack. Both studies depended on hospital admissions. Thus, the differences are not easily explained. The studies simply do not agree with each other. Angst et al. collected data from patients during a period of considerable therapeutic efforts, but Pollock's material came from a time when there was no treatment for mania or depression and no prophylactic treatment. During the period of Angst et al.'s admissions, lithium was used, as was electroconvulsive therapy (ECT), but in Pollock's material the patient episodes predate these modern treatments.

Also in contradistinction (but not as dramatically) to the findings of Angst et al. are the findings of Fukuda et al. (1983), who followed 100 bipolar patients for a period of about 12 years. About 15% of the patients had one episode and another 24% had two episodes. About

8% had more than 15 episodes in the 12-year observation time. In Fukuda et al.'s material, the patients who were admitted in recent times appeared much more likely to have single episode courses than did the patients in the study by Angst et al. The reason for these discrepancies is not apparent.

The course of bipolar illness is variable; some patients have a poly-episodic course (three or more episodes) whereas others have an oligoepisodic course (1 to 2 episodes). A polyepisodic course is related to such factors as an early age of onset, a nonacute onset, a family history of bipolarity, and the administration of ECT. This last associa-tion is of considerable interest, but could just as well be the result of a polyepisodic course as the cause of it. Though somewhat less strong than a specific family history of bipolarity, a family history of remit-ting illness in male sibships and in grandparents is also related to a polyepisodic course. The meaning of the association of ECT with cause and effect in multiple episodes is impossible to determine, but the influence of ECT in causing a remission is clear. Possibly, success-ful treatment with ECT will influence the patient and family to return for subsequent treatment, and this could be the cause of the associa-tion of ECT with more episodes. Both hospital discharge and being asymptomatic in follow-up are strongly related to an oligoepisodic background in bipolar illness (Winokur and Kadrmas, 1989).

Rao and Nammalvar (1977) studied 122 patients with endogenous depression and followed them for 3 to 13 years. Forty-two cases turned out to be bipolar and 21 remained unipolar. The change in bipolarity from depression to mania usually occurred within 3 years, and the number of episodes of depression prior to the onset of mania varied between 1 and 3. Winokur and Wesner (1987) reported on cases who switched from unipolar to bipolar illness and noted that over 40 years about 10% did this. In the Rao and Nammalvar study, there was a much higher percentage of switch and it occurred much earlier.

Ayuso-Gutierrez and Ramos-Brieva (1982) followed 84 bipolar pa-tients and found that manic and depressive episodes were approxi-mately equal in frequency. This study was based on both retrospective and prospective assessments of data of patients who were con-secutively admitted in Madrid.

Akiskal et al. (1983) reported on a bipolar outcome in the course of depressive illness. They noted that a bipolar outcome was predicted by an onset of illness that was less than 25 years, a bipolar family history, a large number of affectively disordered relatives in the ped-igrees, precipitation by childbirth, hypersomnia and retardation in the clinical picture, and treatment with an antidepressive medication.

When any three of those variables were combined, the specificity was 98%.

The question of whether antidepressants precipitate a switch from depression to mania in bipolar illness has been discussed at length in the literature. However, good controlled studies to support this are lacking. Using an epidemiologic method, Angst (1987) showed no evidence of a substantial drug-induced switch to mania in depressed patients treated with antidepressant medication. Likewise, using patients as their own controls, Lewis and Winokur (1982) showed no evidence of any switch to mania on treatment with tricyclic antidepressant medication. Kupfer, Carpenter, and Frank (1988) evaluated the possible role of antidepressants in precipitating mania and hypomania in recurrent depression. They conducted a prospective study and examined the incidence of mania or hypomania in 230 patients with recurrent depression treated with imipramine. Overall, only 2.6% of those individuals developed hypomania and patients who had a history of hypomania (bipolar II depression) did not have a greater incidence of switching than those with a simple unipolar depression. Because bipolar illness is a highly episodic illness, it would be natural to expect a substantial portion of patients who switched just by virtue of the natural history. To make a decision that there is a drug-induced switch, it is absolutely necessary to have reasonable controls. Such controls are missing in most positive studies.

Because bipolar illness often begins in adolescence, it is conceivable that there is some special set of course characteristics that are shown by patients with an early onset. Olsen (1961) studied 28 patients whose first attack of manic-depressive illness occurred before the age of 19. Twenty-six patients had either first or subsequent attacks of mania. Therefore, two of the patients may not have been bipolar. These patients were followed for an average observation period of 25 years, and at follow-up the average age was 41. Olsen noted that until age 18 mania was four times as common as depression, but after that age manias and depressions occurred almost equally in this group with an adolescent onset. The frequency of attacks reached a peak at age 17 and decreased gradually thereafter. These patients had a poor prognosis for social life. Nine of them were considered socially incapacitated and unable to adopt an independent role in the community. Nineteen of the patients had good rehabilitation after their attack, but many became socially incapacitated around the age of 50. Nine patients were never rehabilitated and 10 relapsed after a period of acceptable functioning. It would appear that very early onset bipolar illness carries a rather grave prognosis. Landolt (1957) followed 60 manic-depressive patients, all of the circular type, whose onset occurred between the ages of 15 and 22. These patients showed a positive family history of mental problems in 75% of the cases, and schizophrenic symptoms were observed in about one-third of them. None of those factors affected the prognosis, however.

Of special interest is the fact that nine of Landolt's patients developed schizophrenia, all of the catatonic type. Twenty-seven patients continued to exhibit typical affective symptomatology. Ten of the 60 patients were considered completely recovered (18%). Of special interest are the patients who were said to have developed schizophrenia. Two remained in the hospital and were characteristically withdrawn and hallucinated and were diagnosed as catatonic schizophrenia. Two had their diagnosis changed to schizophrenia, catatonic type, but recovered. Three required further treatment and were considered schizophrenic but were not hospitalized. In general, some of the patients who received the diagnosis of schizophrenia recovered and some went on to chronicity. Whether the chronicity was in all cases of a schizophrenic type is difficult to determine from the follow-up material. Certainly the patients showed chronic social incapacity but, as the Olsen study shows, that is not so uncommon. In two case studies the premorbid history of 2 of the patients was totally different. One patient who had the symptoms of mania had a premorbid personality of humorlessness and self-consciousness with feelings of inferiority. She went on to have chronic catatonic schizophrenia. Another one who completely remitted and went on to an effective life was considered cheerful, outgoing, oversensitive, and warm-hearted, but stubborn. In the case of the early-onset mania, it is conceivable that further study should be directed toward the premorbid personality.

The long-term outcome in bipolar illness has been well studied by Tsuang, Woolson, and Flemming (1979). These investigators traced 100 bipolar patients who were a part of a large family and follow-up study called the Iowa 500 and evaluated them 30 to 40 years after index admission. These patients had a mean age at index admission of 34 and a mean age at follow-up of 65. Seventy percent of the bipolar patients were married or widowed at follow-up, 9% were divorced or separated, and 22% had never married. Sixty-seven percent were employed or retired or otherwise maintained an appropriate occupational status for their age, 8% were incapacitated due to physical illness, and only 2% were occupationally incapacitated due to mental illness. Sixty-nine percent lived in their own home or a relative's home; the remainder (31%) lived in either a nursing or county home or mental hospital. Fifty percent of the bipolar patients had no psychiatric symptoms at last follow-up, 21% had some symptoms, and 29% had symptoms that were considered incapacitating. For the first decade after admission, bipolar patients had a significantly higher mortality rate than would be expected in the general population (three times the expected rate) but in the follow-up (10 to 30 years), the mortality rate was similar to that of the general population.

There is one interesting pattern in the outcome data of Tsuang, Woolson, and Flemming: although half of the group were symptomatic and one-third had incapacitating symptoms, these symptoms did not invariably translate into marital, residential, or occupational disability.

Mortality is one aspect of course of illness that should be discussed. Bipolar patients suffer an increased mortality over that expected in the general population (Tsuang and Woolson, 1979). This increased mortality is particularly high for women in the first decade after admission.

Laboratory Findings

Over the years there have been many efforts to find an unequivocal laboratory test for bipolar disorder. What is needed is a test that is very specific for bipolar illness and sensitive enough to pick up a good proportion of the cases. The problem turns out to be the specificity. Some of the tests that are useful may also be positive for other disorders. For example, the overnight dexamethasone suppression test has been studied in both unipolar and bipolar depressive patients. Of 50 familial unipolar depressive patients, 76% were nonsuppressors. Of 33 bipolar depressive patients, 85% were nonsuppressors. Thus, the test does not differentiate between bipolar and unipolar depressive patients (Schlesser, Winokur, and Sherman, 1980). Interestingly, in this same study 5 bipolar patients were tested in both the manic state and the depressed state. At 8:00 A.M., the morning after being given 1 mg of dexamethasone around 10:00 P.M. the night before, all 5 were nonsuppressors in the depressed state. At the same point, all 5 were normal suppressors in the manic state. However, other studies have shown an abnormal nonsuppressor status in manic patients as well. Still, it may be that nonsuppressor status is less frequent in mania than in bipolar depression.

Potter, Rudorfer, and Goodwin (1987) reviewed extensively a large number of classes of biologic findings in depression. Though many studies separate depressed versus normal individuals, far fewer studies separate bipolar versus unipolar patients. There are positive findings in electrolytes, membrane transports, peptides, neuroendocrine response, neurotransmitter receptors, and metabolites of neurotransmitters and enzymes that separate depressed individuals from controls. However, when one evaluates the differences between bipolar and unipolar patients, the specificity is achieved only in the red blood cell/plasma lithium ratio, serotonin uptake by platelets, and norepinephrine in plasma. Potter, Rudorfer, and Goodwin (1987) rightly pointed out that findings based on fewer than three studies should be considered questionable.

The same problems that exist for the neuropharmacologic, neurochemical, and neuroendocrine evaluations exist for sleep studies in bipolar illness. In depression, short rapid eye movement (REM) sleep latency (time from the onset of sleep to the onset of REM sleep) has been noted. Likewise, there is a reduced amount of slow-wave sleep and increased frequency of rapid eye movements during REM sleep. However, these changes tended to be nonspecific and are seen in depressive patients who have bipolar depression as well as in those with unipolar depression. These data have been reviewed extensively by Wehr et al. (1987).

After many years and no unequivocal findings, one may have to look for a new lead or a new methodology. The candidate-gene strategy might be successful. The candidate gene is one whose role in a disease seems possible even though it may not be proven. Such a candidate gene might be used as a probe to determine whether it is contributing anything to the disease. Thus, if there were a suspected candidate gene in bipolar illness and a specific allele possibly was related to the illness, this possibility could be subjected to investigation in the molecular genetics laboratory. If the specific probe were in truth associated with bipolar illness, it would be an important lead toward unraveling the biologic background of the illness.

Treatment

The assignment of autonomous-illness status to bipolar disorder would be greatly enhanced if there were very specific responses to medication. Lithium seems clearly effective in the prophylaxis of bipolar episodes, but it also seems useful in the prophylaxis of depressive episodes in patients with recurrent depressions (Coppen et al., 1971). Coppen et al. commented that "unipolar and bipolar patients both showed a striking response to lithium prophylaxis." However, some data do exist that suggest there might be a differential acute effect of lithium, with bipolar patients in the depressed state responding better than unipolar patients (Noyes et al., 1974).

Although ECT seems efficacious in bipolar depression, it is equally efficacious in unipolar depression. Abrams and Taylor (1974) found no differences in response to ECT of patients who were similar in severity of illness and clinical psychopathology, though 28 had unipolar depression and 15 had bipolar disorder.

A large number of possibly effective agents might be used to treat manic patients. One evaluation (Jann et al., 1984) cited 31 alternate drug therapies for mania. This did not even include lithium, ECT, or neuroleptic medications. Among the drugs on which there are some existing data were clonidine, fenfluramine, physostigmine, verapamil, carbamazepine, clonazepam, sodium valpoate, and lecithin. There were many others, and not only may some of these have an efficacious effect on mania, but also they may influence depression in a specific way. Currently, carbamazepine looks promising. In one study there were no significant differences between carbamazepine and lithium with regard to efficacy, but carbamazepine appeared slightly less effective for the treatment of acute mania and more effective as a prophylactic treatment (Lusznat, Murphy, and Nunn, 1988). In one study on sodium valpoate, two patients with major depression did not respond to the drug but bipolar manic patients frequently did. Whether bipolar depressive patients would have responded is unknown (McElroy, Keck, and Pope, 1987).

Heterogeneity in Bipolar Disorder

Though the data suggest that bipolar illness is an autonomous illness, it is quite possible that more than one kind of etiology might produce a similar clinical picture.

Electroencephalographic (EEG) studies in bipolar illness have suggested that patients who have manias and a normal EEG are more likely to have a positive family history for affective disorder than those patients who have an abnormal EEG and mania. This has been studied on six different occasions, and in five out of the six studies the above statement was supported. The most recent study is that of Cook, Shukla, and Hoff (1986). These investigators compared 23 bipolar patients with abnormal EEGs with 23 bipolar patients with normal EEGs. The group with normal EEGs was significantly more likely to have affective disorder in a first- or second-degree relative or affective disorder in any relative than was the group with abnormal EEGs. The next most recent study was reported by Rihmer, Tariska, and Csisz (1982). In this study from Hungary, of 13 patients with bipolar illness and an abnormal EEG, 2 showed a positive family history, whereas of 31 patients with bipolar illness and a negative EEG 15 showed a family history ($p < .05$). The only negative study was published by Taylor and Abrams (1980), who did not find different rates of abnormal EEGs between familial and nonfamilial manic patients.

Thus, the vast majority of the available data suggests a dissociation between an abnormal EEG and a family history. It also suggests the possibility that two types of bipolar illness may exist, one of which is transmitted familially and the other of which is associated with a nonfamilial abnormal brain-wave pattern. However, a further possibility exists. The abnormal EEG may be evidence of significant organic factors that bring out a bipolar illness in a person less disposed genetically than the person with the normal EEG. Thus, both genetic and organic factors might be involved. Of some interest is the fact that sodium valpoate, an anticonvulsant, has been reported to be effective in the treatment of recurrent major affective disorders (McElroy, Keck, and Pope, 1987). The presence of a nonparoxysmal EEG abnormality predicted a favorable response to valpoate.

We have already noted that there is some evidence of heterogeneity, in that genetic studies have shown data supporting X-linked transmission as well as autosomal transmission. Though these kinds of transmissions are different, there is no obvious difference in the clinical manifestations of the illness so far as we know. In a study of bipolar patients with a positive family history versus those with a negative first-degree family history, no important clinical differences were found. However, there was a clustering of affective disorders in certain families. Thus, those with a positive first-degree family history were also more likely to have more affective illness in second-degree relatives and more affective disorder in grandparents. This kind of clustering held true in first-degree family relationships also. Those bipolar patients whose parents had an affective disorder showed a greater likelihood for the sibships to contain an affective disorder. This study by Winokur, Crowe, and Kadrmas (1981) showed clear evidence for a clustering of illness in some families. It is possible, of course, that this could be related to a nonfamilial type of bipolar illness, but again it may also be explained by the possibility that bipolar illness is transmitted in a multifactorial way and that some patients might show fewer of these etiologic factors; this would be associated with an increased likelihood of a negative family history. It seems clear that there is an inverse relationship between an abnormal EEG and a positive family history for affective disorder in bipolar patients, as noted above, and it is possible that a high proportion of those patients with a totally negative history would, in fact, have some other kind of unrelated biologic but nonfamilial insult that might be involved in the pathogenesis of the bipolar illness.

Another indication of possible heterogeneity comes from a study of postpartum mania (Kadrmas, Winokur, and Crowe, 1979). Twenty-one patients with bipolar affective disorder occurring during the postpartum period were evaluated. They were compared with an un-selected group of women with bipolar illness as well as a matched control group of 21 nonpostpartum bipolar patients. The postpartum group had significantly more first-rank (Schneiderian) symptoms of schizophrenia and fewer recurrences of illness within a three-year period after index admission. Thus, the postpartum manic patients were different both in clinical presentation and in course from the nonpostpartum manic women. This suggests the possibility that post-partum mania could be a separate and independent illness; however, again, another possibility is that multiple genes cause manias of all kinds and that the postpartum manics are less vulnerable because they have fewer such genes. It would therefore require more stress, that is, something like the postpartum state, to precipitate a mania in these patients. This seems highly improbable, however. A woman who has independent mania and therefore higher vulnerability should have postpartum manias 100% of the time, but in fact a sizable proportion of bipolar women never have a mania in the postpartum state (Winokur, Clayton, and Reich 1969). The idea that postpartum mania is an independent illness remains a possibility.

The final case for heterogeneity concerns bipolar II illness. Pa-tients who suffer major depressive episodes and hypomanias (but not manias) have been considered to have a form of bipolar disorder called *bipolar II* by Dunner, Gershon, and Goodwin (1976). Bipolar II patients have a clear depressive episode and also recall maniclike symptoms of only a brief duration or mild severity. The question remains whether bipolar II illness is simply a milder form of bipolar illness, a depressive illness of a unipolar type, or maybe even a third kind of affective illness. It is useful then to compare it with bipolar illness of an ordinary kind and with unipolar illness. By definition, there are certainly clinical differences from bipolar illness. There seems to be no difference between bipolar I and bipolar II illness in terms of the age of onset of affective symptoms or the age of first outpatient treatment. Nor is there a difference in the number of suicide attempts in a lifetime. However, bipolar I and bipolar II ill-nesses are different in terms of other nonaffective diagnoses. Male bipolar II patients are more likely to receive a diagnosis of antisocial personality. Female bipolar II patients are more likely to receive diag-noses of other psychiatric disorders and to exhibit premenstrual dys-phoria (Endicott et al., 1985). Endicott et al. (1985) concluded that because of differences between bipolar II patients and bipolar I pa-tients, as well as other differences between bipolar II patients and those with recurrent unipolar disorder, there is some reason to con-sider it as a separate illness.

Coryell et al. (1989) looked at the course and outcome over a five-year period. The bipolar II patients remained diagnostically stable. They were much less likely to develop full manic syndromes or to be hospitalized in follow-up. Thus, clinically, they did not change into the more severe form of the illness, bipolar I disorder. Both the bipolar I and bipolar II groups had higher relapse rates than unipolar patients and developed more episodes of major depression, hypomania, and mania.

Coryell et al. (1984) published a family study of bipolar II disorder. As expected, the bipolar I proband group had more bipolar I illness than the other two groups, bipolar II and nonbipolar (unipolar). All three groups had about the same amount of unipolar illness in the family. The surprising finding was that the bipolar II patients had more bipolar II illness. Thus, bipolar II illness appeared to breed true. These data did not support bipolar II illness as a milder form genetically of bipolar I illness. If the bipolar II probands simply possessed fewer genes because of their mildness, then the relatives of the bipolar I probands should have had more bipolar II illness as well as bipolar I illness. This was not found. The preferred explanation might be that bipolar II illness is simply a depression with some hypomanic personality characteristics or that it should be considered separately as another diagnosis in the affective spectrum. The fact that Endicott et al.'s (1985) study suggested an association of bipolar II illness in the proband with antisocial personality as well as other psychiatric disorders and premenstrual dysphoria suggests the possibility that bipolar II disorder may be a mixed kind of psychiatric illness. This is not so unreasonable when one considers that unipolar depression is rather common and the frequency with which it occurs would suggest that other factors might, on occasion, be involved. It would be useful to examine the family histories of bipolar II patients in order to determine if other nonaffective illnesses were in excess in these families. Endicott et al. (1985) did this and found more phobias in the relatives of female bipolar II probands than in the relatives of female bipolar I probands. The other positive finding was an increase of obsessional disorder in the relatives of female bipolar II patients compared with the relatives of female bipolar I patients. Further work on the nonaffective family background of the bipolar II patients would be useful.

Certainly it is possible that some currently unknown proportion of bipolar II patients are simply mildly affected ordinary bipolar patients, whereas another proportion are "true" bipolar II patients who breed true and whose illness bears no relation to bipolar illness.

At this point the available evidence suggests there may be some heterogeneity within the bipolar syndrome that is not easily explainable by the presence of organic factors. It is an area that could use considerably more research.

8   Schizoaffective Disorder

In earlier times, the concept of schizoaffective disorder demanded simply that the patient show an admixture of schizophrenic and affective symptoms. Thus the patients presented with pronounced elation or depression, and at the same time their mental content was considered predominantly schizophrenic and their behavior was bizarre. For practical purposes, because such patients showed delusions and hallucinations in addition to affective symptoms, they were called either *atypical* or *schizoaffective*. Using this definition, 39 patients with schizoaffective psychosis were identified and followed up for one to two years after admission (Clayton, Rodin, and Winokur, 1968). In 85% of the cases at follow-up, the patients either were well or, if they continued to be ill, were not suffering from unequivocal schizophrenia. The family history of these patients showed a high incidence of affective disorder, and those who had a family history of affective disorder were not different from those without such a family history. Of 9 of these patients who were followed up, good documentation was obtained. This suggested a familial relationship with ordinary affective disorder rather than with schizophrenia or schizoaffective illness. Schizoaffective disorder did not breed true in these families. The modal illness was simple mania or depression. The conclusion was that schizoaffective disorder was simply a variant of affective disorder.

This conclusion was controversial because there was a strong belief that schizoaffective disorder essentially was really a variant of a chronic nonaffective psychotic illness, mainly schizophrenia. To this day the subject remains a matter of discussion and differing opinions. The options for classification are clear. Schizoaffective disorder may simply be a variant of ordinary affective disorder, it may be variant of schizophrenia, or it may be a "third psychosis," one that deserves some consideration as a specific or autonomous illness (Winokur, 1984). It poses a special problem because some of the symptoms that are seen in the illness are more often seen in schizophrenia than in affective disorder. The course, on the other hand, is often acute and the illness remits, which suggests a relationship with affective disorder. The crucial factor will probably turn out to be the specificity of the family history.

There have been a lot of studies on schizoaffective disorder, conducted all over the world. As is usual with this kind of situation, there are marked differences in definition, but there is little reason to believe that there are major differences between these numerous terms and definitions. All of the sets of criteria similarly define the concept of schizoaffective disorder. Among the terms that have a great deal in common are *benign stupor, schizophreniform psychosis, cycloid psychosis, reactive psychosis, psychogenic psychosis, remitting schizophrenia, recovered schizophrenia, nonnuclear schizophrenia, nonprocess schizophrenia, acute schizophrenia, atypical schizophrenia,* and *atypical psychosis.* To this tiresome list of diagnoses, one might also add *psychotic affective disorder,* although this diagnosis in recent times has achieved somewhat more specificity because of the concept of mood-congruent and -incongruent psychotic symptoms. In general psychotic affective disorder shows mood-congruent delusions and hallucinations, and in this case, the content of these psychotic symptoms is consistent with either a depressed or a manic mood, more specifically, with guilt, sinfulness, grandiosity, and special powers. Alternatively, a mood-incongruent delusion or hallucination would not be consistent with these kinds of moods. An example would be somebody who believed that his mind or body was controlled by some outside force for no reason related to the patient's mood. These mood-incongruent psychotic symptoms are crucial to the concept of schizoaffective disorder.

In 1978 a good working definition for schizoaffective disorder appeared (Spitzer, Endicott, and Robins, 1978). The schizoaffective disorders were clearly divided into manic and depressive types. To be diagnosed as having manic schizoaffective disorder, a patient had to have a group of symptoms of mania plus at least one symptom suggestive of schizophrenia that was present during the active phase of the illness. Such schizophrenic-type symptoms were essentially mood-incongruent delusions and hallucinations. The signs of the illness had to last one week after onset and the manic syndrome had to overlap temporally to some degree with an active period of schizophrenic-type symptoms. It was also possible to be considered schizoaffective if the following sequence of events occurred. At some time during the illness, the patient might have at least one week when he or she ex-

hibited no prominent manic symptoms but had delusions or hallucinations, or the patient at some point during the period of illness had
more than one week when he or she exhibited no prominent manic
symptoms but had several instances of marked formal thought disorder with blunted or inappropriate affect, delusions, hallucinations of
any type, or grossly disorganized behavior. Thus schizoaffective disorder, manic type, can be diagnosed if there is an admixture of symptoms or if there are periods when the patient shows only manic symptoms and other periods with the patient shows only schizophrenic
symptoms. In the latter case, there is a dissociation of the clinical
states. Part of the usefulness of the definition depended on some
qualifying categories. Schizoaffective disorder, manic type, was divided into a sudden-onset type with a short course and full recovery.
This was called *acute schizoaffective disorder* and was differentiated from
chronic schizoaffective disorder, in which the signs of schizophrenia were
more or less continuously present for at least two years. Also there was
an attempt to decide on the basis of premorbid behavior whether
the illness was mainly schizophrenic; if it was, prior to the onset of
the affective features, the subject exhibited social withdrawal, oc
cupational impairment, eccentricity, emotional blunting, or unusual
thoughts or perceptual experiences. This was contrasted with the
mainly affective type, in which such schizophrenic symptoms developed simultaneously with the affective syndrome and there was good
premorbid social adjustment.

The criteria for schizoaffective disorder, depressive type, are similar, although of course the symptoms for the depressive syndrome
differ from those of the manic syndrome. Again, as in mania the
affective syndrome should overlap temporally to some degree with an
active period of schizophreniclike symptoms. One difference is that
some time during the period of illness the patient may have had more
than one month (as opposed to one week in schizoaffective mania)
when he or she exhibited no prominent depressive symptoms but had
mood-incongruent psychotic symptoms.

Thus schizoaffective disorder, depressive type, can be defined as
either an admixture of schizophrenic and affective symptoms or an
illness in which some periods of illness are typically schizophrenic and
other periods are typically affective in nature. In the latter case, there
is a dissociation of the clinical state, much the same as in schizoaffective disorder, manic type.

These criteria essentially set up two kinds of schizoaffective disorders: one in which there is some alternation between the schizophrenic and the affective states and another in which there is an
admixture. The value of these criteria is that they are specific enough

to be used in further research and also specific enough that a good clinical history would contain information that would allow one to make such a diagnosis.

As one evaluates the preceding Research Diagnostic Criteria for schizoaffective disorder, one may note that they have a great deal in common with the concept of admixture of depressive or manic symptoms with schizophrenic symptoms, similar to what had been true in the past. However, these criteria are clearly more specific in terms of the necessity for mood-incongruent psychotic symptoms to firm up the diagnosis. With these points in mind, we may now further examine the nature of schizoaffective disorder—whether it is simply affective disorder, simply schizophrenia, or an independent psychosis.

First, it is necessary to determine the relationship of schizoaffective disorder to a chronic nonaffective illness, usually schizophrenia. This requires a definition that is used often in this book, that of *secondary depression*. A secondary depression has the same symptom complex as a primary depression. However, the secondary depression occurs after a preexisting nonaffective psychiatric illness that may or may not be present at the time the diagnosis is made (Feighner et al., 1972). Likewise, if a life-threatening or incapacitating medical illness precedes the depression, such a depression may also be considered secondary. Parenthetically, there is no evidence for the existence of a secondary mania over what would be expected by chance. There are some problems in making a diagnosis of secondary depression, because it is often difficult to determine the temporal sequence of the affective episode and the nonaffective illness. Also, clinically the following is occasionally seen: A person is admitted with a depression and, as far as can be noted from either the clinical records or the personal examination, that person up until admission showed only a depression. Then, in a few months the individual will develop a massive set of schizophrenic symptoms that last indefinitely with or without accompanying depressive symptoms. It seems inappropriate to consider that a secondary schizophrenia. On the other hand, it does not fit the definition of a secondary depression, which is dependent on time constraints. A good way to determine the preponderant diagnosis would be most valuable. It would be useful to create some kind of reliable hierarchical scheme. Perhaps an illness that is typically chronic should take precedence and be considered primary; an illness that is typically remitting would be considered secondary. We do not have such a scheme and in this book the term *secondary depression* is used as defined above (the temporal definition). The concept of preponderant psychiatric illness is left for further research.

In a follow-up and family study of schizophrenia, Guze et al. (1983)

presented data relevant to the concept of schizoaffective depression. The follow-up results indicated that schizophrenic patients who met criteria of a systematic sort often experienced intercurrent depressions, but such depressions did not affect the familial incidence of either schizophrenia or the primary affective disorders. Forty-four patients received a diagnosis of definite schizophrenia. In 19 of these patients after a 6 to 12-year follow-up, no affective syndrome was noted, but in 25 there was an intercurrent affective syndrome. None of the relatives of those probands who had intercurrent episodes of depression had a diagnosis of primary affective disorder, but 6.7% of the relatives of probands who had no intercurrent depression had a diagnosis of primary affective disorder—a trivial difference. This last figure was similar to the figure among the relatives of nonschizophrenic probands. There was no significant difference in the amount of schizophrenia between the relatives of probands with an affective syndrome (6 of 66, 9%) and the relatives of probands without an affective syndrome (3 of 45, 6%). In a sense these patients would probably be considered to have a schizoaffective illness. They have both schizophrenic and affective symptoms at the same time, but they are chronic. Thus a certain number of schizoaffective patients will be related to schizophrenia, and these schizoaffective patients will essentially have a chronic illness with secondary depression. Of course, such patients do not fit under the rubric of affective disorder. They truly belong under chronic nonaffective psychoses in a classification.

Of particular interest is the fact that more than half of the schizophrenic patients who were followed up by Guze et al. (1983) showed an affective syndrome intercurrently; thus such a depression is quite common in the course of chronic schizophrenia.

It seems clear that there is a schizoaffective disorder that is, for all intents and purposes, a depression secondary to a chronic schizophrenia. This barely deserves to be called an affective disorder because affective syndromes, particularly depression, are so common they occur as secondary phenomena to a number of things. Notably, Guze et al. reported there was no secondary mania. However, Leonhard, a German psychiatrist (Fish, 1962) has reported an admixture of schizophrenic symptoms and manic-type symptoms, particularly in his group of patients with chronic systematic paraphrenias. Whether these would meet the criteria for having a diagnosis of a manic episode is questionable. Individuals with chronic paraphrenia are overly talkative and often grandiose, but they do not show the panoply of symptoms that are necessary for the diagnosis of mania. That a secondary depression occurs in schizophrenia has been reported before. Winokur (1972a) reported that at admission 41% of 111 schizophrenic patients had depressive affect. Twenty-five percent had depressive affect and three other depressive symptoms, and 20% had depressive affect and four other depressive symptoms, thus coming rather close to meeting the criteria for a depressive diagnosis. As noted, however, this kind of secondary depression barely deserves being considered as an independent affective disorder.

What about the possibility that schizoaffective disorder is a third psychosis?

If schizoaffective psychoses have a genetic etiology and breed true, the case would be very strong for the existence for a third psychosis. A good part of the literature on breeding true concerns cycloid psychoses, which were first defined by Leonhard and have recently been investigated by Perris (1988). Cycloid psychoses are of three types: anxiety-happiness psychosis, confusion psychosis, and motility psychosis. These are acute and the clinical picture is dominated by persecutory, grandiose, religious, and neurotic delusions that fluctuate and change rapidly. Likewise, there are intense feelings of happiness or ecstasy, anxiety, or irritability; hallucinations may be present; and there may be increased or decreased motility. Most important, these illnesses remit, making them unlike schizophrenia and like the affective disorders. Perris (1988) reported that first-degree relatives of cycloid psychotic patients were more likely to show homotypical disorders (i.e., cycloid psychoses) than schizophrenia, bipolar affective disorder, or suicide. Bipolar affective disorder and/or suicide, however, did make up a sizeable proportion of the disorders in the first-degree relatives of cycloid psychotic patients; schizophrenia made up a trivial proportion of the disorders in the first-degree relatives. Another term that seems to have a close relationship with schizoaffective disorder is *atypical psychosis*. Mitsuda (1962) showed a marked breeding true for atypical psychosis in the family members of atypical psychosis patients. Again, there was a rather large number of manic-depressive illnesses in the family members of the atypical psychosis patients, but the familial incidence of atypical psychosis was 3.5 times as high as the familial incidence of manic-depressive psychosis (Fish, 1964; Mitsuda, 1962; Perris, 1988).

The preceding data on cycloid psychosis support the idea of a third autonomous category of illness besides schizophrenia and affective disorder. However, not all of the data in the literature agree, particularly as one gets further away from the specific diagnosis of cycloid psychosis. Tsuang (1979) studied 35 pairs of siblings, each of which had two members with schizophrenia, schizoaffective disorder, or affective disorder. The criteria for schizoaffective disorder were that the patient had either both schizophrenic or affective features together or, alternatively, an affective episode separate from another episode in which there was an admixture of affective and schizophrenic symptoms or only schizophrenic symptoms. The pairs that were observed were schizophrenic-schizophrenic ($n = 5$), schizoaffective-schizoaffective ($n = 4$), affective disorder-affective disorder ($n = 11$), affective disorder-schizoaffective disorder ($n = 8$), and schizoaffective disorder-schizophrenic ($n = 5$). The expected number of schizoaffective-schizoaffective pairs in this particular data set was 10.5, as opposed to the observed number of 4. The results then showed that there was a statistically significant deficiency of schizoaffective-schizoaffective pairs if schizoaffective disorder were regarded as being genetically distinct. Interestingly, there was a total of 13 affective disorder-schizoaffective and schizophrenic-schizoaffective pairs, 62% of which were affective disorder-schizoaffective. This suggests that the affective disorder connection genetically is more frequent than the schizophrenic connection.

Winokur, Scharfetter, and Angst (1985a) evaluated the relatives of 40 patients with schizoaffective psychosis, 34 manic, 6 depressed. Ninety-three proband-relative pairs were available. There was a tendency for the probands and relatives to breed true for the presence of psychotic symptoms, with 53 pairs breeding true and 40 pairs not breeding true. More specifically, there were 33 pairs in which the proband was positive for psychosis and the relative negative and 50 pairs where the proband was positive for psychosis and the relative positive. Though this suggests that there may be some true breeding, it is important to note that in this group of schizoaffective patients there was a marked decrease in psychotic symptoms as the years rolled on and the probands had more episodes (Winokur, Scharfetter, and Angst, 1985b). For the first 8 episodes 58% were associated with psychosis; but by the 17th to the 24th episode, only 27% of the episodes in these schizoaffective patients had psychotic symptoms associated with them. Thus in schizoaffective disorder there seems to be a decrease in the number of episodes with psychosis, and this finding is also true for both bipolar and unipolar affective disorder. Another study of concordance was published by Winokur, Dennert, and Angst (1986). Concordance for psychosis was defined as concordance for either mood-congruent or mood-incongruent symptomatology. More than half of the probands for this group had mood-incongruent psychotic symptoms. This study is particularly interesting because the data came from hospital records for admissions to the same hospital for both proband and family member. There were 22 pairs of proband-relatives in this group: no proband or relative had schizophrenia; all probands had either bipolar or unipolar affective disorder. Eleven pairs were concordant for either the presence or absence of psychosis; 11 were discordant for psychosis. This study could be counted as against the hypothesis that schizoaffective disorder breeds true, but the diagnoses of the probands were affective with psychoses, not specifically schizoaffective.

Of course, it is conceivable that there is a nongenetic type of schizoaffective disorder that might contaminate the breeding-true studies. The breeding-true studies themselves have not solved the problem. Three studies seem to be in favor and three are against.

Support for the concept of a third psychosis, specifically schizoaffective disorder, comes from another source. In Chapter 7, we discussed the possibility that there was some heterogeneity in postpartum mania that set it apart from ordinary or spontaneous postpartum illness. Such patients had schizophrenic (Schneiderian or first-rank) symptoms and were less likely to have subsequent episodes outside of subsequent postpartum periods. If we assume that the postpartum period is a time of special and considerable stress for the woman, and if we assume that postpartum psychosis is simply a manifestation of a multifactorial psychosis for which the genetic background is less than one would expect when the illness manifests itself spontaneously, we would also have to assume that in those patients who had spontaneous bipolar illness there would be 100% manifestation of illness in the postpartum period, because the patients with the higher genetic liability should always fall ill in the period of high and special stress. This does not occur, however. Reich and Winokur (1970) studied a group of 20 bipolar women and 29 female first-degree relatives, all of whom had children and also an episodic affective disorder. The frequency of postpartum breakdowns was significantly greater than the frequency of nonperipheral episodes during the period at risk of 50 to 80 years and during the childbearing years. Postpartum episodes followed 30% of the births of the patient group and 20% of the births of the family group; 40% of the patients with children and 41% of the family members with children and affective disorder had a postpartum episode. These rates are much higher than general population rates. It should be noted, however, that even in such periods of great stress as the postpartum period there are more births that are not followed by a postpartum episode than are followed by a postpartum episode (70% to 80% vs. 20% to 30%). The fact that the expected illness does not follow each postpartum period suggests that there may be embedded in the postpartum manias an independent illness that bears no relationship to spontaneous bipolar illness. Because the postpartum mania is characterized by schizophrenic-type symptoms as well as mania, it fits the category of schizoaffective illness and suggests the possibility of an autonomous disease.

Cadoret et al. (1974) studied 28 "good-prognosis" schizophrenic patients. These patients fit the diagnosis of schizoaffective disorder that was current at the time. These researchers suggested that good-prognosis schizophrenia was heterogeneous and composed of two groups, unipolar and bipolar. The separation was based on clinical differences. The bipolar patients had an earlier age of onset of illness, more episodes, and more "schizophrenic" symptoms.

Clayton (1982) and Coryell (1986) also have suggested that the schizoaffective disorders would best be divided by polarity. In the case of schizoaffective mania, the data suggested that most cases are similar to bipolar patients in symptomatology, course, family history, and response to treatment. Schizoaffective depressed patients were more complex. Clayton noted that schizoaffective depressive patients may have shown blunted affect, a schizophrenic-type symptom. She noted also that there were relevant data from laboratory tests in the schizoaffective depressive disorders. Thus, shortened rapid eye movement (REM) latency was present in the sleep of schizoaffective depressed patients, much the same as in unipolar psychotic depressive patients. Likewise, the dexamethasone suppression test was noted to be abnormal in schizoaffective depressed patients, as it was in patients with major "endogenous" unipolar depression. From Clayton's evaluation, one concludes that it is possible that some of the schizoaffective depressive patients are in fact schizophrenic, whereas others are depressive.

Coryell's review dealt with a good part of the world literature on family and family history studies of probands with schizoaffective disorder. He noted that when the proband groups were mixed, that is, contained both schizoaffective depressive and schizoaffective manic probands, all studies show that the probands with schizoaffective disorder were more likely to have schizophrenia in their families than were probands with affective disorder. Similarly, in three studies that considered schizoaffective depression separately, more schizophrenia was found in the families of schizoaffective depressive probands than in the families of probands with affective disorder. In contrast, in studies of schizoaffective mania separately, no schizophrenia was found among the relatives of the schizoaffective manic probands. These data strongly suggest a difference between schizoaffective depressive and schizoaffective manic probands.

In a large study of schizoaffective mania, Winokur, Kadrmas, and Crowe (1986) compared 164 nonschizoaffective bipolar patients with 66 schizoaffective bipolar patients who met the Research Diagnostic Criteria. First it was noted that there was a marked relationship between catatonic symptoms and Schneiderian first-rank delusions and hallucinations in the schizoaffective patients. Thus 25 of the 66 patients had catatonic symptoms. There was a highly significant relationship between the presence of Schneiderian first-rank symptoms and catatonic symptoms in the same person. Only 10 patients of the schizoaffective manic patients had only catatonic symptoms, but these were included as being ill with schizoaffective mania. There were no differences between the schizoaffective bipolar patients and the ordinary bipolar patients as regards meeting criteria for bipolarity. The course of the illness was the same in both groups. The family history for primary affective disorder in the schizoaffective patients showed a morbidity risk of 12% for all primary relatives; for the other bipolar patients, the morbidity risk was 11%. Thus, there was no difference in morbid risk for affective illness. There was no difference in amount of schizophrenia in first-degree relatives, but the schizoaffective bipolar patients showed an excess of schizophrenia when all family members including parents, grandparents, and third-degree relatives were taken into account. This suggests that in these schizoaffective bipolar patients there was some small proportion of true schizophrenic patients. Probably the most interesting finding was the fact that in the female schizoaffective patients, there was an increase in various kinds of endocrine abnormalities compared with the female patients with ordinary bipolarity. As has been noted, postpartum manic patients are likely to show schizophrenic-type symptoms. Thus they are quite likely to fill the criteria for schizoaffective disorder. There were other endocrine problems that seemed to be associated with schizoaffective disorder in these female patients, but they were poorly defined. Certainly, however, the postpartum state is of interest because it is a period of considerable endocrine change. In any event, it may be that although there is no familial difference, endocrine abnormalities may lead to a schizoaffective status in an ordinary bipolar patient. Alternatively, it is possible that postpartum mania could be a different illness—this would support the concept of a third psychosis.

Procci (1976) also evaluated the literature. Most of the studies he reviewed predated the separation of schizoaffective mania from schizoaffective depression, but his findings were striking nevertheless. Remission of psychosis was seen in 11 of 11 studies. Acute onset was seen in 10 of 11 studies. Good premorbid adjustment was seen in 10 of 11 studies. Depressive hereditary was seen 5 out of 6 studies, and confusion was found in 7 out of 11 studies. Of course, these are the kinds of findings that suggest a strong relationship of schizoaffective disorder with ordinary affective disorder itself.

The course in schizoaffective disorder is usually remitting. Coryell, Tsuang, and McDaniel (1982) and Coryell and Tsuang (1982) studied outcome and family history in 203 patients with psychotic depression. Patients whose psychotic features were mood incongruent had a slightly poorer outcome. In these evaluations, the morbid risks for affective disorder and schizophrenia among relatives distinguished these mood-incongruent patients from nonpsychotic patients but not from patients with schizophrenia. In contrast, depressive probands with mood-congruent psychotic features resembled probands with nonpsychotic depression and differed significantly from schizo-phrenic probands as regards family history. Of importance is that nonpsychotic major depressive patients had a short-term recovery in 69% of the cases, compared with a 44% recovery in major depressive patients with mood-congruent features and a 33% recovery in major depressive patients with mood-incongruent psychotic features. The short-term recovery was clearly less good for the major depressive patients with mood-incongruent psychotic features. The schizo-phrenic patients in this study had only a 7% recovery rate. Thus, the short-term outcome in mood-incongruent depressive patients looks more like that of affective disorder than that of schizophrenia; but as mood incongruence increases, the short-term recovery becomes less. Coryell and Tsuang (1985) evaluated these same patients 40 years after the index admissions. The outcome in the mood-congruent de-pressive patients resembled that of the nonpsychotic group and was significantly better than in the mood-incongruent depressive group. These outcomes were rated on marital, occupational, mental, and residential status. In general, schizophrenic patients did most poorly, and the mood-incongruent depressive patients next most poorly. These data are consistent with the possibility that some of the schiz-oaffective patients are, in fact, related to schizophrenia and others are related to the affective disorders.

As noted earlier, the Research Diagnostic Criteria enable one to determine whether a schizoaffective depressive patient is mainly schizophrenic or mainly affective. This is done by virtue of pre-illness characteristics. Essentially, the patients who are mainly schizophrenic have a prodromal period characteristic of schizophrenia. Coryell and Zimmerman (1988) evaluated schizoaffective depressive patients and rated them using Research Diagnostic Criteria as mainly schizo-phrenic or mainly affective. This rating turned out to be highly pre-dictive of a course of illness. Those rated as mainly schizophrenic were most likely to have chronic illness in follow-up (84%), whereas those diagnosed as mainly affective were far less likely to have chronic illness in follow-up (11%). The follow-up period was for a year, but it was clear that preceding schizophrenia-like symptoms and a history of schizophrenia-like prodromes predicted a more chronic course. In a different group of patients, Coryell et al. (1987) showed an association with chronicity and the schizophrenic-type prodrome as opposed to a nonchronic course in mainly affective-type schizoaffective depression. At 24 months, 72% of the mainly affective schizoaffective depressive patients had recovered, compared with only 50% of the mainly schizophrenic schizoaffective patients. These findings are extremely important in clarifying the schizoaffective diagnosis. Essentially, in schizoaffective depression, a schizophrenic prodrome and a chronic course go together, and this suggests there is a way to separate schizoaffective depressions related to schizophrenia from those that are essentially affective in nature. If, in fact, schizoaffective depression is either schizophrenic or affective, the use of the course may be a reasonable way to separate the types. Grossman et al. (1984) followed a large group of schizoaffective patients and found that the outcome differed from that of either schizophrenia or affective disorder. Schizoaffective patients showed intermediate outcomes with both good posthospital functioning in some areas (like the affective disorder patients) and poor posthospital functioning in other areas (like schizophrenic patients). This was true of both schizoaffective depressed and schizoaffective manic patients. The follow-up in this study lasted one year.

Coryell et al. (submitted) studied both schizoaffective manic patients and schizoaffective depressive patients, all of whom met the Research Diagnostic Criteria. The patients were followed for five years. In the schizoaffective depressive patients, a schizotypal prodome at intake predicted the lack of a remission in follow-up. The dissociation of mood-incongruent psychotic features from the presence of affective symptoms was a very good predictor of the presence of sustained delusions at the end of follow-up. Poor adolescent friendship patterns also were related to a sustained delusional outcome, as was never having married.

In the schizoaffective manic patients, those with a chronic subtype had a poor outcome. In a combined group of psychotic manic patients (mood congruent) plus schizoaffective manic patients, the persistence of delusions at a five-year follow-up was predicted by loosening of associations at intake, the history of any formal thought disorder in the absence of prominent manic symptoms (i.e., dissociation of affective and schizophrenic-type symptoms) and severity of illness at intake.

Some of the findings on heterogeneity are buttressed by an English study (Brockington, Kendall, and Wainwright, 1980). They studied

76 patients presenting with both depression and a schizophrenic or paranoid symptom. The patients were quite heterogeneous. Many followed a typical schizophrenic course, but others followed a course similar to that of affective disorders. The best predictors for poor outcome were development of an illness that occurred against a background of previous psychotic symptoms and the presence of schizophrenic symptoms at some time without a depression (again, dissociation of schizophrenic and affective symptoms). The successful prediction of a poor outcome in association with the development of illness against the background of previous psychotic symptoms suggests data similar to the aforementioned Coryell studies—being "mainly schizophrenic" in the Research Diagnostic Criteria suggested a schizophrenic-type premonitory state, as in the Brockington study. Brockington, Kendall, and Wainwright also looked at response to treatment and found that tricyclic antidepressants were relatively ineffective, neuroleptics were more effective, and electroconvulsive therapy still more effective. They concluded that because of the heterogeneity they were not able to support the hypothesis that schizoaffective patients can be divided clearly into either schizophrenic or affective in diagnosis. Probably the only way to make this decision would be on the basis of a systematic study of the family history that suggests that some patients had an obvious affective family background and others an obvious schizophrenic background. This would also leave an opening for the finding of a third psychosis that bred true.

Table 8.1 presents data on a large sample of relatively acute schizoaffective depressive patients (Winokur, Black, and Nasrallah, in press). In Table 8.1 these are referred to as unipolar depressive patients with mood-incongruent psychotic symptoms. They are compared with unipolar depressive patients without psychotic symptoms and unipolar depressive with mood-congruent psychotic symptoms. The patients with mood-incongruent psychotic symptoms best fit the criteria for schizoaffective disorder, depressed, according to the Research Diagnostic Criteria. In this group of relatively acute onset patients, these three groups in the continuum appear more alike than not. It is of considerable interest that they all respond well to electroconvulsive therapy and all are similar in terms of improvement at discharge. Even the patients with the mood-incongruent psychotic symptoms would be mainly associated with the affective disorders. It would be the schizoaffective, depressed, patients with the more prolonged onset and premorbid schizophrenic-type symptoms who would not belong in this group. Thus, at least in this sample, the schizoaffective, depressed, patients look very similar to other depres-

Table 8.1. Nonpsychotic Unipolar Depressive Patients Versus Depressive Patients with Mood-Congruent and -Incongruent Psychotic Symptoms

Variable	Unipolar Depressive Patients without Psychotic Symptoms	Unipolar Depressive Patients with Congruent Psychotic Symptoms	Unipolar Depressive Patients with Incongruent Psychotic Symptoms (Schizoaffective)	p
N	604	76	60	
Median age at index admission	44	56	34	<.02
Female	64%	68%	73%	N.S.
Duration of hospitalization less than 4 weeks	50%	38%	35%	<.001
Seven or more hospitalizations previously	4%	4%	14%	<.004
Mean age at first illness	37	32	31	<.02
Ill 4 weeks or less at index admission	9%	9%	12%	N.S.
Previous suicide attempts	33%	26%	35%	N.S.
Marked improvement at discharge	61%	68%	57%	N.S.
Electroconvulsive therapy given	44%	67%	50%	<.01
Marked improvement with electroconvulsive therapy	59%	56%	70%	N.S.
DST[a] nonsuppression at 4:00 P.M. (≥ 5 μg/dl)	42%	81%	47%	<.01
Marked improvement or improvement on antidepressants	19%	14%	19%	N.S.
Antipsychotic maintenance	21%	35%	57%	<.001
No relapse in follow-up	50%	31%	52%	N.S.
Follow-up 2 or more years	42%	45%	41%	N.S.
Suicide attempt in follow-up	5%	4%	3%	N.S.
Suicide in follow-up	4%	5%	5%	N.S.
Death in follow-up	10%	14%	5%	N.S.

[a]Dexamethasone suppression test.

sive patients. There are some differences though. The schizoaffective, depressed, patients in this group are more likely to have multiple
hospitalizations, suggesting that they are a more relapsing and remitting group. Also, they were younger at time of admission and at the
onset of illness.

As already noted, schizoaffective manic psychosis seems far more
homogeneous than schizoaffective depressive disorder. Brockington,
Wainwright, and Kendall (1980) evaluated 32 patients meeting criteria for "schizomanic" psychosis. They concluded that most of the
patients should be regarded as manic. Most did extremely well.
Lithium seemed an effective treatment. These patients had a good
prognosis in general, and 24 of the 32 made a full recovery. The
family history data in the study were incomplete; however, as already
noted, studies of schizoaffective mania are usually associated with
a family history of affective disorder, not schizophrenia. Table 8.2
presents comparisons among nonpsychotic manic patients, mood-
congruent psychotic manic patients, and mood-incongruent psychotic manic patients, the last group comprising those who would meet
criteria for schizoaffective disorder according to the Research Diagnostic Criteria. There were few differences between the groups. Outcome was quite good and comparable in all groups; responses to
electroconvulsive therapy were comparable (Winokur, Black, and
Nasrallah, in press). Certainly, the data suggest that the mood-
incongruent psychotic manic patients are similar essentially to the
other types of manic patients.

In studying the patients presented in Tables 8.1 and 8.2, one can
adopt a different kind of methodology. One can look at the mood-
incongruent unipolar and bipolar patients and determine whether
there are differences between them that are similar to the differences
between ordinary unipolar and bipolar affective disorder. Table 8.3
gives such a comparison. The patterns of the bipolar versus unipolar
mood-incongruent patients are similar to the patterns that would be
expected if we were dealing simply with bipolar versus unipolar disease. The unipolar patients are more likely to be female, less likely to
have an acute onset, more likely to be nonsuppressors on the dexamethasone suppression test, less likely to have multiple hospitalizations, and more likely to be older at time of first illness. They are not
different in relapse, follow-up, or outcome.

One can conclude that a substantial proportion of schizoaffective
disorders are related to ordinary affective disorders. However, the
possibility that there may be a third psychosis that is schizoaffective
cannot be disproved with certainty. The schizoaffective manic patients
are clearly associated with ordinary bipolarity, but the schizoaffective

Table 8.2. Comparison of Nonpsychotic Manic Patients, Manic Patients with Mood-Congruent Psychotic Symptoms, and Manic Patients with Mood-Incongruent Psychotic Symptoms

Variable	Nonpsychotic Manic Patients	Mood-Congruent Psychotic Manic Patients	Mood-Incongruent Psychotic Manic (Schizoaffective) Patients	p
N	188	113	88	
Median age, at index admission	34	30	31	N.S.
Female	57%	50%	53%	N.S.
Divorced, widowed, or separated	22%	23%	27%	N.S.
Duration of hospitalization greater than 4 weeks	31%	37%	51%	N.S.
Index hospitalization is first hospitalization	23%	20%	14%	N.S.
Median age at first illness	31	33	25	N.S.
Ill less than 1 month at index admission	37%	46%	51%	N.S.
Previous suicide attempt	12%	15%	17%	N.S.
Organic features present	13%	14%	29%	<.02
Outcome, marked improvement	61%	64%	58%	N.S.
Use of antipsychotic drug	70%	87%	90%	<.001
Marked improvement or improvement with electroconvulsive therapy	69%	65%	78%	N.S.
Follow-up of 2 years or more	40%	40%	42%	N.S.

(continued)

Table 8.2 (*Continued*)

Variable	Nonpsychotic Manic Patients	Mood-Congruent Psychotic Manic Patients	Mood-Incongruent Psychotic Manic (Schizoaffective) Patients	*p*
Suicide attempt in follow-up	1%	2%	10%	<.02
Suicide in follow-up	1%	1%	0%	N.S.
Death in follow-up	5%	3%	3%	N.S.

Table 8.3. Patterns in Unipolar Patients Versus Bipolar Patients with Mood-Incongruent Psychotic Symptoms

Variable	Unipolar	Bipolar
N	60	88
Median age at index admission	34	31
Female	73%	53%
Index hospitalization = first hospital-ization	25%	14%
Four to seven or more hospitalizations	26%	42%
Median age at first illness	29	25
Ill less than 4 weeks at index admission	12%	51%
Proportion receiving electroconvulsive therapy	50%	10%
Marked improvement with electroconvlsive therapy	70%	67%
Proportion receiving lithium	18%	89%
Improvement or marked improvement on lithium	55%	65%
Nonsuppression at 8:00 A.M. on DST[a] (≥5 μg/dl)	28%	9%
Outcome, marked improvement	57%	58%
Follow-up 2 years or more	41%	42%
Relapse in follow-up	52%	45%
Suicide in follow-up	5%	0%
Death in follow-up	5%	3%

[a]Dexamethasone suppression test.

depressive patients are a heterogeneous group, some of whom may have schizophrenia. Those with schizophrenia can usually be identified by virtue of having schizophrenic-type premorbid life-style with difficulty functioning, withdrawal, and incomplete remission of psychotic symptomatology. Thus the schizophrenic-type schizoaffective patients are likely to have chronic illness with exacerbations, and the schizoaffective patients whose illness is related to the affective disorders are likely to have acute illnesses with relatively good premorbid functioning.

9 Neurotic Unipolar Depression: The Generic Syndrome and Its Components

The dictionary defines *neurotic* as an emotionally unstable individual, and a perfectly reasonable definition of neurotic depression would include those patients who suffer from depression in the context of a serious personality disorder and a stormy life. Such a definition would be consistent with the earlier findings described in Chapter 5. Having defined what we mean by neurotic depression, we can now show a way to operationally diagnose such an entity, which diagnosis is based on preexisting characteristics. Neurotic depression is then compared with endogenous depression, which essentially is a diagnosis by exclusion. We then go from the generic to the specific, taking up the two kinds of diagnoses that fit the definition of neurotic depression but are, in fact, separate and autonomous illnesses.

The Basis of the Neurotic-Endogenous Distinction

First, can we justify separating endogenous from neurotic depression on the basis of first defining a neurotic depression and using the remainder as an endogenous group? We are proposing that neurotic depression is composed of two separate groups. The first of these is based on a familial definition. Patients who have a family history of alcoholism have many personality problems and problems in living. This fulfills the definition. Such patients are considered to have depression-spectrum disease. Depression-spectrum disease is a primary depression in an individual who has a family history of alcoholism in a first-degree relative. The second group, which also fits the preceding definition of neurotic depression, is secondary depression in an individual who has a preexisting serious personality disorder (i.e., antisocial personality), has had preexisting alcoholism or drug abuse, or has had a preexisting neurosis such as anxiety disorder or somatization disorder. In the case of both depression-spectrum disease and the secondary depressions, there are many long-standing personality problems and manifestations of an extremely stormy lifestyle. Still the question arises whether it is justifiable to identify such patients first and call the remainder endogenous rather than starting with the endogenous and calling the remainder nonendogenous.

The diagnosis of neurotic depression may be made by the presence of positive findings. The data on depression-spectrum disease that support the concept of a neurotic depression indicate that it is an illness with a chronic stormy, disabling life-style and the presence of associated personality traits, lifelong irritability, and a tendency to complain (Van Valkenburg et al., 1977). Mendels (1968) shows that one group of depressive patients showed "reactive items," in particular neurotic traits of childhood, neurotic traits in adulthood, precipitating factors, early sleep disturbance, inadequate personality, and emotional lability. Such traits are contained in the classic descriptions of neurotic depression. Similarly, Kay et al. (1969a) used a factor analysis in a group of clinically diagnosed patients. They separated endogenous from neurotic syndromes and noted that somatic complaints, blaming others, initial insomnia, and the presence of life events were related to the diagnosis of neurotic depression. Interestingly, in their study, early-morning awakening, loss of weight, and morning worsening were also more frequently seen in the neurotic group. These symptoms are usually considered endogenous. Therefore, it is striking that they were not invariably useful in differentiating the groups in the predicted way. Another study dating back to around the same period is that of Rosenthal and Gudeman (1967). These investigators found that in some of their evaluations neurotic factors were quite discriminating, as were the endogenous factors. Both types of characteristics were useful in separating the patient groups. More recently, Copeland (1983) separated "psychotic" from "neurotic" depression by a discriminant function analysis and looked at a five-year outcome. In this study, neurotic depressive patients were worse in the evening and angry with others more frequently than were psychotic depressive patients. Personality disorder was more frequent in the neurotic depressive patients, and they had an earlier age of onset and fewer episodes of illness. Finally, they responded less well to electroconvulsive therapy (ECT) and had fewer episodes of depression in the follow-up. This is a finding that also has been noted in depression-spectrum disease.

Most studies of neurotic depression have dealt with episode-related symptoms, but there is a need for more studies of personality traits and life events that are indicative of problems in living. Nelson,

Charney, and Quinlan (1980) used another set of diagnostic terms for what essentially is the endogenous versus neurotic dichotomy. In their study, endogenous depression was called autonomous depression, and the neurotic depression was called responsive depression. In any event, these authors rated personality traits and found that histrionic, borderline, and hostile personality traits were frequently related to the responsive or neurotic depressive group. It is important to note that these traits are part of the personality background rather than necessarily indicative of current symptoms.

A study by Davidson et al. (1984) bears directly on the ability to diagnose neurotic depression. These investigators compared the Newcastle Endogenous Depression Diagnostic Index with other sets of criteria, such as the Research Diagnostic Criteria, the *Diagnostic and Statistical Manual of Mental Disorders (Third Edition) (DSM-III)*, the Michigan Diagnostic Index, and the Klein Endogenomorphic Scale. As noted before, the Newcastle scale is of special interest because it includes not only the so-called endogenous symptoms, such as loss of weight, psychomotor change, and nihilistic delusions, but also some of the items that are usually related to neurotic depression. These are blaming others and having an adequate personality. This latter is in favor of an endogenous depression, whereas an inadequate personality would suggest a neurotic depression as would blaming others. Agreement in this study was high regarding the question of whether the patient had an adequate personality. The item about blaming others was less reliable but acceptably so. There was considerable concordance between the other sets of diagnostic criteria and the Newcastle scale; however, for two of them, the *DSM-III* criteria and the Klein Endogenomorphic Scale, there was more agreement between those scales and the Newcastle scale on nonendogenous depressive (i.e., neurotic depressive) patients than on endogenous depressive patients. This strengthens the idea that neurotic depression may be diagnosed equally well as endogenous depression. It does not necessarily deserve to be considered an exclusion diagnosis, as has been the style in recent years. We should not be surprised that there would be considerable reliability in evaluating such factors as inadequate personality. Symptoms of the present illness come and go. Such symptoms as early-morning awakening, loss of weight, and lack of appetite are variable and, as was also noted in the Kay et al. (1969a) study, were more frequently seen in neurotic depression in some cases. This may make it difficult to assess whether the symptom is always present and associated with a particular diagnosis. On the other hand, personality is composed of a relatively stable set of traits, and if one inquires about a trait that has been occurring over a long period of time, its presence or absence during the day of the interview may not make that much difference. The stability of personality problems should be an important asset in making the diagnosis of neurotic depression.

Operationalizing the Diagnosis of Neurotic Depression

Table 9.1 presents the criteria for neurotic depression. It is possible to document the justification for most of the criteria, and this documentation is included in the table.

How might one make a diagnosis of neurotic depression? There are two ways, both of which are operational. The first and simplest way is to employ the definition and determine what kinds of patients might fit the definition. There are two diagnoses that conform to this. The first is depression-spectrum disease. Persons with this disorder show a depressive syndrome meeting all the criteria for a major depressive disorder, have a family history of alcoholism, and may or may not have a family history of depression. There would be no family history of manic-depressive illness (bipolar illness). The other diagnosis that fits the definition is secondary depression. Persons with secondary depression start out by having a substance abuse disorder, a neurotic disorder such as somatization or anxiety, or a marked personality disorder such as antisocial personality. The depression-spectrum patient has had major problems in living over a long period, thus confirming the definition of neurotic depression. In the case of secondary depression, the simple fact of having had a chronic illness manifested by substance abuse, somatization, anxiety, or antisocial behavior is by definition an indication of a stormy life-style and major problems in living.

There is a problem with this operational definition and it exists in the diagnosis of depression-spectrum disease. In some cultures, alcoholism as a familial marker for this kind of illness may be either nonexistent or rare. Data from some Oriental countries and among certain religious groups (e.g., Jews and Moslems) suggest that it may be difficult to find alcoholism in these communities. Thus, there is a need for a set of criteria that lead to a diagnosis of neurotic depression, and that is why these are presented in Table 9.1. These criteria arise from studies of neurotic depression, depression-spectrum disease, and secondary depression in Western countries. The support for using these criteria is presented in Chapters 10 and 11. However, the first step is to determine what happens if we compare the group of patients who have depression-spectrum disease or secondary depression with a group of patients (the remainder would be considered

Table 9.1. Criteria for Neurotic Depression

1. Patient meets Feighner criteria for primary unipolar depression (Feighner et al., 1972)
2. Patient has stormy life-style (at least two of the following) (Van Valkenburg et al., 1977)
   a. Divorce and/or separation (duration of one week or longer)
   b. Fired from job one or more times
   c. Quit job out of pique with no better job to replace it
   d. Multiple conflicts with co-workers, friends, family, or in-laws
   e. History of sexual problems (D'Elia et al. 1974; Van Valkenburg et al., 1977)
3. Patient attributes illness to life event (Kendall, 1968; Kiloh and Garside, 1963)
4. Patient has at least three of the following symptoms
   a. Trouble getting to sleep (initial insomnia) (Mendels, 1968; Rosenthal and Gudeman, 1967)
   b. Feels others are cause of problem (self-pity) (Rosenthal and Gudeman, 1967; Van Valkenburg et al., 1977)
   c. Multiple somatic complaints (Kay et al., 1969b; Rosenthal and Gudeman, 1967)
   d. Demanding behavior (Rosenthal and Gudeman, 1967)
   e. Hostility (rosenthal and Gudeman, 1967)
   f. Depression reactive to circumstances (Rosenthal and Gudeman, 1967)
5. Patient has personality problems
   a. Partner, family, close friend, or associate believes that patient
      1) Has shown lifelong irritability (Van Valkenburg et al., 1977); or
      2) Continually abrogates responsibility (immaturity) (Kiloh and Garside, 1963), or
      3) Is hard to get along with, or
      4) Is a chronic complainer about bodily functions (Kendall, 1968; Kiloh and Garside, 1963) or
      5) Is easily upset (emotional lability) (Mendels, 1968), or
      6) Has major personality problems (inadequate personality) (Kiloh and Garside 1963; Mendels, 1968; Nelson, Charney, and Quinlan, 1980)
   b. Patient scores positively on a systematic personality test (for one or more unstable personality disorders) (Pfohl, Stangl, and Zimmerman, 1984)
6. Miscellaneous (two or more of the following)
   a. Family history of alcoholism (Van Valkenburg et al., 1977; Winokur, 1985b)
   b. Less than two hospitalizations for depression (Van Valkenburg et al., 1977)
   c. Under the age of 40 at onset (Winokur et al., 1978)
   d. Poor response to previous treatment (Rosenthal and Gudeman, 1967; Yerevanian and Akiskal, 1979)

(continued)

Table 9.1 (*Continued*)

e. Multiple (two or more) nonserious suicide attempts (Kendall, 1968; Pfohl, Stangl, and Zimmerman, 1984)
f. No more than four of the following: loss of interest in usual activities, retardation, delusions and/or hallucinations, self-condemnation, diurnal variation, early-morning awakening, and loss of concentration (all marked) (Mendels, 1968; Rosenthal and Gudeman, 1967; Van Valkenburg et al., 1977)

Note: For Items 2 through 6, meeting criteria for four categories makes a *positive* diagnosis, and meeting criteria for three categories makes a *probable* diagnosis of neurotic depression.

endogenous) who have no background of personality problems or a stormy life-style.

Neurotic Depression: The Generic Diagnosis

Several studies suggest a relationship between a clinical diagnosis of neurotic depression as we have defined it and a family history of alcoholism (Winokur, 1985b). In a study that deals directly with the definition of neurotic depression as essentially based on long-standing personality problems, Pfohl, Stangl, and Zimmerman (1984) compared patients who had a depression and a personality disorder with patients who had a depression and no diagnosable personality disorder. These patients were systematically studied with a personality disorder inventory that was a structured interview. Both a family history of alcoholism and a family history of antisocial personality were found significantly more frequently in those patients who had a diagnosable personality disorder in addition to the major depression. Price and Nelson (1986) examined the family history of psychiatric illness in first-degree relatives of depressive patients. The morbid risk for alcoholism in relatives of unipolar, nonmelancholic probands was 16% compared with 5% in relatives of unipolar, melancholic probands. Related to the different morbid risks for alcoholism was the presence of delusions: those patients having delusions showed a decreased likelihood of having a family history of alcoholism. This finding has been supported by the work of Coryell et al. (1982). Psychosis has often been associated with a diagnosis of endogenous or melancholic depression, and consequently the inverse relationship between this symptom and a family history of alcoholism is meaningful. Interestingly, Price et al., (1984b) evaluated the presence of familial unipolar depression in melancholic versus nonmelancholic unipolar probands. The morbid risk for familial unipolar depression in nonmelancholic probands was 23.4%, which, surprisingly, was significantly higher than the morbid risk for unipolar depression in melancholic probands, 13.5% (*p* < .025). However, if one simply looked at the proportion of families with a positive family history for unipolar depression, there was no difference. Forty-eight percent of nonmelancholic probands had a positive family history for depression versus 47.0% of melancholic probands. There could be a difference in the "seriousness" of the depressions in the family members of the melancholic and nonmelancholic probands. In the depressed family members of the melancholic probands, ECT was given more frequently than in the depressed family members of the nonmelancholic probands. This difference was significant.

Thus considerable data suggest that a family history of alcoholism is related to a neurotic depression that tends to be somewhat less severe than an endogenous depression. Neurotic depression tends to lack the melancholia symptoms that are seen in the endogenous type. By virtue of having a long history of substance abuse disorders, neuroses (anxiety disorders or somatization disorder), or antisocial personality, patients with secondary depression automatically meet the definition of neurotic depression. Such preexisting psychiatric diagnoses are heavily associated with many problems in living, markedly impaired interpersonal relationships, and a generally stormy lifestyle. Thus, it is possible to evaluate patients who are diagnosed as having a neurotic depression on the basis of preexisting characteristics such as a family history of alcoholism and the existence of a primary nonaffective illness that was in place prior to the major depressive syndrome.

Winokur, Black, and Nasrallah (1987b) systematically evaluated 2,054 patients who were admitted to a psychiatric hospital with chart diagnoses of unipolar depression, bipolar disorder, manic disorder, involutional melancholia, manic-depressive psychosis, atypical depression, atypical bipolar illness, atypical psychosis, schizoaffective disorder, secondary depression, neurotic depression, cyclothymia, or dysthymia. It was possible to separate out consecutively admitted patients (*n* = 937) who met the *DSM-III* criteria for a major depression, either single episode or recurrent episodes. These were divided into two groups. The first was said to have "neurotic" depression. It contained patients who, in addition to having a major depression, had another preexisting diagnosis, such as a substance abuse disorder, anxiety disorder, somatization disorder, personality disorder, or anti-

Table 9.2. Operationally Defined Neurotic Depression Versus
Endogenous Depression

Variable	Endogenous[a]	Neurotic[b]	*p*
N	536	401	
Female	64%	64%	N.S.
Mean (±SD) age at index	48 (±18)	38 (±15)	<.0001
First illness before age 20	70 (13%)	131 (33%)	<.0005
Index admission is first hospitalization	168 (31%)	100 (23%)	<.05
Previous suicide attempts	161 (30%)	184 (46%)	<.0005
Depressed before index hospitalization less than 6 months	202 (38%)	180 (45%)	<.05
Divorced or separated	59 (11%)	82 (20%)	<.0005
Memory deficit	73 (14%)	33 (8%)	<.01
Suicide thoughts at index admission	221 (41%)	204 (51%)	<.005
Delusions	91 (17%)	38 (9%)	<.001
Fills melancholia symptom criteria (*DSM-III*)[c]	87 (17%)	28 (7%)	<.0005
Duration of index hospitalization less than 4 weeks	283 (53)	255 (64%)	<.001
Marked improvement with electroconvulsive therapy	158/164 (60%)	49/114 (43%)	<.005
No maintenance antidepressant	28%	39%	<.0005
Discharged as markedly improved	336 (63%)	194 (48%)	<.0005
Suicide attempts in hospital or after discharge	16 (3%)	25 (6%)	<.005

[a] Nonneurotic primary depressions.
[b] Depressions secondary to neuroses, substance abuse disorders, and personality disorders plus primary depression with a family history of alcoholism (depression-spectrum disease).
[c] Third edition of the *Diagnostic and Statistical Manual of Mental Disorders*.

social personality. To these were added all patients who had a diagnosis of a major depressive disorder plus a family history of alcoholism. This combined group numbered 401 patients, and they were compared with the remainder, who were called the "endogenous" group.

Table 9.2 presents the comparison. The neurotic group was clearly younger at onset and had more evidence of interpersonal strife as evidenced by more divorce and separation. The onset was earlier in the neurotic group, and the depressive episode was somewhat more acute (less than six months between onset and hospitalization). There was a striking increase in prior suicide attempts in the neurotic group.

Such endogenous symptoms as a disturbed sensorium (problems in memory and orientation), delusions, and the melancholia-symptom criteria of *DSM-III* were more frequently seen in the endogenous group, but suicide thoughts at index were more frequently seen in the neurotic group. The neurotic group was more likely to spend a shorter time in the hospital and less likely to be treated with ECT or, in fact, somatic therapy of any type. The neurotic group was less likely to be discharged as markedly improved, and suicide attempts in the hospital or after discharge were more frequent in the neurotic group.

Thus there were differences in premorbid functioning that were probably manifestations of personality problems. There were some symptom differences. There were some treatment differences and some follow-up differences.

A dexamethasone suppression test was performed in 126 of the endogenous patients and 102 of the neurotic patients, with a cortisol level tested at 8:00 A.M. the next morning. The mean postdexamethasone cortisol for the endogenous group was 5.9 ± 6.3 μg/dl as opposed to 2.5 ± 4.1 μg/dl in the neurotic group. This difference was significant at the .0001 level of reliability. These patients were also tested at 4:00 P.M., and the endogenous group had a higher level at that point also (6.0 ± 6.3 μg/dl vs. 3.7 ± 4.4 μg/dl, (p = 0.009).

For a subset of the same patients (Winokur, Black, and Nasrallah, 1987a), it was noted that melancholic symptoms, delusions, sensorium problems, and nonneurotic depression were associated with abnormal suppressor status (>6 μg/dl). Early onset (<20 years), poor response to treatment and neurotic depression were associated with normal suppressor status (<1.5 μg/dl). As before, neurotic depression in this subset was defined as either depression-spectrum disease or secondary depression. Possibly secondary depressions and the depressions of depression-spectrum disease differ, but we have no data on that.

There is another operational definition for neurotic unipolar major depression currently available (Zimmerman et al., 1987). Conceptualizing neurotic unipolar major depression as a major depressive disorder "occurring in patients with a long standing maladaptive personality patterns characterized by coping and social skill deficits" (p. 30) resulting in disrupted social, occupational interpersonal functioning, Zimmerman et al. have set up a useable set of criteria (see Table 9.3). After surveying the literature, these investigators noted considerable support for the criteria being related to the concept of neurotic depression as they defined it. They separated a large number (n

Table 9.3. Frequency of Neurotic Depression Scale Items in 152 Major Depressive Patients

Item	Neurotic Depressive Patients (% Present)	Nonneurotic or Endogenous Depressive Patients (% Present)
Onset below age 40	92	56
Psychosocial stress	79	21
Inadequate personality	78	21
Nonserious suicide attempt	40	3
Divorce/separation	57	21
Blames others	30	5

Source: Zimmerman M, Coryell W, Stangl D, Pfohl B: Validity of an operational definition for neurotic unipolar major depression. *Journal of Affective Disorders* 12:29–40, 1987.

= 152) of consecutively admitted inpatients with unipolar major depressive disorder into those who had a neurotic depression and those who had a nonneurotic depression. Each of the items used significantly correlated with the total score. Seventy-seven patients with three or more of the neurotic features were classified as neurotic, and 75 of the patients with two or fewer features were classified as nonneurotic.

In the Zimmerman et al. study, there were a number of dependent variables that were assessed blindly according to the neurotic/nonneurotic dichotomy. Significant differences were as follows: the intensity of depressive symptomatology at discharge was higher and the change in intensity with hospitalization significantly less impressive in the neurotic patients. At discharge the general Global Adjustment Scale, which evaluates incapacity, was significantly lower in the neurotic group. It was also significantly lower at the time of admission. In a six-month follow-up, the neurotic group was more likely to be rehospitalized. The neurotic group was less likely to show the melancholia symptomatology of the *DSM-III* diagnosis of major depressive disorder. In the neurotic group, there was a higher family history of both alcoholism and treated alcoholism. Further, the neurotic subtype was significantly associated with dexamethasone suppression test results; in this case they were less likely to be abnormal nonsuppressors. Notably, this study used criteria to diagnose neurotic depression and compared such patients with the remainder, who could be considered melancholic or endogenous. Using this methodology their results supported the validity of neurotic subtyping and also suggested that the distinction between neurotic and nonneurotic depression was "more valid than the melancholia/nonmelancholic dichotomy" (Zimmerman et al., 1987, p. 38). If one compares the criteria in Table 9.3 with those in Table 9.1, it becomes apparent that there are fewer items in the former and thus the scale may be easier to use. Both, however, are essentially grappling with the same problem. Both point to making a diagnosis of neurotic depression on the basis of a preexisting set of personality problems and a stormy life-style. Though the six items in Table 9.3 may not capture the essence of the illness in the same way that the items of Table 9.1 do, they are obviously simpler and perhaps quite practical.

Even though part of the definition of neurotic depression presented here depends on the concept of depression-spectrum disease, there are considerable findings in the literature that bear on specific familial constellations related to the neurotic depression. These familial relationships, however, may not necessarily be genetic. The question of whether such familial background is genetic awaits further research. In any event, the kinds of familial relationships that seem relevant to neurotic depression are as follows:

1. Secondary depression is more frequent in relatives of patients with secondary depression than in relatives of patients with primary depression;
2. Primary depression is equally seen in relatives of patients with secondary and primary depression;
3. Alcoholism and drug abuse are seen equally in relatives of alcoholic patients with secondary depression as in relatives of other patients with secondary depression (excluding alcoholic patients);
4. Phobic disorder is seen more frequently in relatives of alcoholic patients with secondary depression than in relatives of patients with primary depression;
5. Alcoholism is seen more frequently in relatives of panic disorder patients than in relatives of controls;
6. Depressed patients with hysterical personality are more likely to have alcoholic fathers than are depressed patients without hysterical personality;
7. Both clinical and research diagnoses of neurotic depression are associated with more familial alcoholism than are diagnoses of endogenous depression;
8. Familial alcoholism is more frequent in patients with depression and personality disorder than in patients with depression and no personality disorder (Winokur, 1987).

These clinical and familial relationships suggest a generic illness, neurotic depression, that crosses boundaries between alcoholism, anxiety disorders, personality disorders, and primary and secondary depression. If any one familial condition draws together the concept of neurotic depression, it is alcoholism.

A good example of the quality of data that back up these findings is a study by Lazare and Klerman (1968). These investigators showed that depressed women with a hysterical personality more often had alcoholic fathers than did depressed women without a hysterical personality. Most of the preceding associations that are relevant to secondary depression have been presented by Grove et al. (1987b) in a recent comparison of the familial backgrounds of primary and secondary affective disorders. An example of the relationship between familial alcoholism and secondary depression can be found in a study by Harris et al. (1983). These researchers found that the morbid risks for alcohol disorders in relatives of agoraphobic and panic disorder probands were higher than in the relatives of controls. Because secondary depression is seen with higher frequency in these kinds of anxiety disorders, one can note the possibility of a relationship between anxiety disorder patients both with and without secondary depression.

The striking findings in these family history and family studies suggest the possibility that a good familial marker for neurotic illness is the presence of alcoholism or perhaps other substance abuse disorders.

The course and outcome of neurotic depression deserve considerably more research. In the Zimmerman et al. (1987) study, it was noted that rehospitalization in a short period of time (six months) was more frequent in the neurotic group. Over the long period, however, there are some relevant data. Lee and Murray (1988) followed 89 consecutively admitted primary depressive patients from Maudsley Hospital. The follow-up was 18 years. These patients had originally been diagnosed as having neurotic or psychotic depression on the basis of clinical criteria. Psychotic in this case did not necessarily imply the presence of hallucinations or delusions. It was related more to severity of illness. These clinical diagnoses were highly correlated with diagnostic index scores that weighed on the side of either a neurotic or a psychotic depression. These diagnostic items contained such symptoms as delusions, sleep disturbance, duration of illness, the presence of hysterical or anxiety symptoms, childhood neurotic traits, precipitating factors, and demonstrative suicidal attempts. There were 41 diagnostic items in all, concerning personal and family history, phenomenology, and possible precipitants. Using these symptoms, it was possible to give a score that was in favor of either a neurotic or psychotic depression. The scores using these criteria correlated highly with ordinary diagnoses given by attending physicians. Over the course of the 18 years, it was clear that those patients diagnosed as psychotic had a higher risk of readmission than the neurotic patients. More than 80% of the psychotic patients had a readmission, but less than half of the neurotic patients were ever readmitted.

Kiloh, Andrews, and Nielsen (1988) evaluated 145 patients with a primary depressive illness and followed them for an average of 15 years. At index admission, these patients, who were diagnosed as having neurotic depression, had a shorter hospitalization, similar to the neurotic depressive patients represented in Table 9.2. Of interest, in the follow-up period, patients with an index diagnosis of endogenous depression were more likely to need readmission than patients with an index diagnosis of neurotic depression. The original criteria that were used to diagnose them as having neurotic or endogenous depression were those of Kiloh and Garside (1963). It is quite possible that patients with endogenous depression have more serious depressions that necessitate hospitalizations, but not necessarily more depressions. Also, it is possible that patients with the more variable neurotic depression may show more episodes but these are less severe and do not necessitate hospitalizations. The course of neurotic depression in the long run may provide better resolving power for the differential diagnosis of the unipolar depression.

One can operationally define a neurotic depression and create a set of criteria that related to family background, symptomatology, treatment, and course. However, this may be a mixed group of patients and it may be useful to evaluate the components of neurotic depression separately. The two components that we shall evaluate are depression-spectrum disease (Chapter 10) and depressions secondary to neuroses, substance abuse disorders, and personality disorders (Chapter 11). Depression-spectrum disease is a primary depression. Such patients have no other diagnosis except that of a major depressive syndrome. Patients with secondary depression, on the other hand, have preexisting diagnoses of other nonaffective illnesses. Though they both fit under the rubric of neurotic depression, they may be quite separate in other respects.

Although it is necessary to take up depression-spectrum disease and secondary depression as separate entities, it is useful to place the generic concept of neurotic depression into a modern context. A number of other diagnoses have been put forward by researchers that bear considerable similarity to the concept of neurotic depression. For example, Schildkraut (1970) used the terms "chronic characterologic depression" and "situational depression." The chronic characterologic depression would fit the definition of neurotic depression. A series of findings that are consistent with the data on neurotic depression have been noted by Angst and Dobler-Mikola (1985). These investigators used the term "conflictual depression." This is characterized by recurrent brief depressions. "Conflictual depression" is a term that makes a great deal of sense. Patients who suffer from conflictual depression have chronic personality problems that put them in conflict with people to whom they are close. They experience such intermittent relationships as being distressing. Akiskal (1984) and Yerevanian and Akiskal (1979) have used the diagnosis of "character spectrum disorder" to identify the kinds of patients we are considering as having a neurotic depression. Interestingly, character-spectrum disorder shows an increased family history of alcoholism (like depression-spectrum disease). Further, the rapid eye movement latency is normal, as opposed to the reduced rapid eye movement latency that is seen in endogenous depression. Such diagnostic terms as "conflictual depression," "characterologic depression," and "character spectrum disorder" share a commonality with neurotic depression, as does depression-spectrum disease. However, there is no reason to switch to any of them. Psychiatrists over the years have understood what neurotic depression is, and changing the words or the names does not have great promise.

10 Neurotic Unipolar Depression: Depression-Spectrum Disease

Depression-spectrum disease is a primary depression that manifests itself as a depressive syndrome meeting ordinary research criteria. It is a familial diagnosis, and to make it one must identify a family history for alcoholism in a first-degree relative. The term *spectrum* refers to the family, not the proband. In the family, the illness may express itself as alcoholism, antisocial personality, or depression. A patient with depression-spectrum disease may or may not have other primary depressions in the family. Such a person will not have any mania in the family. The original diagnosis was made on the basis of a familial background of either alcoholism or antisocial personality, but most of the subsequent studies suggested that alcoholism was the more likely marker. Some of the data on early-onset depressions overlap with the data on depression-spectrum disease. It is helpful to compare depression-spectrum disease with familial pure depressive disease (FPDD), which is an ordinary depression in an individual who has a family history of depression but no family history of mania, antisocial personality, or alcoholism. FPDD has generally been considered to be similar to endogenous depression in that it is familial and breeds true. Thus, the data presented in this chapter are to a large extent a comparison between depression-spectrum disease and FPDD, the latter being the benchmark that invites comparison.

The data suggest that depression-spectrum disease may manifest itself differently in men and women. Women who come from families in which alcoholism is present are likely to be depressed and not alcoholic. Men, on the other hand, are likely to be alcoholic. They may have a secondary depression to the alcoholism, but clearly the primary illness is alcoholism. These differences in expression according to sex are not invariable. Because depression-spectrum disease is dissimilar from other major depressions in having an earlier age of onset, some relevant comparisons have been made between early- and late-onset unipolar depressions. FPDD has an early onset like depression-spectrum disease; however, if one includes all depressive patients, even those with no family history of any kind, the patients whose depression is not depression-spectrum disease have a later age of onset. Thus the early studies of familial subtyping compared early- and late-onset depressions and found that the former had a high degree of familial alcoholism compared with the latter. The patients whose depression was not depression-spectrum disease were combined into a group said to have "pure depressive disease"; a later development was to separate pure depressive disease into FPDD and sporadic depressive disease, the latter showing a totally negative family history (Winokur, 1982).

Depression-spectrum disease is a diagnosis made on the basis of both a clinical criterion as well as a familial criterion. A person with depression-spectrum disease must fill reasonable research criteria for a primary unipolar depression (e.g., Feighner et al., 1972). Moreover, such a person must have a family history of alcoholism and/or antisocial personality in a first-degree relative. A change from simple clinical criteria to a combination of more complex clinical and familial criteria produces some difficulty in understanding. Consequently, an algorithm is offered for diagnosis.

An algorithm is a step-by-step procedure for accomplishing some end. In this case, the algorithm identifies a set of familial diagnoses. It is as follows: starting with patients who meet criteria for a definite depression, we eliminate those with a definite secondary depression at any time, those with a personal history of a definite mania, and those with a history of mania in a first-degree relative.

Of those first-degree unipolar depressive patients, the familial subtypes are as follows:

1. Depression-spectrum disease—at least one first-degree relative has alcoholism or antisocial personality; a first-degree relative may or may not have a unipolar depression.
2. FPDD—at least one first-degree relative has a depression and no first-degree relative has either antisocial personality or alcoholism.
3. Sporadic depressive disease—no first-degree relative has alcoholism, a depression, or antisocial personality.

The Development of the Concept of Depression-Spectrum Disease

The concept of depression-spectrum disease originated from a study of 100 consecutive unipolar depressive admissions (Winokur et al.,

Table 10.1. Morbid Risk for Depression in Parents, Siblings, and Children of Early- Versus Late-Onset Depressive Probands

	Proband					
	Onset before Age 40 ($n = 54$)			Onset after Age 40 ($n = 46$)		
Relative	Ill	At Risk	Morbid Risk[a] (%)	Ill	At Risk	Morbid Risk (%)
Female	20	69	29	21	130	16
Male[b]	7	69	10	15	135	11

[a]An estimate of the probability that a relative will develop the disease if he or she survives the risk period for the disease. The risk period is the same for both groups, and the age of the relatives at time of last observation was taken into account.
[b]Male relatives versus female relatives of early-onset group: χ^2 (1) = 6.63, $p < .01$.

Table 10.2 Proportion of Alcoholism and/or Sociopathy in First-Degree Relative Separated by Age of Onset and Sex of Probands

Proband	Relatives	Ill (%)	p
Female ($n = 31$)	183	10 $\rbrack$	N.S.
Male ($n = 69$)	81	6	
Early onset ($n = 54$)	105	17 $\rbrack$	<.0005
Late onset ($n = 46$)	159	3	

Note: Early onset is before age 40; late onset is at age 40 or older.

1971). Specific familial relationships were found in this study. Regarding methodology, this was one of the early studies that used a family history obtained from the patient as well as a family member and a personal interview of all available first-degree family members. A structured interview was used. Tables 10.1 and 10.2 present some of the important relationships that were discovered. When the probands were separated by sex and age of onset (under versus over 40 years of age), it was noted that the early-onset female probands were more likely to have female relatives ill with affective disorder than male relatives. Most important, alcoholism, antisocial personality, or both were seen more frequently in early-onset depressive patients than in late-onset depressive patients. These findings suggested that female patients with early-onset depression might have a particular type of depressive illness, at least as regards familial relationships.

Table 10.3. Familial Findings in 1,255 Depressive Probands from Six Studies

Study	Familial AD: EO > LO probands	Familial Alc: EO > LO probands	AD in family of LO M;M relatives ≥ F relatives	AD in family of EO F;F relatives > M relatives
Winokur et al. (1971) (N = 100)	+	+	+	+
Winokur et al. (1971) (N = 345)	+	+	+	+
Woodruff, Guze, and Clayton (1971) (N = 139)	+	+	−	+
Winokur (1972b) (N = 242)[a]	+	+	+	+
Marten et al. (1972) (N = 204)	+	+	+	+
Winokur et al. (1973) (N = 225)	+	+	+	−

Note: AD = affective disorder, EO = early onset, LO = late onset, Alc = alcoholism and/or antisocial personality (mainly alcoholic in these studies), M = male, F = female.

[a] In this study EO is younger than 40 and LO older than 50; in all other studies EO is younger than 40 and LO is older than 40.

The consistency of these findings was evaluated in six separate studies that encompassed 1,255 probands (Winokur, 1974b). Of interest is that several investigators were involved in these studies and, in fact, some of the data that come from these studies predate the original finding. Table 10.3 presents these findings and the specific studies. In all studies, early-onset probands had a higher amount of familial affective disorder than late-onset probands. Likewise, in all studies familial alcoholism was seen more frequently in early-onset than in late-onset probands. In five out of six studies, late-onset men showed more affective disorder in male relatives than in female relatives, and in five out of six studies, early-onset women showed a higher amount of affective disorder in female relatives than in male relatives. These data suggested that it was possible to split off from the mass of unipolar depressions a type of unipolar depressions that had both an early age of onset and a very specific family history, mainly alcoholism and/or antisocial personality. Most of the studies actually dealt with the family history of alcoholism rather than antisocial personality because alcoholism was more likely to be recorded. Thus there were two depressive illnesses. One was depression-spectrum disease and the other was pure depressive disease. In the course of time, pure depressive disease was split into FPDD, in which an individual has a family history of depression only and no alcoholism or antisocial personality, and sporadic depressive disease, in which the individual has no family history of depression, alcoholism, or antisocial personality. The most distinct type was depression-spectrum disease. This was an affective illness that was diagnosed primarily on the basis of the family background, although it was necessary for the patient to fulfill reasonable research criteria for a unipolar depression (Feighner et al., 1972). Essentially what appeared to come from the data were the following principles. There were early-onset unipolar depressive women who came from families in which alcoholism and/or antisocial personality existed. When they had such families, female patients tended to be depressive whereas male patients tended to have alcoholism or antisocial personality.

Confirmation for the strong relationship of familial alcoholism to depression in women came from a different direction. In a family study of 259 alcoholic probands, it was clear that male relatives were most likely to have alcoholism and female relatives most likely to have a primary depression. These data on the relatives are presented in Table 10.4 (Winokur et al., 1970). This study involved a personal examination of more than 500 relatives of alcoholic probands. The criteria for alcoholism were those of Jellinek (1962) and the World Health Organization, which defined alcoholism in such a way that it had to interfere with one's life as evidenced by the presence of one of the following problems: job, police, domestic, or health problems related to drinking either antedating or concomitant with other psychiatric disorders. Depression was defined by the criteria of Cassidy et al. (1957), and the patient had to manifest the symptom criteria for an affective disorder without preexisting alcoholism, antisocial personality, anxiety neurosis, hysteria, or schizophrenia. Also, the periods of affective illness had to have been followed by symptom-free periods, that is, remission with no residual illness. The vast majority of affectively ill relatives presented in Table 10.4 had unipolar depression. Only two of the alcoholic probands had a mania, and only two of the interviewed, affective disordered first-degree relatives had a mania. It seemed obvious that the affective disorder usually seen in alcoholic individuals and their families was not bipolar psychosis. To further validate the concept of depression-spectrum disease, one can select either early-onset depressive women or patients who have a family history of alcoholism and/or antisocial personality. There are studies that deal with both methods. The simplest method is to use the familial definition and to separate patients who have a family history of

Table 10.4. Morbid Risks for Depression and Alcoholism in 507 Personally Examined Relatives of 259 Alcoholic Probands

Morbid risk	Male Probands ($n = 156$) (%)	Female Probands ($n = 103$) (%)
Male relatives		
for alcoholism	40	48
for depression	8	12
Female relatives		
for alcoholism	5	5
for depression	35	53

alcoholism and/or antisocial personality. This group can be compared with patients with FPDD. FPDD is, in a sense, the benchmark for the concept of an endogenous depression. Much of what follows involves comparisons of these two types of depression, although it is perfectly reasonable to compare depression-spectrum patients with both those patients who have FPDD and those who have sporadic depressive disease.

Further Studies of Family Background

Because the definition of depression-spectrum disease depends on family history, it is redundant to look for specific family history findings. What one can do is to evaluate the literature for confirmatory studies and make certain predictions on the basis of the family history findings presented above. This would prevent the circularity that would be inherent otherwise.

The relationship of age of onset in unipolar affective disorder to risk of alcoholism and depression in parents was investigated by Cadoret, Woolson, and Winokur (1977). This study included five separate series of unipolar depressed patients, and incidences were computed for alcoholism and affective disorder among the parents of these patients. The incidence of alcoholism was computed only for fathers, and the incidence of alcoholism and depression in parents was computed separately for male and female probands. Early-onset unipolar illness was considered to be related to the concept of depression-spectrum disease. Early-onset illness was separated from late-onset illness at age 40. A break-point model showing a marked and significant decrease in family history of alcoholism at age 40 would be in favor of the possibility that there were two kinds of ill-

nesses, both of which manifested themselves as depression (phe-
notypically equivalent) but were related to different etiologic factors
(familially and/or genetically different). On the other hand, if there
was a uniform decrease in risk for alcoholism in a relative when plot-
ted against the age of onset in the probands, the likelihood would be
that there was a simple difference in the number of genes involved (if
it were genetic) or in some combination of environmental, or genetic
and environmental, factors. For both male and female probands,
there was a nonsignificant break point in the incidence of familial
depression at onset of age 40 for the proband. However, for the
women but not for the men, there was a significant break point at the
proband's onset at age 40 for rate of alcoholism in fathers, supporting
the possibility of two separate unipolar illnesses, one associated with
familial alcoholism and the other not. Thus the possibility of heterogeneity, with two etiologically unrelated types of unipolar depressive
illness, was supported by the finding that risk for alcoholism in relatives appears to show two discrete periods of risk.

Mendlewicz and Baron (1981) looked at morbidity risks in subtypes of unipolar depressive illness and found significant differences
between early- and late-onset forms. Patients with an early-onset unipolar depression had greater familial morbidity for depression, alcoholism, and antisocial personality (taken together) than did patients
with a late-onset unipolar depression. There was an excess of unipolar depression in female relatives of early-onset unipolars compared
with female relatives of late-onset probands, regardless of the proband's sex. Alcoholism and antisocial personality (taken together)
were significantly more frequent in parents and siblings of early-onset
versus late-onset probands. Of importance is the fact that the sex of
the proband was not as significant as the age of onset. The authors
stated that their data showed familial genetic differences between
early and late-onset forms of unipolar illness and partially confirmed
the concept of two subtypes of unipolar depression.

As noted before, Akiskal's character spectrum disorder shares
many of the characteristics of depression-spectrum disease with unstable personality characteristics. Alcoholism is a common familial
finding in these kinds of patients (Akiskal, 1984). Also, Yervevanian
and Akiskal (1979) and Pfohl, Stangl, and Zimmerman (1984) separated patients with major depression and no personality abnormality
from those with major depression plus personality disorder. There
was a significant increase in familial alcoholism as well as antisocial
personality in those patients with a primary depression and personality disorder. Price and Nelson (1986) showed a significant increase
in familial alcoholism in relatives of unipolar nonmelancholic pro-

bands compared with relatives of unipolar melancholic probands.

Zimmerman, Coryell, and Pfohl (1986) assessed the validity of familial subtypes of primary unipolar depression. Depressive patients were separated according to the algorithm presented at the beginning of this chapter. Patients with a family history of alcoholism were compared with patients with FPDD and were found to be more likely separated and divorced, more emotionally reactive, less retarded, and less anhedonic. Patients with depression-spectrum disease experienced significantly more life events during the year before hospital admission than patients with FPDD. Of considerable importance is the fact that the familial subgroups differed only in the frequency of nonindependent events; familial subtyping was not associated with events independent of the patient's behavior. The differences between FPDD and depression-spectrum disease were generally significant whether one used a low or high diagnostic threshold for the familial subtyping (Zimmerman, Coryell, and Pfohl, 1985). A high threshold was defined as alcoholism in a relative only if the relative were treated, the diagnosis of antisocial personality required presence of legal problems, and a high threshold for depression required that a relative had been hospitalized for depression. A low threshold simply meant that the person met criteria for a depression, alcoholism, or antisocial personality. Zimmerman, Coryell, and Pfohl concluded that the findings supported the hypothesis that depression-spectrum disease was a variant of neurotic depression, whereas FPDD overlapped with endogenous depression.

One of the major questions about depression-spectrum disease is whether it is genetic. It is certainly familial: as noted before, alcoholism runs in the families of depressive patients and depression runs in the family of alcoholic patients. However, this does not prove a genetic etiology. To conclude that depression-spectrum disease is truly transmitted in a genetic fashion, it is necessary to use either an adoption methodology or a linkage study. If adopted children of alcoholic individuals were more likely to have depression than a control group, this would go a long way toward proving a genetic factor. The reverse would also be true. If alcoholism in adoptees was more frequently seen when the adoptees came from biologic families containing depression than if they originated from families with no depression, the possibility of a genetic cause would be strengthened a great deal.

Goodwin et al. (1977a, 1977b) investigated adoptees whose parents have alcoholism. Women born of alcoholic parents and raised by their biologic alcoholic parents showed a significant increase in depression over that of controls, but women of alcoholic parents brought up by adopted parents did not show this increase. This might be interpreted as indicating that an environmental factor only is involved or that there is some kind of interaction between an environmental factor and a genetic etiology. Interestingly, severity of depression might have been related to a family history of alcoholism in this study. A definite depression was seen in 12% of the adopted-out daughters of alcoholic parents, but in only 4% of the adopted-out daughters of controls, a threefold difference. A "possible" depression was seen more frequently in the adopted-out daughters of controls (28%) than in the adopted-out daughters of alcoholic parents (16%).

Von Knorring et al. (1983) reported on a Swedish adoption study. They found a significant excess of biologic mothers with substance abuse in depressive adoptees. However, this study made multiple comparisons, and it is conceivable that the significant finding was simply due to the large number of comparisons that were made. One might expect some comparisons to turn out significant by chance alone. Studying depressed adoptees in Denmark, Wender et al. (1986) found that there was an increase in alcoholism in the biologic relatives of the depressive adoptees compared with control adoptees.

In sum, there are currently three adoption studies that are relevant to the question of a genetic etiology in depression-spectrum disease. Though each study suggests the possibility that a genetic factor may be relevant, a final assessment cannot as yet be made.

Another way to investigate the possibility of a genetic contribution to depression-spectrum disease is to perform a linkage study. Linkage occurs when two genes, each responsible for a separate trait, are close enough on the chromosome that they assort in a dependent fashion. Linkage analysis is a useful tool in determining the etiology because it would be unlikely that linkage between a behavioral trait and a known genetic marker could result from environmental effects. Hill et al. (1988) analyzed the possibility of linkage in 14 families that contained depression-spectrum disease. Twenty-four genetic markers were assessed for linkage in these families. Illness in these families was considered to be primary, major, minor, intermittent, or schizoaffective depression; alcoholism; or antisocial personality. All of these illnesses were considered to be part of the same illness. Thus depression-spectrum disease was part of a familial illness that manifested itself in different ways. Hill et al. evaluated previous linkage studies in depression-spectrum disease. Data in the literature suggested linkage between depression-spectrum disease and the third component of complement gene and α-haptoglobin. There were other studies that excluded specific loci, but only the third component of complement gene and α-haptoglobin had been suggestively positive in prior evaluations. Hill et al. found evidence for linkage between the various clinical entities subsumed under depression-spectrum disease families and orosomucoid, a gene located on chromosome 9, more specifically, 9q. In this study, individuals with nonaffective diagnoses (diagnoses other than the ones listed above) were considered to be unaffected. The data did not confirm the linkage findings with the third component of complement gene and α-haptoglobin that had been previously reported. The method used to determine linkage was a robust sibpair method. In fact, this study provided support for previous evidence for linkage of depression-spectrum disease with the orosomucoid gene (Wilson et al., 1989). Wilson et al. study evaluated 27 families considered to have depression-spectrum disease. Thirty genetic markers were assessed using the robust sibpair and the lod score methods. Evidence for linkage with orosomucoid on chromosome 9q was found regardless of whether only individuals with unipolar depression, alcoholism, or antisocial personality were considered to be affected or whether individuals with any psychiatric disorder were considered to be affected. Because a large number of markers were used in both studies, it is quite possible that a positive linkage finding would have occurred by chance in either of them. Finding linkage with orosomucoid locus in both studies, however, strengthens the possibility that the linkage is real, rather than chance.

To summarize the familial findings, it seems clear that depression and alcoholism run together in families more than would be expected by chance. Patients with primary depression who are related familially to alcoholic individuals can often be identified by virtue of the fact that they have marked personality problems in addition to a primary depression. The adoption studies suggest the possibility that the familial concurrence may be genetic, but certainly more work has to be done on this possibility. The linkage studies suggest a specific linkage of the variants of depression-spectrum disease with a known genetic marker, but once again this cannot be taken as conclusive. Replication is needed.

Personality Problems

Recognizing that personality problems, a stormy life-style (many unpleasant life events), and a family history of alcoholism have been frequently associated, we should assess character and behavioral difficulties in patients who have been diagnosed as depression-spectrum disease on the basis of a first-degree family history of alcoholism. These patients should be compared with other depressive patients who do not have the same familial background. Such data are plentiful.

Table 10.5. Characteristics of Depressed Women Ages 30
to 50 according to Family History of Alcoholism

Characteristic	Women with Family History of Alcoholism ($n = 49$)		Women with No Family History of Alcoholism ($n = 78$)		$p <$
	n	(%)	n	(%)	
Fear	30	(61)	32	(40)	.025
Demanding behavior	16	(33)	8	(10)	.005
Need for reassurance	4	(8)	0	(0)	.02
Lifelong nervousness	19	(39)	14	(18)	.01
Lifelong complaining	11	(22)	5	(6)	.01
Lifelong irritability	13	(27)	5	(6)	.01

Winokur (1985b) reported on some personality characteristics of depressed patients who were separated according to a family history of alcoholism. All of these patients were female, and they were partially controlled for age at index admission. Table 10.5 presents these data. A family history of alcoholism was associated with a variety of unstable personality characteristics, including lifelong irritability and nervousness, a need for dependent relationships, and the presence of demanding behavior.

In a comparison of 105 female depression-spectrum disease patients and 86 female FPDD patients, evidence of a stormy life-style was more frequent in the former (Winokur, 1979c). There was a history of sexual problems in 32% of the patients with depression-spectrum disease, as opposed to only 15% of the FPDD patients ($p < .01$). Further, this was supported by a history of divorce or separation that appeared in 20% of the depression-spectrum disease patients, as opposed to only 6% of the FPDD patients ($p < .01$).

Van Valkenburg, Lilienfeld, and Akiskal (1987) compared 99 patients who had depression-spectrum disease with 121 patients who had other kinds of depression. The former were significantly more likely to be chronically nervous, worrisome, irritable, labile, bad tempered, immature, dependent, hostile, and self-pitying. Likewise, they were significantly more likely to have unstable and tempestuous relationships with others. Discriminant analysis confirmed that these variables were not associated by chance. Some of the symptoms, the aforementioned chronic personality problem, lifetime diagnoses, and family history correctly classified 88% of the 220 patients as suffering from either depression-spectrum disease or other depressions. The methodology of this study, however, was even more complex than had been previously reported. Van Valkenburg, Lilienfeld, and Akiskal attempted to broaden the definition of depression-spectrum disease to include secondary depressions. Their rationale for doing this was that they considered depression-spectrum disease to be secondary to underlying personality pathology. By including secondary depression, the authors expected the characterologic manifestations to emerge more floridly, and in fact this is what happened. Note that this definition is similar to the definition of neurotic depression that has already been presented in this book, because both patients with secondary depression and patients with primary depression who have depression-spectrum disease can be considered as having neurotic depression. The separation in the study by Van Valkenburg, Lilienfeld, and Akiskal was mainly on the basis of the family history of alcoholism. By using this expanded definition of depression-spectrum disease (to include secondary depression as well), these researchers found a significant increase in anxiety disorder in the patients with depression-spectrum disease compared with the other patients. Of course, this was not totally unexpected considering that some of the patients in that study had a primary diagnosis of anxiety disorder. Suffice to say that depression-spectrum disease and secondary depression have a lot in common. (Secondary depression is discussed in Chapter 11.)

Zimmerman, Coryell, and Pfohl (1986) found that patients with depression-spectrum disease were more likely that patients with FPDD to have history of marital separation or divorce. Personality disorder in this study was assessed by a structured interview. There was no significant difference in the number of diagnosable personality disorders in the two groups of patients, but the proportion of patients with depression-spectrum disease showing a personality disorder was higher than that of FPDD patients. This was true whether a low threshold for diagnosis (65% vs. 44%) or a high threshold (58% vs. 41%) was used. The depression-spectrum patients experienced significantly more life events during the year before hospital admission than the patients with FPDD, but this occurred only in the frequency of nonindependent events; thus familial subtyping was not related to events that were independent of the patient's personal behavior.

Clinical Picture

Because a familial diagnosis depends on meeting prespecified criteria for a major depressive illness as well as a specific family background, there will be relatively few differences in symptoms between depression-spectrum disease and FPDD, but there are some reported differences. The diagnosis of neurotic/reactive depression that was used by the hospital clinicians was more likely associated with a family history of alcoholism than the clinical diagnosis of endogenous depression. Perris, von Knorring, and Perris (1982) as well as Winokur (1985b) have shown this. Perris, von Knorring, and Perris divided unipolar depressive patients into two groups. One presented with a reactive/neurotic depressive illness, which was an illness that occurred in close relation to a psychologically understandable precipitating factor in a person with a neurotic personality development. The comparison group comprised endogenous depressive patients, each of whom had had three or more depressive episodes. These patients were then cross-diagnosed with either FPDD or depression-spectrum disease. Of 15 patients diagnosed as having depression-spectrum disease (i.e., a family history of alcoholism) 12 (80%) had a cross-diagnosis of reactive/neurotic depression. Of 42 patients with FPDD, 16 (38%) had a cross-diagnosis of reactive/neurotic depression. Thus, the clinical diagnosis of neurotic/reactive depression in the hands of clinicians showed a relationship to depression-spectrum disease.

In a study comparing 105 women who had depression-spectrum disease with 86 women who had pure depressive disease, the one symptom that clearly separated the groups was loss of interest in usual activities. The FPDD patients were more likely to show this than the patients with depression-spectrum disease. The latter showed a trend toward more hypochondriasis and anxiety symptoms, and the former showed a trend toward more complaints of diurnal variation. In this study there were no differences in the presence of psychotic symptoms or in the presence of sensorium defects (Van Valkenburg et al., 1977).

In Zimmerman, Coryell, and Pfohl's study (1986) of familial subtypes, there was a trend for more depression-spectrum disease patients than FPDD patients to have made a nonserious suicide attempt. There were no differences in symptom severity. However, patients with depression-spectrum disease were more reactive to pleasurable environmental stimuli than the FPDD patients. This is similar to the symptom of losing interest in usual activities that separated the depression-spectrum disease from FPDD patients in the Van Valkenburg et al. (1977) study. Using only high-threshold diagnoses in this study, endogenous depression according to the Research Diagnostic Criteria was diagnosed significantly more often in the FPDD patients than in the patients with depression-spectrum disease. Likewise, melancholia symptoms in the *Diagnostic and Statistical Manual of Mental Disorders (Third Edition) (DSM-III)* were more frequently diagnosed in the FPDD patients than the depression-spectrum disease patients. Thus using research criteria for endogenous symptomatology or melancholia shows essentially the same thing as the clinical diagnoses of the clinicians. An endogenous depression or some variant of it is more frequently seen in FPDD patients. It is important to reiterate, however, that these differences were really only seen with high-threshold diagnoses. Research Diagnostic Criteria for definite endogenous depression and *DSM-III* criteria for melancholia did not separate the groups with the low-threshold diagnoses. Coryell et al. (1982) separated patients into those with FPDD and those with depression-spectrum disease and evaluated the presence of delusions. Delusions were more frequently seen in the former (47%) than in the latter (5%).

Epidemiology

The frequency of the familial subtypes in the general population is unknown, simply because nobody has ever attempted to evaluate it. On the other hand, in a hospital population starting with a diagnosis of unipolar depression, depression-spectrum disease was seen in 17% of a consecutive series, FPDD in 25%, and sporadic depressive disease in 32% (Winokur et al., 1978). There was a discard group of about 25% in which the family history was not sufficient because the illness of the family member was not diagnosable, or affective disorder or alcoholism had occurred in an extended family member but not in a first-degree family member. Presumably, given the best of all possible worlds and clear definitions, one should be able to diagnose all unipolar depressive patients in a sample with one of the familial subtypes.

Course of Illness

The mean age of onset of illness in depression-spectrum disease is 38 years, the same as for FPDD patients. Whereas depression-spectrum disease and FPDD patients tend to have the same age of onset, sporadic depressive disease patients have a significantly older onset, 47 years. Dividing the depression-spectrum disease patients into those who first became ill before the age of 30, those who became ill at ages 30 to 49, and those who became ill at the age of 50 or older, the percentages are 29%, 48%, and 22%, respectively. For the FPDD pa-

Table 10.6. Course of Illness for Depression-Spectrum
Disease and Familial Pure Depressive Disease

Characteristic	Depression-Spectrum Disease (%)	Familial Pure Depressive Disease (%)	$p <$
First admission	57	41	.05
Complete recovery, no relapse	48	31	.05
At least one relapse	23	48	.005
Ill at last report	13	28	.025
Subsequent hospitalization	26	44	.025

tients the corresponding percentages are 25%, 57%, and 17%, respectively (Winokur et al., 1978). These ages of onset refer only to female patients.

The course of the illness at admission and afterward in female patients is presented in Table 10.6. All of these female patients were admitted over a period of several years. The average length of follow-up in these two groups was 2.6 years in the patients with depression-spectrum disease and 2.9 years in the FPDD patients. It seems clear from these data that the FPDD group was more likely to have subsequent episodes that required hospitalization. In this sense, they were rather similar to patients with endogenous depression who have been evaluated by previous investigators and are discussed in Chapter 5 of this book. Episodes prior to index admission were also more frequent in the FPDD group.

Not all studies are in agreement with these findings. Zimmerman, Coryell, and Pfohl (1986) found no significant difference between number of prior hospitalizations in patients with depression-spectrum disease when compared with FPDD patients. As above, the age of first psychiatric treatment was the same between the two groups.

The follow-up data in Table 10.6 come essentially from chart material. They suggest that depression-spectrum disease is significantly less likely than FPDD to have subsequent hospitalizations and also relapses. Chart data are always heavily dependent on rehospitalization and therefore may be a measure of severity of relapse as well as occurrence of relapse. The data suggest that, like endogenous depression, FPDD is subject to more severe relapses (Lee and Murray, 1988).

There are few follow-up studies dealing with familial subtypes. Smith and North (1988) followed the female probands on whom the original concept of depression-spectrum disease was formulated. These women were systematically interviewed 11 years after they entered the original study and were reported by Winokur et al. (1971). Twenty patients with FPDD were followed and were compared with 14 depression-spectrum patients. The index characteristics were similar, although 64% of the depression-spectrum patients were hospitalized for the first time, compared with only 45% of the FPDD patients. Regarding episodes, however, only 36% of the depression-spectrum disease patients had a hospitalization for their first episode as opposed to 60% of the FPDD patients. Again, this suggests that the patients with depression-spectrum disease may have more episodes but less hospitalizations, indicating the possibility of a difference in severity of episodes between depression-spectrum disease and FPDD. Almost twice as many of the patients with depression-spectrum disease were admitted for suicide threat or attempt. There were no significant differences in the course over the follow-up periods, but there was information on only 18 FPDD patients and 11 depression-spectrum disease patients. In any event, only 9% of the latter, compared with 22% of the former, had no subsequent episodes. In contrast, in follow-up the FPDD patients were hospitalized in 58% of the cases, as opposed to only 36% of the depression-spectrum disease patients. Thirty percent of the depression-spectrum disease patients made a suicide attempt in follow-up; only 19% of the FPDD patients made such an attempt. A chronic course was seen in 33% of the FPDD patients and only 9% of the patients with depression-spectrum disease. The mean longest period of depression for the former was 84.9 weeks, whereas for the latter it was only 19.6 weeks. Thus not only the severity, but also the length of the episode, is greater in FPDD. The number of depressive episodes during the follow-up was twice as high (3.7) in the depression-spectrum disease patients as in the FPDD patients (1.6), suggesting that the former had more short, nonincapacitating episodes than the latter. The patients who had depression-spectrum disease received additional diagnoses in 27% of the cases, and in each case the diagnosis was alcoholism. Note that when they were accepted for the study they were not alcoholic. Among those who had ever married, 60% of subjects with depression-spectrum disease had a poor marital history (two or more divorces or repeated arguments with separations) compared with only 27% of the FPDD subjects. The subjects with depression-spectrum disease were more likely to have relinquished responsibility for the care of one of their children (22%) than were FPDD subjects

(8%). Unsatisfactory relationships with parents, especially with mothers, were more often reported by subjects with depression-spectrum disease subjects (45%) than by FPDD (7%). Likewise, the former were more likely than the latter to report problems in relationships with their fathers (27% vs. 7%). This study is useful because it gives us a microscopic picture of the course of illness in depression-spectrum disease, particularly as compared with FPDD.

Laboratory Findings

In general, laboratory findings are more abnormal for FPDD patients than they are for patients with depression-spectrum disease. Consequently, it seems more appropriate to present those findings in Chapter 13 in the discussion of FPDD as a subtype of endogenous depression. There is one study, however, that suggests that depression-spectrum disease may show pathologic biologic findings. Rosenthal et al. (1980) performed lumbar punctures on patients who had major affective disorders. None met the diagnostic criteria for alcoholism. There were 10 patients who had at least one first-degree relative and 3 with least one second-degree relative with a history of alcoholism. These subjects' illness would fit the definition of depressive-spectrum disease. Most subjects with alcoholic relatives had a major affective disorder in their family also. Depressive subjects with alcoholism in a first-degree relative had significantly lower levels of cerebrospinal fluid 5-hydroxyindolacetic acid and 3-methoxy-5-hydroxylphenylglycol than did patients without such a family history. There was no difference in levels of homovanillic acid. The authors pointed that the findings support previous studies that linked alcoholism to abnormal serotonin metabolism. They suggested that the findings also provide evidence for the usefulness of the family history in subtyping the depressions.

Treatment

Treatment generally has been evaluated in neurotic depression as a generic diagnosis. There are few data that deal directly with treatment in depression-spectrum disease. However, some data are available. Avery and Winokur (1977) reported a study on the efficacy of electroconvulsive therapy (ECT) and antidepressant medication in depression. In some unpublished data from that study, patients were evaluated according to a family history of alcoholism. The patients with a family history of alcoholism were less likely to respond favorably to ECT or any kind of antidepressant treatment than those who lacked such a family history. In 37 patients with depression-spectrum disease, there was a 32% rate of no improvement with various anti-depressant treatments. This could be compared with 72 patients with FPDD, 13% of whom showed no improvement. The difference was significant ($p < .05$). The data then suggest that depression-spectrum disease is associated with a poorer response to what has ordinarily been considered effective treatment in the affective disorder. In the Pfohl, Stangl, and Zimmerman study (1984), patients with major depression were compared on the basis of whether or not they had a concomitant or concurrent personality disorder. Those major depressive patients with a personality disorder had a significant increase in both familial alcoholism and antisocial personality. Improvement was defined as a 50% drop in the Hamilton Depression Rating Scale at discharge, and there was a significant difference between patients who had only a major depression and those who had a major depression plus a personality disorder. Those with only major depression had a 50% improvement rate with antidepressant medication, as opposed to only 16% of those with concurrent depression and personality disorder. There was no significant difference in response to ECT in this particular study. Seventy-nine percent of those with depression only improved, whereas 75% of those with depression and personality disorder improved. There may have been some unrecognized circumstance that provided differential treatment. Thus 14 of 37 patients with only depression received ECT. This 38% could be compared with the 20% (8 of 41) of patients with concurrent major depression and personality disorder who received ECT. At discharge from hospital, 59% of those with depression only had a 50% drop in Hamilton Depression Rating Scale versus only 24% of those with depression and personality disorder ($p < .01$). Global assessment was significantly better for those patients with depression only than it was for those with depression and personality disorder. Sixty-two percent of those with depression only had a 15% increase on a global assessment score versus 37% ($p < .05$) of those with both depression and a personality disorder. Thus, although these patients with depression plus a personality disorder were not selected for having depression-spectrum disease, in fact they fit the diagnosis of depression-spectrum disease in many cases and certainly fit the diagnosis of neurotic depression. It is notable that such patients did worse than those who did not have a concurrent personality disorder.

Similar findings have been reported by Coryell and Zimmerman (1984). In a search for predictors of response to ECT in depression, they found that a family history of alcoholism and a normal dexamethasone suppression test independently predicted a poor outcome with ECT. Notably, the presence of melancholic symptoms was not as good a predictor as familial subtype or dexamethasone response.

As noted from the preceding material, there are data to suggest that depression-spectrum patients differ from FPDD patients on many of the items that are used to define a disease according to a medical model. We suggest that depression-spectrum disease is a diagnosis that deserves more study and may very well be a clear and autonomous entity. The fact is that depression-spectrum patients have many problems in living and many personality conflicts. As we develop better personality disorder diagnoses, it may be that depression-spectrum patients can fit into the category of secondary depression. Until that time, it is best to regard them as patients with primary depression, a stormy life-style, and major personality problems and to diagnose them separately.

11 Neurotic Unipolar Depression: Secondary Depression

A secondary affective disorder has been defined as an affective syndrome currently occurring in a patient who has suffered a preexisting, diagnosable, nonaffective, psychiatric illness (Woodruff, Murphy, and Herjanic, 1967). In contrast, a primary depression occurs in a person who has never had any psychiatric illness, except possibly a previous episode of depression. Woodruff, Murphy, and Herjanic compared 54 patients who had primary affective disorder with 18 patients who had secondary affective disorder. The patients who had secondary affective disorder had preexisting psychiatric conditions, such as hysteria, probable hysteria, anxiety disorder, alcoholism, antisocial personality, and obsessional illness. In this study only one of the patients with secondary affective disorder had obsessional illness. How were the patients with primary depressions different from those with secondary depressions? There were only two significant differences in the symptomatology. The patients with secondary depression complained of middle insomnia more than did those with primary depression. The most significant difference, however, was the feeling that the illness represented a definite change—not one's old self at all—from before the depression. This was seen significantly more frequently in the primary depression patients. Thus, the secondary depression patients saw their depression as part of a long and ongoing process. There were some nonsignificant differences that were notable. The primary depression patients more often showed motor retardation and increased latency of speech at time of examination. Thirty-seven percent of the patients with primary affective disorder demonstrated one or both of these symptoms, but only 11% (2) of the patients with secondary affective disorder demonstrated one or both of these symptoms. Over time relatively few symptom differences have been demonstrated in primary versus secondary depression.

151

This is because to enter any study an individual must show a diagnosable depression, and consequently the amount of symptomatologic overlap between individuals with primary and secondary depressions should be considerable.

We propose that depressions that are secondary to substance abuse disorders, anxiety disorders, somatization disorders, and marked personality disorders fit the definition of neurotic depression. This is because all of these primary nonaffective conditions are associated with considerable interpersonal conflict and a stormy life-style. Some definitional problems remain, however. As noted from the study by Woodruff, Murphy, and Herjanic, secondary depression in a hospital population was rarely associated with obsessional disorder. An obsessional disorder is relatively infrequent and the personality problems are not similar to those in antisocial personality and substance abuse, anxiety, and somatoform disorders. Therefore, we have chosen not to include depression secondary to obsessional disorder as a neurotic depression. Because they are relatively infrequent, they do not pose that much of a problem. A far larger problem is illustrated by the following scenario.

An individual at the age of 20 meets the criteria for a depression but has no symptoms of anxiety attacks (panic attacks). The patient is diagnosed as having a primary depression. Within several months, however, the individual develops anxiety attacks and is followed for the next 10 years, showing these attacks during the entire period. The patient meets the criteria for panic disorder with agoraphobia. On occasion during the 10-year follow-up, that person shows a full panoply of depressive symptoms and is diagnosed as having a major depression on a few occasions. The dominant or preponderant symptomatology over the entire period of observation is mainly anxiety disorder. Should such an individual be diagnosed as having a secondary anxiety disorder because it followed the depression? Should there be some provision made in the definition of a secondary phenomenon to take into account the preponderant or dominant illness? We believe the latter is the case, but such a definition has not yet been presented; nor is there any research bearing on the problem. Therefore, in this particular classification, we are using the usual concept of secondary depression. A secondary depression is one that follows another well-established nonaffective illness. The definition is thus based on a temporal sequence, with the depressive episode coming after the nonaffective illness. One could also make the case that another problem in definition is what to do with those patients who develop a major medical illness and then develop a secondary depression. We believe those patients do not belong in the group of neurotic depressive patients, and they are included in the chapter on reactive depressions. In this chapter, as a subcategory of neurotic depression, we consider those patients who, after having had an unequivocal diagnosis of somatization disorder, anxiety disorder, personality disorder, or substance abuse disorder, develop a depression. There has been a start on a broader definition of secondary depression. Patients who have at least one depressive episode before and another after developing a nonaffective condition could be called "complicated" secondary depression. In fact, there are some data on this on this complex set of temporal circumstances (Grove et al., 1987a).

In general, secondary depressions may be compared with primary depressions. Primary depressions have been considered more closely aligned to endogenous depression, though, as noted in Chapter 10 depression-spectrum disease is a primary depression but fills the characteristics of a neurotic depression. Thus, comparing primary depression and secondary depression does not always mean one is comparing endogenous depression and neurotic depression. However, in general the comparison is meaningful to the endogenous/ neurotic separation.

Early studies of secondary affective disorder showed that 53% of nonaffectively disordered inpatients had a depressive affect. However, if one approached a systematic diagnoses in these patients using a threshold of depressive affect and four other depressive symptoms, about 26% met those criteria (Winokur, 1972a). In general, it made little difference whether the primary diagnosis was schizophrenia, psychoneurosis, acute brain syndrome, alcoholism, chronic brain syndrome, or personality disorder. The amount of secondary depression defined as depressive affect and four other depressive symptoms in these groups varied between 20% and 34%. Suicide trends and attempts were frequently seen in the patients with secondary depression. The sex differential depended on the primary diagnoses. If the primary diagnosis was alcoholism or drug addiction, there were more men; if the primary diagnosis was one of the psychoneuroses, women predominated. In an attempt to assess family history in a group of hysteric patients with secondary depression, 8% of siblings and parents showed alcoholism or depression. In those hysteric patients without secondary affective disorder, 9% showed alcoholism or depression. Thus having a secondary depression did not change the family history in these patients. Hysteria was diagnosed in a similar fashion to the concept of somatization disorder in the *Diagnostic and Statistical Manual of Mental Disorders (Third Edition-Revised) DSM-III-R)*. Of considerable importance is that in the case of these patients, it may have been the secondary depression that precipitated the admission to a psychiatric hospital.

A relevant study is that of Guze, Woodruff, and Clayton (1971). These patients were taken from a series of consecutive outpatient clinic admissions. The most frequent conditions associated with secondary depression were anxiety neurosis, antisocial personality, alcoholism, and drug dependency. The approach to diagnosis in this study is of considerable interest. The disorder that began the earliest according to the patient's history was called the first diagnosis; if a patient presented a history consistent with anxiety neurosis complicated after several years by depression, anxiety neurosis was considered the first disorder and the depression was considered secondary. The high frequency of personality disorders and neuroses associated with the secondary depressions indicates a marked overlap with the concept of neurotic depression. This study showed an absence of mania among the secondary affective disorder cases, indicating that there was a low likelihood of secondary mania existing as a viable diagnosis. In general, patients with secondary depression were younger at onset of illness and at time of interview than those with primary depression.

Another early study that is relevant to the primary/secondary distinction is the follow-up study of Kay et al. (1969b) on "endogenous" and "neurotic" syndromes of depression. These patients were followed for a period of five to seven years. Patients were selected who had a chart diagnosis of endogenous depression, neurotic depression, or involutional melancholia. In the follow-up, there were clearly more readmissions for the endogenous group, with the neurotic group showing a course of prolonged ill health. In a sense, this suggests a more episodic course with recovery and exacerbations in the endogenous group and a more constant, chronic course of symptoms in the neurotic group. In the neurotic depressive patients, somatic complaints were significantly correlated with all measures of outcome except readmission. In those patients who had prolonged ill health, the existence of somatic complaints predicted such a course. The set of symptoms entitled "somatic complaints" included complaints of bodily dysfunction or pain or abnormal sensations. These complaints were neither delusional nor bizarre. These somatic complaints were much more frequently seen in the patients who were clinically diagnosed as neurotic depressive than in those diagnosed as endogenous depressive. Also, somatic complaints boded poorly for a good prognosis. In fact, between the concept of a neurotic depression and the presence of somatic complaints, there was little from which to choose.

Both were useful and both were about equally unfavorable for a prognosis. They predicted an adverse course referred to as "prolonged ill health." The relevance of this finding to the concept of secondary depression is clear. It is entirely possible that the patients who were said to have neurotic depression, in fact, had a depression secondary to a somatization disorder that manifested itself by multiple somatic complaints. The study did not give the kind of information that would allow us to make a diagnosis of a secondary depression, but certainly this is reasonable considering the importance of the somatic complaints.

In addition to the older studies described above, there have been new findings reported in the literature. These new findings are often best presented in comparisons between primary and secondary depression. Of course, it is entirely possible that a depression that is secondary to an anxiety disorder may very well be different in many ways from a depression secondary to alcoholism or somatization disorder. There have been relatively few attempts to describe clinical differences between the depressions secondary to various disorders. However, this may be the ultimate direction that the distinction between primary and secondary depression should take.

Generally, most studies have simply compared patients who showed secondary depressions with those who had primary depressions. Usually patients with secondary depressions include those with such primary diagnoses as personality disorders, somatization disorders, anxiety disorders, and the substance abuse disorders. Because there are relatively few patients who have depression secondary to obsessional disorder, we do not deal with this directly. Depressions that are secondary to medical disorders are discussed in Chapter 12.

The epidemiology of secondary depression is difficult to ascertain. Winokur (1988) evaluated the proportion of patients with a primary diagnosis of either anxiety disorder or panic disorder who had a secondary depression. The rates varied between 33% and 75%. These data reflect findings from psychiatric settings. In the Robins et al. (1984) epidemiologic study, the lifetime prevalence rate for a major depressive episode varied from 3.7% to 6.7% in the community. Because the differences between 33% and 75% and 3.7% and 6.7% are large, we can assume that depression is very likely a secondary phenomenon in anxiety disorder. On the basis of chance alone, the rate of anxiety disorder and depression existing in the same person would be the rates of anxiety disorder and depression multiplied by each other. Depression in anxiety disorder should then be a small proportion. As it happens, the high rate of depression in anxiety disorder patients suggests that the anxiety disorder simply manifests itself at some time by a set of depressive symptoms. In a community study of 67 panic disorder patients, 45% had a depression. Thus it seems clear that the high prevalence of major depression in a clinic population of anxiety disorders is reflected also in the community (Boyd et al., 1984). Not only is depression secondary to anxiety disorder of considerable importance, but depressions secondary to other disorders associated with problems in living, such as neuroses, alcoholism, drug abuse, and antisocial personality, are not trivial complications.

Using the findings of a six-year follow-up of subjects with a history of nonaffective disorders that met Research Diagnostic Criteria, Coryell (personal communication, 1990) projected who would develop a depression. This projection was based on the assumption that observed age-specific risks would persist over the next 40 years. Of these nonaffective-disordered subjects, 93% had a primary diagnosis of substance abuse disorder, anxiety disorder, or antisocial personality. According to Coryell, 83% of men and 100% of women would develop a depression that met the Research Diagnostic Criteria by age 29. This suggests that a secondary depression may be even more prevalent than previously thought.

Demographic and clinical variables separate primary from secondary depressions rather clearly. Table 11.1 presents these data. In general, one may note that compared with primary depressive patients, secondary depressive patients are more likely to be divorced or separated, less likely to have psychotic symptoms such as delusions, less likely to show the *DSM-III* complex of melancholia, and more likely to make suicide attempts both before and after discharge (Black, Winokur, and Nasrallah, 1987a). In a specific study of psychotic symptoms, Black and Nasrallah (1989) showed that patients with secondary depression were less likely to show any hallucinations and were less likely to show either auditory or visual hallucinations. Regarding delusions, both mood-congruent and mood-incongruent delusions were less likely seen in patients with secondary unipolar depression. For definite psychosis, which meant that the individual had unequivocal delusions and/or hallucinations, 19% of the patients with primary depression showed this compared with only 9.3% of the patients with secondary depression. Thus the presence of psychotic symptoms differentiates primary from secondary depression.

Winokur, Black, and Nasrallah (1988) compared patients who had depression secondary to substance abuse with those who had depression secondary to somatoform disorders, anxiety disorders, or personality disorders. Of course, those with depression secondary to substance abuse were more likely to be male than the other group. Sixty-four percent of patients with depression secondary to substance

Table 11.1. Demographic and Clinical Variables in Primary Versus Secondary Depressive Patients

Variable	Primary Depressive	Secondary Depressive
N	763	324
Age at index	45	41
Female	66%	58%
Divorced/separated	20%	28%
Precipitating event	49%	64%
Delusions	18%	9%
DSM-III[a] melancholia	16%	6%
Prior suicide attempts	33%	45%
Age of onset > 40	37%	23%
Episode duration > 1 yr.	17%	26%
Suicide attempts after discharge	5%	12%
DST[b] nonsuppression at 8:00 A.M. and/or 4:00 P.M.	97/183 (53%)	20/78 (26%)

Note: All differences are significant at the .001 level except percent female (*p* < .05) and percent divorced/separated (*p* < .01).
[a]Third edition of the *Diagnostic and Statistical Manual of Mental Disorders.*
[b]Dexamethasone suppression test.

abuse showed previous suicide attempts, as opposed to 41% of those with depressions secondary to the other disorders. Suicidal thoughts, organic features, and age at index were not clearly different between the groups, though onset of illness after the age of 40 was seen in only 9% of depressions secondary to substance abuse but 16% of depressions secondary to the other disorders.

Weissmann et al. (1977) evaluated symptom patterns in primary and secondary depression. More specifically, this study dealt with primary depressions, depressions secondary to opiate addiction, and depressions secondary to alcoholism. There was also a group of depressions secondary to schizophrenia, but this poses another problem and need not be dealt with here. The symptom pattern of secondary depression was similar to that of primary depression but generally less severe. As in other studies, secondary depressions in opiate addiction and alcoholism were rather common. Specifically, when compared with patients with primary depression, patients with depressions secondary to opiate addiction were less obsessional, less depressed, less anxious, and less hostile as well as less psychotic. When the patients with depression secondary to alcoholism were compared with patients with primary depression, the former were less compulsive and less depressed. Pottenger et al. (1978) followed up the depressive symptoms in 61 alcohol-abusing individuals after one year. These depressive symptoms were rarely treated with antidepressant medication. After the year, 59% of the alcoholic patients were clinically depressed, even though the patients had attended a standard treatment program for alcoholism. There was no significant change in depressive symptoms between intake and one-year follow-up. Thus, in depression secondary to alcoholism, depression is a persistent state.

Bibb and Guze (1972) compared a group of patients with depressions secondary to hysteria (Briquet's syndrome) to a group of patients with primary depression. They determined that the depressed mood, often complicated by alcohol or drug abuse or suicidal behavior, was the usual reason for admission in these secondary depression patients. Cross-sectionally, the depressive symptoms of the depressions secondary to the somatization disorder and the primary depressions were really not much different. However, patients with secondary depression and hysteria were less likely to receive electroconvulsive therapy. Also, the history of previous hospitalizations and operations was far higher in the patients with depression secondary to hysteria than in patients with primary depression. Patients with secondary depression in this study were more likely to have had previous drug reactions, such as reactions to penicillin, narcotics, or any drug. They were more likely to have a history of alcohol or drug abuse. Of course, these things can be expected in a person who has many personality problems and problems in interaction with both the medical care system as well as the community. In essence then, those patients whose depression is secondary to somatization disorder truly fill the definition that has been given for neurotic depression.

Grove et al. (1987a) compared 327 patients who had primary depression with 191 patients who had secondary depression. In this study there were also 51 "complicated" depressive patients who had at least one depressive episode before and another after developing the nonaffective condition. The complicated cases have the earliest onset, the longest duration, and the greatest severity in the index episode. Comparing the primary depression patients and the noncomplicated secondary depression patients, the former were more likely to show weight gain and have diurnal variation, with their mood worse in the morning. Patients with secondary depression were more likely to show subjective anger, overt irritability, and suspiciousness. Interestingly, only 7% of those with secondary depressions had received electroconvulsive therapy, as opposed to 18% of the primary depression patients, and incapacitation with prior episodes was seen more frequently in the primary than in the secondary patients. Sixty percent of the primary depression patients had never had a hospitalization prior to index. This could be compared with patients with secondary depression, who had no hospitalization in 51% of the cases, and patients with complicated secondary depression, who had no hospitalization in only 41% of the cases. Multiple hospitalizations was more frequently seen in the cases of complicated secondary depression. Grove et al. concluded that the data do not discriminate between two possible hypotheses, that secondary and complicated depressions are basically depressions that happen to occur in a nonaffectively ill person or are different disorders that are distinguished clinically by characteristics related to severity.

The largest and most comprehensive family and family history study on primary versus secondary affective disorders was reported by Grove et al. (1987b). Table 11.2 presents their data. Again, these concern a large group of primary depression patients ($n = 327$), a group of secondary depression patients ($n = 191$), and a set of complicated secondary depression patients ($n = 51$). The data were derived from personal interviews of relatives (family study method) and a systematic family history. For the family study material, there was no difference in the amount of familial major depression among primary, secondary, and complicated secondary depressions. The percentages of relatives ill with major depression were, respectively, 32.9%, 30.6%, and 33.7%. For antisocial personality, there was a significant difference even when the probands with depression secondary to antisocial personality were removed. Thus .7% of relatives of patients with primary depression, .7% of relatives of patients with secondary depression, and 3.9% of relatives of patients with complicated secondary depression showed antisocial personality. There was also a significant difference in phobia in the relatives of secondary depression patients. Thus, even when one evaluates the relatives of nonphobic secondary depressive patients, the difference is found, with the percentages being 3.2%, 6.6%, and 5.4%, respectively, for primary, secondary, and complicated secondary depression. Likewise, generalized anxiety disorder was more frequently found in relatives of both groups of secondary depression patients: in secondary depression 9.6% of the relatives showed generalized anxiety disorder, and in complicated secondary depression 12.5% of the relatives showed it, but only 6.7% of relatives of primary depression patients showed this disorder.

Using material gleaned from both family history and family study, again there was no difference between the three groups in terms of familial primary depression. However, using the combined methodology, alcoholism was found to be higher in the relatives of non-

Table 11.2. Family History and Family Study Findings in Primary, Secondary, and Complicated Secondary Depression

Finding	Primary (Proband N = 327)		Secondary (Proband N = 191)		Complicated (Proband N = 51)		p =
	n Relatives	(%)	n Relatives	(%)	n Relatives	(%)	
Rates of illnesses in interviewed relatives (family study)							
N relatives interviewed	715		333		104		
Major depression, primary	179	(25)	66	(20)	21	(20)	.134
Major depression, secondary	56	(8)	36	(11)	14	(14)	.086
Antisocial personality (proband does not have antisocial personality)	5	(1)	2	(1)	4	(4)	.008
Phobia (proband is nonphobic)	23	(3)	18	(7)	5	(5)	.055
Generalized anxiety disorder	48	(7)	32	(10)	13	(13)	.061
Rates of family-history—defined illness in all relatives							
N relatives	2,142		1,178		297		
Major depression, secondary	131	(6)	103	(9)	18	(6)	.014
Alcoholism (proband is not alcoholic)	202	(10)	55	(14)	6	(7)	.033
Drug use (proband is not a drug user)	43	(2)	29	(3)	12	(5)	.008

alcoholic patients with secondary depression than in the primary depression group. Thus, familial alcoholism was seen in 14% of the relatives of the patients (alcoholic patients excluded) with secondary depression, 9.9% of the relatives of patients with primary depression, and 7.2% of the relatives of patients with complicated secondary depression. Drug use disorder was also more frequent in the relatives of patients with secondary depression or complicated secondary depression than in the relatives of patients with primary depression.

Looking specifically at patients with primary depression and those with depression secondary to alcoholism, and using the family study method, antisocial personality was most frequently seen in patients with complicated secondary depression but was about equal in the patients with secondary depression and those with primary depression. Generalized anxiety was again found more frequently in the relatives of patients with secondary depression. Among patients with primary depression the percentage of relatives with generalized anxiety disorder was 6.7%, among patients with secondary depression it was 9.9%, and among patients with complicated depression it was 15.3%. The increase in familial generalized anxiety disorder was specifically related to probands with depression secondary to alcoholism. Table 11.3 presents these data. Antisocial personality using the family history method was more frequently seen in the relatives of both secondary depression and complicated secondary patients than in relatives of primary depression patients. In summary, probably the most interesting set of findings is that in the families of patients with secondary depression anxiety disorders were more frequently seen than in the families of patients with primary depression. This was true even when the probands with depression secondary to anxiety disorders were eliminated. Likewise, antisocial personality seemed to be related to secondary depression, even when patients with antisocial personality were eliminated from the secondary depression group. This set of data suggests a general tendency for anxiety disorders, antisocial personality, and alcoholism to run in families of patients with secondary depression.

The course of the illness separates primary from secondary major depression rather well. Coryell, Zimmerman, and Pfohl (1985) evaluated 110 patients with primary depression and 38 patients with secondary depression. Of the latter, 82% had depression secondary to somatization disorder, alcoholism, antisocial personality, anxiety disorder, or other drug abuse. The first hospitalization in the patients with secondary depression was somewhat earlier than that of the patients with primary depression, and the index episode for the patients with secondary depression was longer than that for the patients

Table 11.3. Rates of Illness in Interviewed Relatives and All Relatives (Family History) of Primary Depression and Alcoholic Probands

	Primary Depression		Depression Secondary to Alcoholism		Complicated Secondary Depression		
	n Relatives	(%)	n Relatives	(%)	n Relatives	(%)	p =
Interviewed relatives							
N	715		202		72		
Secondary major depression	56	(8)	18	(9)	12	(17)	.040
Antisocial personality	5	(1)	1	(1)	4	(6)	.000
Generalized anxiety	48	(7)	20	(10)	11	(15)	.020
Family-history–defined illness							
N	2,142		784		214		
Primary major depression	298	(14)	79	(10)	34	(16)	.011
Drug use	44	(2)	42	(5)	13	(6)	.000
Antisocial personality	50	(2)	32	(4)	7	(3)	.038

with primary depression. At discharge there had been significantly more improvement in the patients with primary depression: they showed a greater improvement on the Global Assessment Scale, which evaluates both symptomatology and incapacity. Most of the patients were followed up after a six-month period. Recovery was defined as at least eight weeks with none of the criteria depressive symptoms. At six months, twice as many primary depression patients (32%) than secondary depression patients (16%) had recovered. Patients with secondary depression in the six-month follow-up had a far higher proportion of weeks in which they showed a full depressive syndrome, and their weekly symptom level was higher. In terms of proportion of weeks during which patients felt they were back to their normal selves, this occurred in 45% of the weeks for the patients with primary depression but only 21% of the weeks for the patients with secondary depression. In the final week of the six-month assessment, patients with primary depression were better as regards symptoms as well as capacity for productive living.

This study suggests what has been noted before—that patients with secondary depression are less likely to have a clearly episodic illness with marked improvement in between. Coryell (1988) noted that in addition to the fact that there is a lower recovery rate in secondary depression compared with primary depression, secondary depression is less episodic and shows a higher relapse rate. Black, Winokur, and Nasrallah (1987a, 1987b, 1987c) showed data on course, some of which are presented in Table 11.1. Episode duration was higher for patients with secondary depression and these patients were more likely to make a suicide attempt after discharge. There was no significant difference in the number who died during follow-up, the number of deaths due to suicide, or the percentage of deaths due to suicide. For naturalistic treatment in the hospital, of those who received total adequate therapy there was a significant difference between the primary depression and the secondary depression patients: 68% of the primary group recovered versus 40% of the secondary group. The group of secondary depression patients in these studies included patients whose depression was secondary to medical illness. Those with depressions secondary to psychiatric syndromes did even less well (recovery in these patients was only 36%).

Zorumski et al. (1986) studied 58 persons with major depression. In 91% of the patients with primary unipolar depression, there was partial or complete remission of depressive symptoms, whereas this occurred in only 56% of the patients with secondary depression. It seems clear that the patients with primary depression showed a more troublesome illness as regards chronic symptomatology.

There have been a number of studies of laboratory findings in primary versus secondary depression. Coryell (1988) assessed 13 separate studies that examined nonsuppression in the dexamethasone suppression test in secondary versus primary depression. The diagnostic specificity was extremely good in favor of the separation. Of the 13 studies, only one was not in favor of a larger percentage of nonsuppressors in the primary group. Coryell et al. (1983) assessed the results in the dexamethasone suppression test according to the primary/secondary distinction. There was a marked difference between primary and secondary depression when multiple tests were considered. The use of multiple dexamethasone suppression tests doubled the sensitivity of the test in primary depression. Thus, with multiple tests none of the patients with secondary depression became nonsuppressors, but 14.3% of the patients with primary depression were nonsuppressors at baseline and this increased to 48% at the end of multiple tests. All of the tests in this case were defined as four tests, three after the index test. In another study, Coryell, Gaffney, and Burkhardt (1982) attempted to compare the current validity of two alternative subclassifications of major depression: the distinction between primary and secondary depression and the *DSM-III* separation of melancholic and nonmelancholic depression. The distinction between primary and secondary depression was valid. Forty-four percent of the patients with primary depression were nonsuppressors on the dexamethasone suppression test, whereas none of the patients with secondary depression had abnormal test results. On the other hand, the comparison between *DSM-III* melancholic versus *DSM-III* nonmelancholic depression was not validated. In fact, it went opposed to the prediction. Thirty-five percent of the depressed patients without melancholia were nonsuppressors, as opposed to 27% of the patients with melancholia.

Though most of the literature supports the separation of primary from secondary depression using the dexamethasone suppression test, there are some negative findings. Giles et al. (1987a) showed no significant difference in the amount of abnormal nonsuppression between primary and secondary depression patients. Further, these investigators found there was no difference in mean rapid eye movement latency between primary and secondary depression: 38% of the patients with primary depression showed a shorted latency (65.0 minutes or less), as opposed to 52% of the patients with secondary depression. Akiskal (1983), on the other hand, showed a shortened rapid eye movement latency in primary depression and a latency in secondary depression that was similar to that of controls.

There is one other promising laboratory finding. Patients with major depression show a significantly lower number of tritiated imipramine binding sites on platelets (Pecknold et al., 1987). This has been reported before and was confirmed by Pecknold et al. They also evaluated the tritiated imipramine binding sites in 43 patients with panic disorder. The number of binding sites in the patients with panic disorder did not differ significantly from that in normal controls, and even in those panic disorder patients who had concurrent major depression or a past history of depression there was no difference from normal controls. These probably would be secondary depression, secondary to the panic disorder, and in these the imipramine binding finding showed normality. According to the authors, these results suggest that the two syndromes, major depressive disorder and secondary depression to anxiety disorder, may have distinct neurochemical substrates.

Treatment differences between primary and secondary depression have been reported. Black, Winokur, and Nasrallah (1987b) presented data showing that short hospitalizations were more typical of patients with secondary depression. Though there were no differences in receiving antidepressants, the patients with primary depression were far more likely to be treated with electroconvulsive therapy during an episode than were the patients with secondary depression. Response to treatment was quite different between the two groups. Seventy-three percent of the patients with primary depression recovered with electroconvulsive therapy, but only 52% of the patients with secondary depression recovered. Fifty-six percent of the primary depression patients recovered with adequate antidepressant treatment, versus only 30% of the secondary depression patients. For adequate therapy either electroconvulsive therapy or antidepressant) 68% of the primary, as opposed to only 40% of the secondary, patients recovered. As noted before, when the depressions secondary to a medical illness were removed, the recovery rate in the remaining patients with depression secondary to psychiatric illness went down to 36%. For inadequate therapy, 53% of the primary, as opposed to 45% of the secondary, patients recovered. This was not a significant difference. Coryell and Turner (1985) evaluated desipramine therapy in subtypes of nonpsychotic major depression. Patients with secondary depression were somewhat more likely to respond to placebo and were significantly less likely to complete the entire course of treatment. The distinction between primary and secondary depression, but not that between endogenous and nonendogenous depression, predicted clinical status after desipramine therapy. After six weeks, 44% of the patients with primary depression were recovered, compared with 0% of the patients with secondary depression.

We may summarize the preceding studies by saying that certainly patients with primary depression differ from those with secondary depression in a variety of ways, including clinical picture, course of illness, presence of laboratory tests, and effects of treatment. The nature of secondary depression is interesting. It is possible that secondary depressions are in fact reactive depressions to chronic problems in living and personality conflicts. This possibility arose in a recent study of secondary depression, panic disorder, and agoraphobia. Lesser et al. (1989) found that the agoraphobic group contained the highest proportion of subjects who showed a current major depressive episode at the time of the study. They also had been ill with their panic disorder for the longest period of time. These authors suggested that "many of the secondary depressions seen in our subjects seem to be akin to demoralization . . . perhaps the consequence of living the constricted life of someone with panic disorder" (Lesser et al., 1989, p. 56). It is not possible to determine whether a depression secondary to a psychiatric disorder that is chronic and incapacitating is in fact reactive. Of course, another possibility is that the symptomatology and pathophysiology of the primary disease overlap with those of the primary depressive disease.

Using a temporal definition (i.e., which came first, the depression or the other illness?), the concept of secondary depression appears simple. However, it is likely that there are many cases in which depression is primary and followed by other well-formed syndromes. A good example of this is primary depression, mainly in women, which is then followed by fully formed alcoholism (Shuckit et al., 1969). This kind of complex relationship suggests that further research would be useful in clarifying the primary-secondary distinction.

12 Reactive Unipolar Depression

At the end of chapter 11, we raised the specter of reactive depression, a subject that has created all kinds of mischief in psychiatry. For one thing, a reactive depression is often considered synonymous with a neurotic depression, but, in fact, the definitions are different. A reactive depression is a depressive state that is produced by an external situation or stress. A neurotic depression is a depression that begins in an individual who has had a long history of problems in living, that is, a "neurotic" life-style. A reactive depression implies a clear etiology. A neurotic depression implies no such etiology but is diagnosed on the basis of preexisting characteristics. Could the problems in living create the kind of stress that produces a reactive depression? Possibly, but the fact remains that although the neurotic depression is secondary to the chronically unstable life-style, one can never be sure that it is reactive.

There is some difficulty in assessing the importance of life events in the cause of affective illnesses. It is often difficult to determine whether an environmental stress was caused by the individual or whether the stress caused the individual to become depressed. The way out of this dilemma is to simply evaluate independent life events, such as the death of somebody close. However, these are not as common as some of the stresses that might not be independent, and it would be difficult to get a large sample. Nevertheless, this is one way to assess stressful events. The other problem is exactly when an affective episode starts. Physicians are very good at telling whether a patient is suffering from a depression but not as good in determining the time of onset. Some kinds of affective episodes, for example, depressions and manias in bipolar patients, occur precipitously and are more easily dated. On the other hand, a depression starting a few months after a birth of a child would be far more difficult to date. Did it occur relatively shortly

after delivery, or only after the recovery period from the pregnancy
had been passed and the mother had to take full charge of the child?
Or did it occur several months after delivery as a result of a forced
change in life-style? Determining onset is not a problem with postpartum psychosis, which clearly occurs very shortly after delivery and is
often manifested by delusions, hallucinations, and grossly manic or
depressed behavior, but it is a problem in the case of a mild to moderate depression in a woman who has had a child in the last few months.

Another problem is that research into life events as a cause of
depression may suffer from a halo effect. Patients, their families, and,
for that matter, many investigators believe that undesirable life events
and stress can cause a depression. It is possible that in the clinical
evaluation this belief may influence an individual's recording of the
importance of the life event. Finally, in addition to the problems of
dating life events, dating the onset of depression, and the halo effect,
there is the fact that life events are extremely common. To show how
commonplace such events are, over the years I have asked medical
students to raise their hands if something extremely upsetting happened to them in the prior two weeks. Usually a quarter to three-
quarters of the class respond affirmatively. Should they have become
depressed, it is not inconceivable that they would have attributed the
depression to such occurrences. Had they not become depressed, it is
conceivable that they might have trivialized these occurrences and
therefore not reported them.

Probably the best way to determine the existence of a reactive depression is to study fairly major common stressful life events or uncommon natural and unnatural disasters. Such occurrences are plausible precipitants of a depressive state. If such a depressive state is
found more frequently than would be expected by chance, the evidence at least supports the existence of a reactive depression. No
doubt the best studied phenomenon is the syndromal response to a
normal bereavement. Quite simply the data show that a reactive depression does exist. Clayton, Desmarais, and Winokur (1968) systematically interviewed relatives of a series of deceased hospital patients.
Three symptoms (depressed mood, sleep disturbance, and crying)
occurred in more than half of the subjects. Such symptoms as fear of
losing one's mind or loss of interest in church or job were rare occurrences. These are of interest because they are commonly seen in
hospitalized depressive patients. Such symptoms as trouble concentrating and anxiety attacks were seen in a sizeable minority of the
patients. In a subsequent study, Clayton, Halikas, and Maurice (1972)
reported on 109 widows and widowers who had suffered a recent
bereavement. A set of criteria for the diagnosis of depression was

presented that included feeling sad, depressed, or despondent and four or five of the following symptoms: loss of appetite, weight loss, sleep difficulties, fatigue, restlessness, loss of interest, difficulty concentrating, marked guilt feelings, wishing to be dead, or suicide thoughts. This cluster had to succeed the death of the spouse. Thirty-five percent of the subjects received a diagnosis of depression. Besides those symptoms, such symptoms as feeling hopeless and feeling a burden were also more frequent in the depressed bereaved compared with the not depressed bereaved. There were no significant differences between the depressed and not depressed in taking sleep medication, taking tranquilizers, or seeing physicians. A family history of a psychiatric illness (i.e., a primary affective disorder or alcoholism) was not related to being depressed in this group. These patients were followed up and at the end of 13 months, 17% of the widows and widowers showed a depression (Bornstein et al., 1973). A subject depressed at one month postdeath had a significantly higher risk of also being depressed after one year. Those depressed after one year were compared with the nondepressed group on the variables of seeing a doctor since the death, seeing a doctor for symptoms related to grief, and taking sleeping medicine and tranquilizers since the death. There were no significant differences between groups. However, the depressed group had significantly more cases of general poor health. Clayton et al. (1974) compared the symptoms in the depressed patients from the bereavement study with patients from an independent study of primary affective disorder (see Table 12.1). The groups were matched for age and sex. The patients with primary depression were from a study by Woodruff, Murphy, and Herjanic (1967). Of particular interest is the fact that the constellation of symptoms differed between the primary depressed and the bereaved depressed patients. Suicidal thoughts, retardation, worthlessness, and loss of interest and friendship were rare in bereavement depression but common in primary depression. These symptoms are commonly related to the concept of endogenous depression.

The dexamethasone suppression test was abnormal in 60% to 70% of severe and/or psychotic depression patients as well as in patients with major depression with melancholic features. Abnormality ordinarily is defined as nonsuppression (less than 5 µg/l) at 8:00 A.M., 4:00 P.M., and 11:00 P.M. following a 1-mg dose of dexamethasone at 11:00 P.M. the night before (American Psychiatric Association Task Force, 1987). This test has also been used in an acute grief reaction with depressive symptoms (Das and Berrios, 1984). Of 21 bereaved first-degree relatives, only two were nonsuppressors and their grief scores were no higher than those of the 19 normal suppressors. These find-

Table 12.1. Comparison of Symptoms of Primary Depression and Depression following Bereavement

Symptom	Primary Depression[a] (%)	Bereavement Depression[b] (%)
Significant differences		
Rather be dead	50	—
Suicidal thoughts	47	—
Retardation	38	—
Burden	44	—
Hopeless	65	6
Worthlessness	53	3
Loss of interest in friends	47	6
Poor concentration	91	44
Terminal insomnia	82	29
Anorexia	91	47
Weight loss	85	41
Mood worse in morning	41	15
Fatigue	82	44
Visual blurring	29	3
Guilt	53	26
Loss of interest in reading, sports, or television	71	44
Loss of other interest	29	6
Thinking slowed	56	59
Irritability	53	26
Cries easily	59	94
Nonsignificant comparisons		
Depression	91	79
Loss of interest in job	35	29
Suicide attempts	9	—
Angry	18	3
Derealization	—	6
Depersonalization	3	—
Auditory hallucinations	3	—
Visual hallucinations	—	3
Initial insomnia	59	50
Headache	35	29
Dyspnea	21	12
Anxiety attack	24	12
Constipation	38	18
Abdominal pain	15	3

[a]$N = 34.$
[b]$N = 34.$

170

ings suggest that a reactive depression to bereavement may be qualitatively different from the depression of a hospitalized depressed patient.

Another life event that might qualify as a precipitant for depression is a major medical illness. In a study of depression in medical inpatients, Moffic and Paykel (1975) concluded that these depressive states were appropriate to their life circumstances. In other words, they could be considered reactive. Hong et al. (1987) studied patients with end-stage renal disease and suggested that the depression associated with this illness was reactive in nature. Carney et al. (1987) systematically interviewed patients with newly diagnosed coronary artery disease and found that 18% were currently experiencing a major depression that met criteria of the *Diagnostic and Statistical Manual of Mental Disorders (Third Edition-Revised) (DSM-III-R)*. Such a high rate of depression, specifically associated with a recent diagnosis, strongly suggests that the depression was reactive in nature. Wells, Golding, and Burnam (1988) compared a sample of the general population who had chronic medical conditions with another sample who did not have such concurrent conditions. In this large epidemiologic study, people with chronic medical conditions were more likely to have lifetime substance abuse disorders and to have recent affective and anxiety disorders. Medical conditions such as arthritis, cancer, lung disease, neurologic illness, heart disorder, and physical handicap were particularly associated with psychiatric disorders. Persons who were being treated for heart disease had a higher prevalence of a recent psychiatric disorder than did those not under care for a chronic medical condition. A major point of this study was that the authors found a high prevalence of both recent and lifetime affective disorders among persons with chronic medical conditions. Noyes and Kathol (1986) reviewed the relationship of depression and cancer. They cited a series of surveys of inpatient populations that suggested that the prevalence of depression was higher among cancer patients than it was in the general population. Estimates of depression for cancer inpatients ranged from 17% to 45%, compared with a six-month prevalence of depression of 2% to 4%, in the general population. There is some controversy in the literature about the amount of depression. Bukberg, Penman, and Holland (1984) found that 42% of oncology inpatients could be diagnosed as having a major depression according to *DSM-III* criteria. Of these, 24% had severe symptoms and 18% had symptoms of moderate severity. The controversy occurs because Derogatis et al. (1984), using the same criteria, found only 6% of cancer patients to have major depression. However, 47% of the patients received psychiatric diagnoses. The majority had adjustment disorders, which included 12% with depressed mood and 13% with mixed emotional features. Possibly some of these would overlap with *DSM-III* major depressions.

In addition to the association of depression with cancer, there is also a strong association of suicide with cancer. In a review of the risk of suicide among persons with cancer, Noyes and Kathol (1986) cited three studies from cancer registries. In a Finnish study, there was an increased risk for suicide, with the highest risk being associated with gastrointestinal cancer. The risk was higher in patients with non-localized tumors and those not undergoing treatment. In a Connecticut tumor registry study, there was a significant greater risk in men soon after diagnosis, but the risk in women was not higher than that of the general population. In a New York state cancer registry study, again a greater risk for suicide was found than would be expected. Also, the risk was greater among younger patients. Stewart, Drake, and Winokur (1965) evaluated 60 severely ill medical patients, and 20 manic-depressive, depressed patients. Among the medically ill patients, one in five patients had a clinical depression following the onset of an illness that was likely to be fatal or lead to severe disability. The depressions associated with medical illness differed from that of the hospitalized depressives in that the former did not have suicidal tendencies, had fewer symptoms, and did not have previous episodes of depression or family histories for depression.

Winokur, Black, and Nasrallah (1988) evaluated a series of depressed inpatients, some of whom had depression secondary to psychiatric illnesses (substance abuse disorders, somatoform disorders, anxiety disorders, or personality disorders). These were compared with patients who had depressions secondary to medical illness. Patients with depressions secondary to psychiatric illnesses had an earlier age of onset, were more likely to have suicidal thoughts or to have made suicide attempts, and were less likely to have memory problems. They were less likely improved with treatment and more likely to relapse on follow-up. They had more alcoholism in their families than patients whose depressions were secondary to medical illnesses. Also, patients who had depressions secondary to medical illnesses were more likely to have no family history of alcoholism or depression. The medical diagnoses in those who had depressions secondary to medical illness encompassed such illnesses as cardiovascular disease, cancer, chronic obstructive pulmonary disease, kidney disease, and severe parkinsonism. Data are presented in Table 12.2, and all comparisons are statistically significant, except for the family history comparison of depression only. Of note is the fact that alcoholism was more frequent in patients with depression secondary to psychiatric disorders

Table 12.2. Comparison of Depression Secondary to Psychiatric Disorders and Depression Secondary to Medical Illness

Finding	Secondary to Psychiatric Disorders (N = 289)	Secondary to Medical Illnesses (N = 112)
Older than 50 at index admission	21%	60%
Index admission is first psychiatric admission	25%	56%
Older than 50 at onset of psychiatric illness	14%	55%
Sensorium defect	8%	17%
Thoughts of suicide	55%	36%
Previous suicide attempts	48%	26%
Marked improvement at discharge	38%	50%
Deceased in follow-up	7%	28%
No relapse in follow-up	72/147 (49%)	42/64 (66%)
Family history excluding probands with depressions secondary to alcoholism or drug abuse		
Depression only	18%	18%
Alcoholism	36%	19%
Neither alcoholism nor depression	47%	64%

than in patients with depression secondary to medical illnesses, even though the depressions secondary to alcoholism and/or drug abuse had been removed from the comparison. The increased death rate in follow-up favoring patients with depression secondary to medical illness was related to the seriousness of the medical illness and also to the older age of that group. The significant difference in relapse in follow-up showing that patients whose depression was secondary to medical illness did better is interesting. It suggests that depressions secondary to medical illness are reactive depressions and as the patients come to terms with their medical problems, they may return to adequate functioning, whereas patients who have depression secondary to psychiatric disorders have a chronic course of personality difficulties and adverse life events.

Though there are many caveats in life event research, it seems clear that the results of numerous controlled studies support the idea of an excess of life events occurring in conjunction with depressive illness (Brown et al., 1973; Paykel, 1982). Paykel noted that careful interview techniques can produce reliable and valid information. Such circumstances as deaths and interpersonal separations have been studied extensively. Paykel reviewed 11 separate studies that reported on recent separations, and in 6 of these studies depressive patients reported more separations than the control groups. The control groups included both general population and other psychiatric patients. Interestingly, there was no excess of separations when medical patients were used as controls. In general, Paykel noted that these studies suggest that recent separations are important in depression, but the relationship is not overwhelming, because in most of the studies a substantial portion of the depressive patients did not report recent separations.

A good example of the difficulty in separating cause from effect in terms of depression and life events is divorce (Briscoe and Smith, 1973). Although divorce appears to be a plausible cause of depression, it is equally possible that depression may precipitate divorce.

Life stress as a causal factor in depression has really not been able to separate patients with neurotic depressions from those with endogenous depressions, and it is possible that a precipitating factor in depression may not be very important in defining the "non-endogenous" group. Paykel (1979, 1982) suggested that precipitating factors are seen in all kinds of depressions. Precipitated depressions (reactive) showed relatively few differences in symptomatology from unprecipitated depressions, which might be considered more "endogenous."

Another term for a reactive depression is "situational depression." A situational depression is a depressive illness that develops after an event or in a situation that is likely to have contributed to a depression at that time (Hirschfeld, 1981; Hirschfeld et al., 1985). Hirschfeld and co-workers compared situational major depressions with nonsituational major depressions. In this study there was no difference in clinical characteristics or family history. Bronisch and Hecht (1989) studied 22 patients with a situationally provoked *DSM-III* major depression (adjustment disorder). These patients were selected from a sample of inpatients who had been admitted for treatment to a crisis intervention unit at the Max Planck Institute of Psychiatry in Munich. They were compared with a sample of patients with major depression. The subjects with adjustment disorder had less severe depressive symptomatology, less social dysfunction, and a faster remission rate. Of some interest is the fact that Avery and Lubrano (1979) reevaluated responsiveness to imipramine or electroconvulsive therapy in a large Italian treatment study (the DeCarolis study). Precipitating events did not distinguish responsiveness to these treatments, but patients who were diagnosed as having "neurotic depression" may have responded considerably less well.

The role of precipitating factors in depression is still unsettled. A totally different methodology could at least tell us whether a significant reactive depression might exist. That methodology would take into account that certain things that happen to people are stressful enough that they might be able legitimately to make a claim to etiologic significance. Thus instead of starting with a depression and looking at precipitating factors, perhaps we ought to start with the life event and look to see whether an illness occurred after the life event. As an example, the death of a close person might reasonably be expected to cause a bereavement that might show the symptoms of a depression. Likewise, a chronic stress, such as a serious medical illness, might be evaluated in order to determine if depression were more likely associated with that. Other possibilities that might cause a depression are major natural calamities or significant economic changes that influence the community in a deleterious fashion. Should such events be related to an increase in depressive illness, we would at least be able to say that a reactive depression to them does exist. It would still not tell us a great deal about the importance of reactive depression in clinical psychiatry, but it would have considerable theoretical difference.

Probably the best studied major stress is the death of somebody close, but in addition to bereavement and serious medical illness other possible etiologic causes for depressive episodes might be natural and unnatural disasters. The natural disaster would be one that was not under human control, for example, a tornado, an earthquake, or a forest fire. An unnatural disaster would be one that humans at least potentially could control, such as radioactive spill at a nuclear plant (e.g., Three Mile Island in Pennsylvania) or a series of economic depressions or farm foreclosures. Bromet and Schulberg (1987) reviewed some epidemiologic findings from disaster research. In the Three Mile Island nuclear accident, the mothers of young children showed a twofold increase in rate of major depression and/or generalized anxiety during the year after the disaster. In essence, these were considered reactive depressions. Some vulnerability factors were related to the development of a psychiatric problem, including proximity to the nuclear plant, a history of psychiatric problems in the past, and having poor social support from friends and relatives. The volcanic eruption of Mount St. Helen was also studied (Shore, Tatum, and Vollmer, 1986). These investigators compared the community exposed to the eruption and severely affected by it with a similar nonexposed community. Psychiatric disorder was diagnosed by administering a systematic interview. The three most common conditions found were depression, generalized anxiety, and posttraumatic stress disorder. Bromet and Schulberg (1987) concluded that these epidemiologic studies of disasters confirm a significant increase in psychiatric morbidity that occurs after the event. More specifically, one may note that depression is one of the psychiatric conditions that are seen in excess of what might be expected.

Unnatural disasters are related to affective illness as well. These may be approached from the statistics on suicide. Lunden (1977) has published international figures on suicide rates during economic depression, farm foreclosures, and war. The suicide rates during economic depression and in a period during which there were a lot of farm foreclosures were high. During war time, they were low. Wasserman (1984) showed that the national economy is inversely related to national suicide rates. The average monthly duration of unemployment from 1947 to 1977 and a business index from 1910 to 1939 are both statistically related to the monthly suicide rate and suggest that in most cases a downturn in the economy is causally related to an increase in the suicide rate.

The cycles that are presented are not simple, however. They are complicated by the possibility that there may be differences between the sexes, differences between urban and rural populations, and differences between people at risk with varying past histories of psychologic difficulties. In a study of female unemployment and attempted suicide, Hawton, Fagg, and Simkin (1988) pointed out that rates of attempted suicide among unemployed women were 8 to 11 times higher than those of employed women and were particularly high in women who were unemployed for more than a year. However, many more of the unemployed women who attempted suicide had a history of prior psychiatric difficulties, were suffering from alcoholism, and had made repeated suicide attempts. One explanation for this is that the secondary consequences of unemployment increased the risk of suicide behavior. However, another possible interpretation is that these women were already predisposed to psychiatric difficulties and hence women who attempted suicide might have been more likely to become unemployed. In any event, it is not a simple matter. The complexity of the relationships has been also noted by McFarlane (1986, 1989). In a group of firefighters who were exposed to an Australian bush fire disaster, he found that 36 of them presented for psychiatric treatment. Of these, 13 had a major depression or some variant of this. In following up these people for as long as 29 months, he determined that "neuroticism" and a past history of treatment for a psychologic disorder were better predictors of posttraumatic morbidity than the degree of exposure to the disaster or the losses sustained. Thus, the question of whether the traumatic event played a central causal role was unanswered. However, as already noted, such events as bereavement and medical disease clearly seemed to be related to the precipitating event as an etiologic factor in a depressive syndrome.

In patients who have reactive depressions, one of the questions that arise is whether they see physicians and whether they are treated. Because the depression seems to be a rational or plausible response to a life stress, it is less likely that either the family or the patient will seek care. Evaluating depression in surviving widows and widowers, Clayton, Halikas, and Maurice (1972) found that 29% of the depressed survivors took sleep medication, 42% took a tranquilizer, and 42% saw or called a physician since the death, but only 18% saw a physician for symptoms related to grieving. These same patients were followed up after 13 months. Ninety-four percent of the depressed bereaved had visited a physician since the death, but only 25% visited a physician for symptoms related to grieving—not much higher than the figure for shortly after the death. As regards response to treatment in a reactive depression, the data on depression secondary to medical illness are of importance, as may be seen in Table 12.2. Such patients do better than other kinds of secondary depression patients with psychiatric treatment, and they have less likelihood of relapse.

Another term used for reactive depression is *situationally induced depression*. Garvey, Schaffer, and Tuason (1984) compared the response to pharmacologic treatment in patients with a situational depression with that of patients who showed a depression that was not situationally induced. There was no difference in response to antidepressant medication after four to six weeks of treatment. However, there may be differences in the course of illness in these two types of depression and a similar outcome may be due to different factors.

There is no question that a reactive depression that meets criteria exists. How important it is clinically is difficult to estimate. Certainly, a large percentage of patients who suffer reactive depressions do not visit physicians or health care providers for the symptoms of their reactive depression. Nevertheless, some do, and it is important to recognize a reactive depression as a significant affective entity.

13 The Endogenous Unipolar
Depressions

It is altogether fitting that we anchor the classification of the affective disorders with a discussion of endogenous unipolar depression. In general, the diagnosis of a unipolar endogenous depression implies considerable severity. Most of the studies on endogenous depression have been done from a base of hospitalized patients. The term *endogenous* implies an origin from within the body; clearly, it suggests a biologic substrate or cause.

Until 1966, when a series of studies suggested the possibility that bipolar and unipolar affective disorders might be separate illnesses, the studies on endogenous depression included both bipolar and unipolar depressions. Since that time, however, most studies have separated the unipolar from the bipolar depressions. Bipolar and unipolar depressions have a great deal in common, but unipolar depressions are found more frequently in the population as well as in the hospital. An exact breakdown of the frequency of the two conditions is not known. Helgason (1961), in an epidemiologic study of psychiatric illness in Iceland, found 320 patients whose diagnosis included the term *depressive*. Of these, 31 had either only manic attacks or manias and depressions. Of the remaining 289 patients who were solely depressive, 118 were considered psychotic or surely endogenous. Thus, 40% of the patients who had depressive states only would have fit into a category of endogenous. Of some importance is the fact that of the endogenous affective disorders including bipolar and unipolar (31 + 118), unipolar depression was four times more frequent than bipolar depression.

Spicer, Hare, and Slater (1973) calculated the number of patients who had their first admissions for either bipolar illness or psychotic depression. In England and Wales from 1965 to 1966, 4,764 male patients were admitted for psychotic depression and 1,056 for mania.

Thus, among these first admissions, men with psychotic depression were 4.5 times as frequent as men admitted for manic illness. Psychotic depression was diagnosed in this study in 10,208 women; mania was diagnosed in 1,500 women. Thus, women were 6.8 times as likely to become ill with psychotic depression as with manic illness. Of course, about 10% of depressed patients who present at first admission will go on to have a mania, but this would not account for the marked preponderance of endogenous unipolar depression over bipolar illness. Interestingly, in the case of psychotic or endogenous depression, women were twice as likely to be given this diagnosis as men. All of these data refer specifically to patients admitted to psychiatric hospitals.

It is notable that the first admission data suggest there are approximately as many neurotic depressive individuals as there are psychotic depressive individuals admitted to British hospitals. The age at index, however, is quite different. Eighty percent of the psychotic depressive men are admitted for the first time after the age of 40, whereas only 53% of the neurotic depressive men are admitted at this late age. Sixty percent of the psychotic depressive women, but only 40% of the neurotic depressive women, are admitted at age 40 or older. These data suggest that psychotic depression has a later onset than neurotic depression.

Though most of the data on endogenous depression come from hospitalized patients, Watts (1957), a British general practitioner, made the case for a mild endogenous depression that was seen primarily in the office of the community physician. He noted that though 60% of such patients appeared with a complaint of nervous and psychiatric symptoms, the remaining 40% presented with possible organic disease. Noting that severe depression was expressed in the triad of symptoms comprising difficulty in thinking, depressive affect, and psychomotor retardation, he suggested that in patients with mild endogenous depressives such symptoms have to be sought because they are not obvious. The difficulty in thinking was expressed first as a feeling of tiredness or exhaustion in one patient, but ultimately the patient found that he could not concentrate enough to enjoy a book, though he was able to get something from newspaper reading. Further, the difficulty in thinking sometimes was expressed as an illogical approach to a problem. Though patients with a mild endogenous depression do not look depressed, they admit to being in low spirits, their sense of humor goes, and they believe that they are not themselves. They feel isolated and misunderstood. In 100 cases of mild endogenous depression, Watts reported that early-morning awakening was evident in only 44% of the patients, but that far more had some other kind of sleeping difficulty. Psychomotor retardation was manifested mainly by minor habit changes and withdrawal from ordinary social circumstances. As Watts put it, "The pianist never opens her piano, and the keen gardener lets his weeds grow unheeded" (1957, p. 7). That the endogenous depression should be sometimes mild seems eminently reasonable. Certainly, the concept of endogenous should not necessarily be based on the severity of the depression. This strengthens the idea that in the algorithm for diagnosis the neurotic depression should at first be eliminated as a possibility by separating those patients with marked personality difficulties and stormy life-styles and leaving the remainder as the endogenous group. This then keeps us from making a diagnosis of endogenous depression essentially on the basis of severity. It depends more on the absence of previous symptomatology and characteristics.

The concept of the mild endogenous depression can create a problem for epidemiologic studies of endogenous depression itself. Bebbington et al. (1989) calculated the risk of minor depression before age 65 in a community survey. The risk for such a depression was 46% for men and 72% for women. This is, of course, extremely high. The episodes that were considered were characterized by "persistent and unalleviated depression of mood, usually lasting more than a month, and in a majority of cases leading to treatment at least by the family doctor" (Bebbington et al., 1989, p. 394). Many of these depressions could have been endogenous depressions, but there is no way to know what this proportion might be. Until there is an unequivocal method for identifying an endogenous depression, we will be confronted by a high frequency of the depressive syndrome in the general population and the inability to determine confidently which ones are endogenous, reactive, or neurotic.

There are other approaches to the concept of endogenous depression. One term that has been used is *autonomous depression* (Nelson, Charney, and Quinlan, 1980). According to Nelson, Charney, and Quinlan, an autonomous depression is a depression that exhibits a lack of responsiveness to environmental events during hospitalization and prior to much treatment. The nonautonomous group of patients would be those who respond in the first week of treatment with improvement. Such nonautonomous patients appear to respond to the psychologic support provided by the hospital. In line with the concept of endogenous depression, the autonomous group in this study was older, less often separated and divorced, and more likely to show lack of reactivity, delusions, agitation, ruminative thinking, loss of interest, loss of weight, trouble concentrating, self-reproach, retardation, somatic concerns, anorexia, and anergia. Patients with autonomous depression showed a significantly higher number of prior episodes of depression. Regarding personality, they were more likely compulsive and less likely histrionic, borderline, or hostile. Essentially Nelson, Charney, and Quinlan have presented a study that overlaps with the studies on endogenous depression.

Another term that has relevance to the concept of endogenous depression is *delusional depression*. On the basis of the finding that delusional depressions are less responsive to treatment with tricyclic antidepressants than are nondelusional depressions, Glassman and Roose (1981) entertained the possibility that a delusional depression may represent a distinct clinical entity. In their study of hospitalized patients with major affective disorder, they found that delusional patients were more likely to have fewer previous episodes, to have more psychomotor retardation, and to respond less to hospitalization or milieu treatment than nondelusional depressive patients. In a sense these patients look somewhat similar to the patients who have autonomous depression, but they are not totally similar. The autonomous depressive patients had more prior episodes than the non-autonomous patients. The delusional patients had fewer prior episodes than the nondelusional patients. However, comparisons between the studies may not be feasible because the delusional patients of the Glassman and Roose material were essentially the same age as the nondelusional patients, whereas in the research on autonomous depression there was a marked difference in age at index admission, with the autonomous patients being considerably older. In any event, the treatment results are different. The delusional patients are less likely to respond to placebo and may need either a combination of tricyclic and antipsychotic medication or electroconvulsive therapy (ECT) for a positive response to treatment (Kroessler, 1985). The lack of response to placebo, however, suggests another possibility besides that of a distinct clinical entity. It is entirely possible that delusions are more frequently seen in endogenous depressions than in nonendogenous depressions, and consequently the lack of response to placebo associated with the presence of delusions may simply mean that endogenous depressions are more reliably diagnosed when delusions are present, and delusional depressions may not respond to ineffective treatment. Coryell and Tsuang (1985) evaluated the prognostic importance of delusions in depression and found that delusional patients had a relatively poor short-term outcome regardless of whether they received somatic treatment. However, in a long 40-year follow-up, there were no differences between delusional and nondelusional groups in terms of marital, residential, occupational status, or psychiatric symptomatology.

At this point it would appear that the presence of delusions in the course of a depression does not define a separate illness. In psychiatric diagnosis, we need all the help we can get in nailing down a specific illness, and the presence of delusions may be very useful as a factor in arriving at the diagnosis of endogenous depression. Support for the viewpoint that delusional depression is not a separate illness comes from a study by Price et al. (1984a) in which the family history in first-degree relatives of delusional cases was compared with the family history of nondelusional inpatients, both groups of which met criteria in the *Diagnostic and Statistical Manual of Mental Disorders (Third Edition) (DSM-III)* for major depression with melancholia. The morbid risks for psychiatric illnesses did not differ between the two groups. More specifically, there was no difference in family history of unipolar depression, nonaffective psychosis, or hospitalizations for affective disorder.

The clinical symptomatology in endogenous depression has already been discussed (see Table 5.1). Not every study supports the high frequency of specific symptoms with the diagnosis of endogenous depression. Nelson and Charney (1987) evaluated a large number of studies that used a variety of methods, including factor analysis, cluster analysis, discriminant function analysis, and symptom frequency studies. The following symptoms showed a strong or moderate association with the diagnosis of endogenous depression: retardation, lack of reactivity, severe depressed mood, depressive delusions, and loss of interest. No matter what type of methodology was used, the preceding symptoms seemed associated with the diagnosis of endogenous depression. Such symptoms as agitation, self-reproach, decreased concentration, diurnal morning worsening, and early-morning awakening showed a slight to moderate association. Other symptoms such as weight loss, midmorning awakening, suicidal thoughts or attempts, and difficulty falling asleep showed a slight to no association with endogenous depression. The methodology of the study made some difference. Thus, in the cluster analysis study, self-reproach was strongly associated with endogenous depression, but in the discriminant function study there was only a slight association. Those symptoms with a strong to moderate association also showed a strong to moderate treatment response, and those symptoms that showed a slight association showed a slight treatment response.

There is a new methodology, called grade of membership analysis. The grade of membership model makes no assumption of independence across diagnostic groups. It permits patients to have varying grades of membership in more than one group and simultaneously show characteristics of these groups. However, it does present a higher probability that symptoms may be more typical of membership in one group than another. In a study of 190 patients with research diagnoses of major and minor depression, Davidson et al. (1988) explored depressive typologies. The data yielded five groups as the most satisfactory solution. One group corresponded to classical melancholia or endogenous depression. It occurred in older, stable inpatients who did not have anxiety symptoms. The pure type of this group was characterized by severe depressed mood, pathologic guilt, frequent suicide attempts, early awakening, and initial insomnia. Psychomotor retardation was found in 94% of the cases. Loss of weight was common, but diurnal variation and anorexia were unusual. External validators showed that this pure type occurred in men mostly, it rarely occurred below age 30, and all of the cases were inpatients. Diagnoses on this pure type were 66% endogenous and 93% primary. The authors remarked that this pure type corresponded to the concept of endogenous depression and that inasmuch as other cluster analytic and multivariant studies usually agree on this kind of depressive group, it should be considered a well-validated diagnosis.

Studies on the course of illness in endogenous depression are best divided into those with short-term follow-up and those with long-term follow-up. Paykel, Klerman, and Prusoff (1974) followed a group of depressed patients for 10 months. These patients came from outpatient settings, day hospitals, and inpatient treatment units. They were divided into endogenous and neurotic. After 10 months the endogenous patients were more likely to be well on the global illness rating. Their social adjustment was more likely noted as good, and they were more likely to have remitted and had no relapse. In follow-up the endogenous patients were less likely to have made suicide attempts. Zimmerman, Black, and Coryell (1989) investigated modern criteria (*DSM-III-R* and *DSM-III*) for melancholia in a group of consecutively admitted nonpsychotic depressed inpatients. Melancholic patients tended to be hospitalized longer, but for the next 6 months after discharge, there were no significant outcome differences between melancholic and nonmelancholic patients. There were nonsignificant trends suggesting that the nonmelancholic patients may have had a more favorable course. Using *DSM-III* melancholia criteria, 63% of the nonmelancholic patients were recovered at discharge, versus 47% of the melancholic patients. Further, the melancholic patients had higher scores on assessments of depressive symptoms. The clinical global rating for melancholia was significantly higher than that for the nonmelancholic patients. Although the studies by Paykel, Klerman, and Prusoff (1974) and Zimmerman, Black, and Coryell (1989) do not agree with each other, it is impossible to determine how much of this lack of agreement may be due to the original selection of patients. In the study by Paykel, Klerman, and Prusoff, the patients came from three different types of treatment centers—outpatient, inpatient, and day hospital—whereas in the study by Zimmerman, Black, and Coryell, the patients were all inpatients but were specially selected in that all of them had nonpsychotic depressive episodes. Further, by changing the definition of melancholia from *DSM-III* to *DSM-III-R*, there were changes in follow-up findings. Thus even so robust an item as course of illness may be highly sensitive to selection of patients and to diagnostic criteria.

There are a variety of longer follow-ups. Nyström (1979) presented the course of illness after 10 years in a group of 83 patients with moderately severe depression. Twenty percent of these patients had been totally free from depressive symptomatology during the 10 years, but 5% had been chronically depressed. Personality problems of an unstable sort, for example, hysteroid personality, were related to unfavorable outcome. Such patients, though moderately severe in illness, quite possibly have a neurotic depression. Fifty-six patients in this series had well-defined periods of depression. Thirteen had one period. Nine had two periods, 9 had three periods, 5 had four periods, and 20 had five or more periods.

Angst (1986) followed 173 cases of major unipolar depression for approximately 20 years. These patients had been admitted to a psychiatric hospital between 1959 and 1963 and were followed up every 5 years. Table 13.1 presents some of the data from the follow-up. In addition to these data, Angst evaluated the clinical state at the time of the last follow-up. The outcome was better for this set of unipolar patients compared with bipolar patients. Forty-two percent of this unipolar depressive group showed a "burning out" of episodes or recovery. Recovery was defined as an illness-free period of at least 5 years since termination of the last episode. Some possibility exists that over the years episodes become less frequent and, in later life, disappear. Ciompi (1969) followed 555 subjects into old age. He noted that the depressions reached a peak in frequency and severity between ages 45 and 65. In this period, 70% of the first admissions occurred, as well as 75% of the subsequent suicides. With advancing age, he noted that about a third of the depressed patients whose illness started before age 65 had less frequent and less severe attacks. About a third of the formerly depressed patients had no relapse at all after the age of 65. This suggests that there is a certain amount of burning out of the depressive propensity with age. In a study of more than 600 unipolar depressive patients, Angst et al. (1973) found that the mean number of episodes in that sample was five to six. They noted also that

Table 13.1. The Course of Unipolar Major Depression
(*DSM-III* Criteria)

Males	22.5%
Median age	68 yrs.
Median age at onset	45 yrs.
Median length of observation	21.3 yrs.
Median length of illness	15.9 yrs.
Time spent in illness	21%
Median number of episodes	4
Median length of episodes	5.3 mos.
Median length of cycles	4.7 yrs.
In episodes	7%
Full remission	30%
Organic brain syndrome	16%
Suicide	10%
Recovered	42%
Chronic	13%
Positive family history (parents)	17%

Source: Angst J. 1986. The course of major depression, atypical bipolar disorder, and bipolar disorder. In Hippius H, Klerman G, Mattussek N (eds.): *New Results in Depression Research* (pp. 26–35). Berlin: Springer-Verlag.
Note: DSM-III = third edition of the *Diagnostic and Statistical Manual of Mental Disorders*. N = 173.

unipolar depressive patients show a periodic course, that the majority of episodes were short—note exceeding three months—and that episode length was more or less constant through a patient's life but cycle length and thus the length of the intervals became progressively shorter. The number of episodes might well be limited and become fewer with age, they also noted.

Chronicity is an important phenomenon in endogenous depression. In an archival follow-up of 225 depressive patients, chronicity was assessed over a period of one month to 20 years (Winokur, 1974a; Winokur and Morrison, 1973). Chronicity was defined as being ill from index admission to the time of last follow-up, whenever that might have been. It included patients who made a social recovery but continued to have subsequent symptoms as well as patients who were both socially and symptomatically unrecovered. Age of onset was not related to chronicity, but age at index admission was. With increasing age, women were more likely to manifest chronicity. On the other hand, men were more likely to show increasing numbers of episodes with increasing age. One significant finding was that for a 2 to 20-year

Table 13.2. Family (Genetic) Studies in Endogenous Depression

| | Family History of Affective Disorder | | | | | |
| | Index Cases | | | Controls | | |
Type of Study	Ill (N)	At Risk (N)	Ill (%)	Ill (N)	At Risk (N)	Ill (%)
Blind family history assessment (Winokur et al., 1972)	123	859	14	32	584	6[a]
Blind family study interviews, unipolar depression (Winokur, Tsuang, and Crowe 1982)	34	305	8.2	25	344	4.6[b]
Psychiatric hospital records (Winokur, Tsuang, and Crowe, 1982)						
All illnesses	30	606	5	2	322	0.6[b]
Unipolar depression only	13	606	2.1	1	322	0.3[b]
Twin study (Bertelsen, Harvald, and Hauge, 1977)	12	28	43	3	16	19[c]
Adoption study (Wender et al., 1986)						
Affective disorder	17	316	5.4	8	346	2.3[d]
Suicide	11	316	3.5	1	346	0.3[d]

[a]Controls were parents and siblings of schizophrenic probands.
[b]Controls were parents and siblings of psychiatrically well surgical patients.
[c]Controls were dizygotic twin pairs; index cases were monozygotic twin pairs.
[d]Controls were biologic relatives of adoptees with no record of psychiatric illness, alcoholism or substance abuse, or attempted or completed suicide; index cases were biologic relatives of adoptees with hospitalized nonbipolar affective disorders.

follow-up period 19 patients were chronic. However, if one evaluated the subgroup who were followed 10 to 20 years, only 2 patients remained chronically ill. That is, of 108 patients who were followed for 2 to 20 years, 41 were followed from 10 to 20 years and only 2 of the 41 had chronic illness. It was thus possible to conclude that chronicity seemed to have a limited life and, if one followed a depressive patient long enough, remission would occur. Similar findings have been reported by Lee and Murray (1988) on the follow-up of endogenous inpatients at Maudsley Hospital. In this follow-up, recovery occurred even after 15 years of illness, and readmissions occurred even after 12 years of wellness. Readmissions were related to an endogenous subtype diagnosis, and the more likely a person was to have an endogenous depression, the more likely the person would have a poor outcome. A very poor outcome was seen in 50% of endogenous patients; such an outcome was defined on the basis of marked incapacity in living, many readmissions, and suicide.

In general, then, endogenous depression manifests itself by episodes with readmissions and periods of relative wellness. Although some patients are chronically ill, this is essentially a limited affair. Chronicity may go on for years but not for the entire lifetime. What seems clear in all studies is that patients with unipolar endogenous depression have multiple readmissions, though conceivably in late life these will diminish.

The family background in endogenous depression is quite distinct. Starting with hospitalized depressive patients, which in some sense controls for severity of illness, there are data showing that a family history obtained by a clinician at time of admission to the hospital reveals an increased number of depressed relatives in the depressive patients compared with controls. This finding holds up even if one personally interviews relatives of unipolar depressive patients and compares them with the personally examined relatives of controls. Some of these data are presented in Table 13.2.

These are not the only data that support a specific family background in unipolar depression. There are numerous studies in the literature at the present time. Of considerable interest is the fact that if one compares the presence of hospital records for psychiatric illness as well as for unipolar depression specifically, one finds more of these records among family members of unipolar depressive patients than among family members of controls. On the basis of hospital records, the ratio of ill family members of unipolar probands to ill family members of controls is much higher (8.3:1 and 7:1) than the ratio of depression in relatives of unipolars to depression in relatives of controls based on family history or family study (2.3:1 and 1.8:1).

In a modern twin study, there is clear evidence for increased concordance in unipolar monozygotic pairs compared with unipolar dizygotic pairs. Finally, in a modern adoption study of a large spectrum of affective disorder patients, there is an increase in unipolar depression in the relatives of the depressed adoptees versus the relatives of the control adoptees. This is also true for the finding of suicide. Actually, the finding presented in Table 13.2 is conservative. If one increases the number of patients who may have unipolar depression by increasing the sample to include those patients who had an "affective reaction," there is a marked increase in affective illness and suicide in family members over what is reported in Table 13.2. However, even though these patients with affective reaction were hospitalized, there was some question as to whether they truly belonged in the unipolar depression group. There is another set of controls in the adoptive relatives of 71 affective index cases and 71 controls. There is only one case of unipolar depression out of 180 adoptive relatives of index cases and only one case of unipolar depression in the adoptive relatives of the control adoptees. In general, then, if one combines all of the control groups (ns = 344, 180, and 169), there are a total of 693 controls; for these controls, there are three cases of unipolar depression and four suicides. The percentage of cases of unipolar depression in the adoptive relatives is 0.4%, as opposed to the 2% that is seen in the biologic relatives of the 71 affective index cases. For suicides, the percentage is 0.6% for relatives of controls versus 3.8% for biologic relatives of the affective index cases.

One can conclude from family history studies, record studies, twin studies, and adoption studies that a familial factor and probably a genetic factor exist in unipolar depression. This is extremely important in that it gives us a distal etiology—genetic—and also may give us a lead on how to best identify certain kinds of patients for both treatment and research.

Biologic Studies in Endogenous Depression

A probable genetic etiology in endogenous depression strongly suggests that in the long run there will be significant biologic findings associated with this diagnosis. These biologic findings will occupy the space between the distal (genetic) etiology and the clinical picture. Thus, the biologic findings are related to a more proximal etiology. The literature on biologic findings in unipolar depression is very large. Essentially, we are dealing with neuroendocrine findings, psychopharmacologic findings, and findings in sleep pathology.

Within the last decade or so, the dexamethasone suppression test (DST) has come to the fore as a way of validating the diagnosis of endogenous depression (melancholia) and helping with the diagnosis. The test is simple enough to be done in a clinical laboratory and involves a dose of 1 mg of dexamethasone given at 10:30 P.M. to 11:30 P.M. The plasma cortisol level is then determined at 8:00 A.M., 4:00 P.M., and 11:00 P.M. the following day. During these periods a plasma cortisol level over 5 μg/dl is considered abnormal (American Psychiatric Association Task Force, 1987; Carroll et al., 1981). Carroll et al. reported that the DST identified melancholic or endogenous patients with a sensitivity of 67% and a specificity of 96%. The sensitivity is the true-positive rate or nonsuppression among those with the index diagnosis. Arana, Baldessarini, and Ornsteen (1985) evaluated 85 reports and some unpublished material on the sensitivity of the DST in major depressive illnesses. The sensitivity was 44.1% among 5,111 patients with major depressive illnesses. For melancholic or endogenous patients, the sensitivity was 50.2%, and for patients with psychosis it was 67.3%. Not all studies agree with these sensitivities. Some studies show no difference between endogenous and neurotic patients, but most do. There is a problem with specificity in some of the studies that were reviewed by Arana, Baldessarini, and Ornsteen. Specificity is the true-negative rate or suppression among those lacking the index diagnosis, or 100% minus the false-positive rate. In some studies dementia has shown an unusually high nonsuppression rate. However, it is the sensitivity that is important to us in this evaluation. Given the fact that a sample has a depressive syndrome, will the DST be able to identify the endogenous group? Coryell (1984) concluded that the test had modest sensitivity and therefore was not usable as a screening test over all psychiatric patients. However, as a confirmatory test, if a suspicion of an endogenous depression was strong, it was very useful. He found that nonsuppression was specific to endogenous depression in most of the reports, even though there were considerable differences in the usually applied definitions.

As an example of the power of the DST using various diagnoses, Kasper and Beckman (1983) showed that 52% of patients considered endogenously depressed by the International Classification of Diseases criteria were nonsuppressors, 51% of patients considered to have major depression by Research Diagnostic Criteria were nonsuppressors, and 53% of patients considered to have endogenous depression by Newcastle criteria were nonsuppressors. Asnis et al. (1981) evaluated DST nonsuppression and cortisol secretion. These investigators suggested that nonsuppression of dexamethasone reflects abnormality of cortisol hypersecretion in depression and that the DST was a specific but not terribly sensitive indicator of hypersecretion.

The DST is a complex phenomenon. Probably, one must control for weight loss, influence of age, concentration of plasma dexamethasone, influence of various drugs, and other metabolic factors. Though the DST seems clearly a state phenomenon (related to the depressive episode in an endogenously depressed patient), there is some reason to believe that it may reflect a trait phenomenon. Kathol (1985) compared eight normal subjects with seven recovered depressive subjects who had been DST nonsuppressors when depressed. He found that the mean urinary free cortisol levels were significantly higher for recovered depressive patients than for controls in the summer and fall as well as for the entire year. In addition, patients who had recovered from depression lost their circannual pattern of cortisol secretion, and there was a positive correlation between depressive symptoms and urinary free cortisol levels in recovered patients but not in controls. If this finding is replicated, it suggests an abnormal trait in endogenous depression.

Amsterdam et al. (1989) assessed abnormalities in hormonal responsiveness at multiple levels of the hypothalamic-adrenal-cortical axis in depressive illness. These investigators evaluated the adrenocorticotropic hormone (ACTH) stimulation test in depression. There were no differences in baseline cortisol concentrations between melancholic depressed patients, nonmelancholic depressed patients, or control subjects. After ACTH infusion, the melancholic depressed patients showed a higher peak in cumulative cortisol response than patients without melancholic features. Also, DST nonsuppressors had higher cumulative cortisol responses than DST suppressors. When patients were divided on the basis of both diagnostic features (with or without melancholia) and dexamethasone response (nonsuppressors and suppressors) the melancholic nonsuppressor group demonstrated higher mean cortisol values for all of the kinds of measurements that were made after ACTH infusion. Compared with other patient subgroups or healthy controls, the authors suggest, this group of DST nonsuppressor melancholic patients represents a diagnostically homogeneous subpopulation who are more likely to demonstrate endocrine abnormalities at several sites within the hypothalamic-pituitary-adrenal axis. They also assessed the question of heightened adrenal cortisol responsiveness after corticotropin-releasing hormone stimulation. They found that cumulative ACTH response was significantly lower in melancholic (endogenous) patients than in controls. By the use of computer-assisted tomography, they evaluated adrenal gland volume in depression. Depressed patients had higher serum cortisol levels than controls. DST nonsuppressors also had higher serum cortisol levels than DST suppressors. Although the mean adrenal volumes for depressed patients were not significantly larger than those of the control subjects, 8 of the 16 patients (50%) and only one of the controls (9%) had an adrenal volume in excess of the 95% distribution of the normal control value. Finally, the authors evaluated enhanced adrenal cortisol sensitivity to submaximal doses of ACTH. Their findings supported the hypothesis of enhanced adrenal cortisol sensitivity to ACTH in patients with melancholic symptoms.

The neuroendocrine findings are very striking in endogenous depression. Not only do they give us better knowledge of the proximal physiology, but they contain leads for further research.

There have been other findings related to the endocrine status of the depressed patient. Impaired thyroid-stimulating hormone response to thyrotropin releasing hormone has been found in endogenous depression. Kirkegaard and Carroll (1980) studied thyroid-stimulating hormone and adrenal cortisol disturbances in patients with endogenous depression and found that the abnormalities were dissociated. The decreased response to thyrotropin-releasing hormone was not related to serum or cerebrospinal fluid cortisol or to urinary secretion of cortisol. Thus there may be a series of neuroendocrine abnormalities in depression, some of which may be related and others not related. Not all studies have shown such a dissociation between thyroid abnormalities and hypothalamic adrenal cortical abnormalities. Considerably more work in this field would be useful.

Somewhat related to endocrinology is the concept of seasonal affective disorder. This is a depression that meets the Research Diagnostic Criteria for a major depressive episode. The depression regularly occurs during the fall and winter, and alternates with nondepressed periods during spring and winter. Such patients have no other major psychiatric disorders, and there are no clear psychosocial variables accounting for the regular changes in mood (Rosenthal and Wehr, 1987). That there might be an endogenous depression that regularly occurs during the winter is an attractive hypothesis, particularly because it has been reported to respond to light therapy (phototherapy). The timing of the phototherapy for effectiveness is at variance in some studies, as is the question of response to dim versus bright light (Pichot and Jensen, 1989; Wehr et al., 1986). The etiologic theory that is currently entertained in seasonal affective disorder might be called the melatonin theory, which posits that the symptoms are due to either an abnormality in melantonin excretion or an abnormal brain response to melatonin. Melatonin is secreted from the pineal gland and related in a circadian fashion to light impinging on the retina. Light suppresses production of melatonin. However, Wehr et al. (1986) pointed out that suppression of melatonin was not critical for an antidepressant affect.

There are also problems with the diagnosis of seasonal affective disorder (Pichot and Jensen, 1989). Whereas some investigators have suggested that seasonal affective disorders usually are bipolar, others have reported that they are unipolar. The criteria used from one study to the other are not invariably similar. Some suggest that the illness is a mild depression; others suggest that the illness is a severe inpatient depression. In any event, it is possible that seasonal affective disorder is a specific endogenous illness, but more rigorous data must be collected on this possibility.

Another set of findings related to the biology of endogenous depression concerns sleep variables. Kupfer (1976) reported a shortened rapid eye movement (REM) latency in endogenous depression. He found that with the exception of drug withdrawal states (such as those caused by withdrawal of a central nervous system depressant or amphetamine withdrawal) or narcolepsy, a shortened REM latency was related to an endogenous depression. Likewise, REM latency was positively correlated with the amount of slow-wave sleep. Rush et al. (1986) evaluated 16 patients for the presence of sleep abnormalities. Thirteen of these patients were reassessed after they had been clinically remitted for six months and were no longer on any medication. When these patients had been symptomatic, they exhibited a reduced REM latency (11 of 13 patients). After remission, 8 of the 11 continued to exhibit reduced REM latency. Of the 13 patients, 11 showed a unipolar depression. These unipolar patients, when retested after clinical remission for six months, generally showed reduced REM latencies (8 of 11). Whether this continuation of sleep abnormalities may be interpreted as a trait finding is unknown, because it is possible that they were simply slow to normalize or that they might have been on the verge of having a recurrence of depression. Of the 9 unipolar patients whose illness was considered specifically endogenous, the REM latency was shortened to 52 minutes when the patients were admitted to the study, and it was still quite short (64 minutes) after they had been well for six months. Stage 4 sleep remained unchanged in this study from illness to wellness.

Giles et al. (1986) studied clinical symptoms and related them to REM latency reduction. The symptoms of endogenous depression that were related to a reduced REM latency were terminal insomnia, pervasive anhedonia, unreactive mood, and appetite loss. Such symptoms as morning worsening of mood, psychomotor activity change, significant weight loss, excessive self-reproach, or loss of interest did not discriminate between reduced and nonreduced REM latency categories. As already noted, Giles et al. (1987b) reported a replication study that was consistent with earlier reports: reduced REM latency was higher in those with endogenous depression, as was the incidence for dexamethasone nonsuppression.

Patients with endogenous depression have been compared with healthy controls on the basis of [^{3}H]imipramine binding in platelets. Wägner et al. (1985) evaluated 63 severely depressed hospitalized patients. Most of these ($n = 48$) were unipolar cases. All of the patients had been drug free for a month, at least as regards antidepressants. There were 53 healthy controls. The [^{3}H]imipramine binding sites in platelets were decreased in the depressed patients as compared with the controls. These observations have been made in the past by a variety of investigators. The bulk of the literature supports a low number of binding sites in endogenous depression. Interestingly, such a low number of binding sites has also been observed in postmortem studies of brain from suicide victims (Stanley, Visgilio, and Gershon, 1982).

Evidence of a neurophysiologic type also supports the existence of different types of depression. Shagass (1981) reviewed studies on the discrimination of psychotic from neurotic depression. He noted that in patients with psychotic depression response to ECT was better, salivary secretion was low, and blood pressure response to mecholyl (the Funkenstein test) was prolonged if the blood pressure was elevated. The sedation threshold using the electroencephalogram was normal. The sedation threshold using the galvanic skin response was low. The stimulation threshold was high. The growth hormone response to amphetamine, clonidine, desipramine, or insulin was reduced, and evoked cortisol potentials were abnormal.

It seems clear that there are a number of biologic findings that are abnormal in patients with endogenous depression. These add credibility to the validity of endogenous unipolar depression as a separate illness.

The treatment reflects the biologic differences. ECT is more effective than tricyclic antidepressants in depressed patients with delusions. Tricyclic antidepressants seem less effective than a combination of tricyclic and neuroleptic drugs in patients with delusional depression. In a sense, the presence of delusions is a good marker for an endogenous depression, and thus these findings are relevant to a differentiation between endogenous and nonendogenous unipolar depressive illness.

Familial Pure Depressive Disease

If the concept of endogenous depression is the anchor for a classification in the affective disorders, the diagnosis of familial pure depressive disease (FPDD) is the prototype of an endogenous depression.
FPDD is an illness that meets criteria for depression and occurs in an
individual who has a family history of unipolar depression in a first-
degree family member. Such a person has no family member ill with
alcoholism, antisocial personality, or mania. FPDD may be the benchmark against which all other groups of depression that are considered
endogenous might be compared. It is important to note that in the
algorithm that identifies FPDD all patients with secondary depression
must be excluded, as should all unipolar depressed patients who have
a family history of alcoholism, antisocial personality, or mania. Likewise, all patients who have a negative family history for any of these
familial illnesses should be removed and put into a group who would
be considered to have sporadic depression. Thus, FPDD is a diagnosis
made by exclusion of other patients who have a specific family history
other than simple unipolar depression. The relevance of FPDD to
endogenous depression may be perceived immediately by reviewing
the material in Table 13.2. It seems quite clear that unipolar endogenous depression has a marked family (genetic) background.

There are no epidemiologic studies of FPDD that have been accomplished with a community sample. Most of the findings are relevant to
comparisons between depression-spectrum disease and FPDD. They
reflect the differences between neurotic depression and endogenous
depression.

To briefly recapitulate some of the findings on depression-spectrum
disease discussed in Chapter 11, these patients are more likely to be
separated and divorced, are more emotionally reactive, are less retarded, and less anhedonic, and are less likely to show a loss of interest
in usual life circumstances than FPDD patients. Patients with FPDD are
less likely to show unstable personality characteristics, such as lifelong
irritability, nervousness, dependency, and demanding behavior. The
course of depression-spectrum disease differs from that of FPDD, at
least in some studies, in that FPDD patients are more likely to have
hospitalizations and episodes. In this way, they are similar to the patients with endogenous depression who have been reported by Lee and
Murray (1988). Hospitalizations in particular separate FPDD from depression-spectrum disease, with the former more likely to show them.
Zimmerman et al. (1988) presented data that FPDD patients have a
more favorable hospital course and report less symptoms during a six-
month follow-up than patients with depression-spectrum disease or

sporadic depressive disease. More specifically, FPDD patients were hospitalized longer, less likely to be discharged after just one week of hospitalization, more likely to be treated with ECT, and more likely to have a reduction of symptomatology as assessed by the Hamilton Depression Rating Scale than the patients with depression-spectrum disease. At six months, the FPDD patients were more likely to have either no depressive symptoms or one or two depressive symptoms. In general, they reported less symptoms than other groups. Smith and North (1988) reported similar kinds of data in their longer follow-up. The FPDD patients were more likely to have no subsequent episodes but were more likely to be hospitalized during follow-up. They were less likely to show suicide attempts but were more likely to have a chronic course. DSD patients were more likely to have depressive episodes during follow-up. It is clear that there is a difference between depression-spectrum disease and FPDD patients in follow-up in number of episodes and hospitalizations, the former having more episodes but the latter having more hospitalizations.

A sample of patients who were admitted between 1934 and 1940 and had no specific treatment for depression were evaluated on the variable of chronicity (Winokur, 1974a). Chronicity was defined as the individual's showing symptomatology over the course of one or more years. If the individual continued to have symptoms even if he or she were socially recovered, the individual was still considered chronically ill. Chronicity in this study was inversely associated with an alcoholic father. Thus if the depressed patient were admitted and had an alcoholic father, it was unlikely that he or she would remain chronic, or, alternatively, if the patient were chronically ill, it was unlikely that he or she would have an alcoholic father.

Though the course of FPDD seems clearly different from that of depression-spectrum disease, the major findings that separate the two groups have to do with biologic variables. Table 13.3 presents a compilation of such findings. Many of the studies have not been replicated (i.e., glucose sensitivity to insulin after recovery, earlier nadir in circadian cortisol curve, and postdexamethasone 24-hour ACTH concentration). However, the REM latency and the DST data have been repeated many times, and, though not all studies are in agreement, the majority are. The tritiated imipramine binding has also been repeated on a number of occasions; and, though the differences between FPDD and depression-spectrum disease have not always been significant, the trends have often been in the same direction. One of the more provocative findings in the sleep study of familial depressives has been reported by Giles et al. (1989). This study is of considerable interest because it combines both a familial as well as a biologic

Table 13.3. Biologic Differences between Familial Pure Depressive Disease and Depression-Spectrum Disease

Finding	Familial Pure Depressive Disease	Depression-Spectrum Disease
Defining factors		
Family history of depression	Yes	+/−
Family history of alcoholism and/or antisocial personality	No	Yes
Biologic families		
Nonsuppressor on dexamethasone test, sensitivity of test	47%	24% (Arana, Baldessarini, and Ornsteen, 1985; Lewis and Winokur, 1983)
Glucose sensitivity to insulin after recovery	Low	Normal (Lewis et al., 1983)
Tritiated imipramine binding to platelet membranes	Low	Normal (Lewis and McChesney, 1985)
Early nadir in cortisol circadian curve	Yes	No (Winokur, Pfohl, and Sherman, 1985)
Dexamethasone nonsuppressors after more than one test	83%	14% (Winokur, Pfohl, and Sherman, 1985)
Postdexamethasone 24-hour adrenocorticotropic hormone concentrations	Higher	Lower (Winokur, Pfohl, and Sherman, 1985)
Rapid eye movement latency	Low	Normal (Giles et al., 1986; Yerevanian and Akiskal, 1979)

variable. Giles et al. compared the relatives of probands with reduced REM latency with the relatives of probands with nonreduced REM latency probands. She found a lifetime prevalence of major depression of 52% in the relatives of probands with reduced REM latency as opposed to 29% among the relatives of probands with nonreduced REM latency. Major depression then occurred almost 1.8 times more frequently among the relatives of patients with reduced REM latency. There was a marked similarity in polysomnographic variables between the patients with reduced REM latency and their relatives. This occurred even though none of the relatives were depressed at the time of assessment. Giles et al. concluded that the polysomnographic alterations "may be stable antecedents of the onset of depression" (1989, p. 127).

Relevant to the separation of depression-spectrum disease from

FPDD is a consideration of the characteristics of affective disorders that seem to go together. Winokur, Black, and Nasrallah (1987a) evaluated DST nonsuppressor status and its relationship to specific aspects of the depressive syndrome. Abnormal endocrine function was related to melancholic symptoms, delusions, and memory deficit, but normal suppressor status was related to an early age of onset, absence of delusions, absence of memory deficit, absence of melancholia symptoms, and the presence of a diagnosis of secondary depression or depression-spectrum disease. Thus certain clinical aspects were doubtlessly clustering in FPDD patients.

Data indicating linkage of FPDD with genetic markers have been reported. In a study of 24 genetic markers, Hill et al. (1988) presented an indication of linkage between FPDD and the MNS blood system. This study used the sibpair method to analyze linkage. Using the same sibpair method of linkage analysis, Tanna et al. (1989) also reported evidence in favor of linkage with the MNS system, which is on chromosome 4. Both findings were significant, but probably the most important thing is that they were replications of each other. Because multiple evaluations were reported with multiple markers, such findings do not come close to definitely proving linkage, but they do suggest that there is some value in another study of FPDD and the MNS locus. There was no strong agreement between the sibpair and lod score methods when used on these same families for the MNS locus. This constitutes a problem, but at the present time we may not know enough about the power of the two linkage methods to interpret contradictory results.

Sporadic Depressive Disease

Another familial subtype, sporadic depressive disease, might lay some claim for consideration as an autonomous endogenous depression. Sporadic depressive disease manifests itself as a depression that meets criteria for a primary depressive syndrome, but there is no family history of depression. Of course, there is also no family history of alcoholism, antisocial personality, or mania. Thus, familially it is a diagnosis made by exclusion. A sporadic familial background is usually related to a later onset of depressive illness (Winokur, 1979a). In three out of four sets of data that represented separate studies, those patients with a positive family history were far more likely to have an onset of their unipolar depression before the age of 40. Interestingly, the one set of data that did not conform to this pattern was composed of a consecutive set of depressive patients who were picked up for study in the late 1960s. The three studies that did conform to the pattern were composed of patients admitted to the Iowa Psychiatric Hospital in 1934 to 1940, patients admitted for care in Sweden before 1950, and patients admitted to a psychiatric hospital in St. Louis in the early 1960s. Of course, it is possible that over the years there has been a change in admission policies and in types of hospitalized affectively ill patients, which might account for the difference between the studies.

In any event, most data suggest that patients with a late onset of depression are more likely to have a negative family history for affective disorder than patients with an early onset. This immediately calls to mind the diagnosis that was in vogue several years ago, involutional melancholia.

Involutional melancholia was described by Huston and Locher (1948) as an illness that occurs in middle life and thereafter without evidence of either organic intellectual defects or a affective episode. Such a melancholia was characterized generally by agitation and depression, and the content was marked by self-condemnation, hopelessness, and a tendency toward hypochondriasis. There is a large literature on involutional melancholia, and part of it deals with a family history of psychiatric illness. Unfortunately, some of the older studies, which show remarkably positive findings, did not separate the bipolar from the unipolar types of affective disorder. Thus, unlike in sporadic depressive disease, the difference between the family history in involutional psychosis and that in manic-depressive disease may depend to some extent on the early-onset bipolar illness.

Keeping this in mind, we may evaluate Kallman's (1954) data, which showed that siblings of patients with involutional psychosis were ill at the rate of 6% but siblings of patients with manic-depressive psychosis had an 18% affective illness rate. He also compared concordance in dizygotic and monozygotic twins for manic-depressive psychosis. Concordance was 24% for members of dizygotic twin pairs and 93% for members of monozygotic twin pairs. This may be compared with the rates for involutional psychosis, in which concordance was 6% for members of dizygotic twin pairs and 61% for members of monozygotic twin pairs. Thus it is clear that, at least in a mixed group of bipolar and unipolar depressive patients, family histories are higher than in the patients with involutional psychosis, and twin concordance is also higher (Kallman, 1954). Similar findings were presented by Stenstedt (1952, 1959). He found that the risk of morbidity for endogenous affective disorders among the siblings and parents of involutional probands was 6.1%, but the risk of morbidity for siblings of manic-depressive probands was 14.1%; among parents it was 7.5% and among children of probands it was 17.1%. Again, interpretation of these data is somewhat compromised by the fact that the manic-depressive group contained both bipolar and unipolar patients.

Using a break-point model, Hopkinson and Ley (1969) found that if the probands became ill before the age of 40, the risk for first-degree relatives varied between 21% and 32%, but if the probands became ill after the age of 40, the risk varied between 11.8% and 13.5%. This is a striking difference in family history of affective disorder depending on whether the proband became ill before or after the age of 40. Again, Hopkinson and Ley did not separate bipolar from unipolar patients, and it is not possible to determine whether this would have made any difference. These researchers demonstrated that the age-related incidence of manic-depressive disorders showed a bimodality for both sexes with a point of rarity around the age of 40. Slater (1938) likewise showed this bimodality for men and women. Looking at the patients in a large study, Slater showed an early-onset syndrome that would have its peak between the ages of 30 and 39 and a later onset syndrome having its peak 10 years later. These findings suggest, but do not prove, the possibility of a two separate disorders, one with an early onset and the other with a late onset.

In an evaluation of age of onset versus percentage of total proband group in 243 unipolar probands, however, Winokur (1979b) showed no evidence of bimodality in men, women, or the two sexes taken together. This would argue against the idea that a sample of consecutively admitted unipolar depressive patients show bimodality in age of onset with a point of rarity occurring around the age of 40.

A good part of the validity of the concept of involutional melancholia depends on clinical characteristics that might separate early-onset from late-onset unipolar depressions. To determine this, one would need to separate the age of onset from the age at index admission because some differences might have to do with the pathoplastic effect of aging rather than the time when the illness first manifested itself. Such a study, taking into account both age at onset and age at index episode, has been reported by Pichot and Pull (1981). These investigators compared the symptomatology of 103 women and 27 men, showing an onset of depression before the age of 50 with the symptomatology of an equal number of subjects showing depressions occurring later. Thus, they were able to eliminate the effect of age at index, matching the early- and late-onset groups on the variable of age at the time of index examination. Observed differences were that the late-onset patients showed more hypochondriasis, retardation, and hallucinations and fewer guilt feelings. Not all of these findings were true in both sexes, however. Pichot and Pull noted that they had not distinguished between unipolar and bipolar groups and so again took up the problem, this time separating the sample into unipolar and bipolar groups. They found only one significant difference. The patients with late-onset or involutional melancholia depression showed fewer suicidal thoughts than the unipolar patients with early-onset depression.

Winokur and Morrison (1973) also compared old, early-onset depressive men and women with old late-onset men and women. Thus there was a control for the effect of age in that the patients differed only on the basis of age of onset. Chronicity increased with age at index examination. In particular, chronicity was associated with increasing age in women. There was no true effect of age of onset if age at index was controlled. Likewise, in these groups there was a positive association of age with subsequent admissions in men but not women. Here too the association was with age at index, not age at onset of illness. This suggests that the course of patients with late-onset unipolar depression or involutional melancholia is not different from that of patients with other depressions as long as there is a control for age at time of observation (Winokur, 1974a). In these studies of the Iowa 500, there was a 10% admixture of bipolar illness in the sample of 225 depressive patients. It is unlikely that this small proportion would change the aforementioned findings.

The early ideas about involutional depression connected it with menopause in women. Winokur (1973) studied 71 women who had an affective disorder before, after, or during menopause to determine whether they were at greater risk for depression during menopause than at other times of the life span. The difference was not significant. There was a 7.1% risk of developing an affective disorder during the menopause and 6% risk at other times. Winokur and Cadoret (1975), reviewing a variety of studies, concluded that few data support the concept that the menopause is particularly relevant to depressive illness. Menopause did not appear to be associated with any increase in either depressive psychosis or suicide. Nevertheless, there were some notable differences. Climacteric depressions were milder and less psychotic, and the family history of such patients may have been lower than the family history of patients who had depressions around the same age period but were not suffering from a change in menstrual status, that is, menopause. Certainly these findings do not provide any confidence in the idea that the climacteric is an etiology for involutional depression.

As regards treatment, involutional psychosis has long been known to respond extremely well to ECT. Huston and Locher (1948) studied two groups of patients with involutional psychosis, one of which was treated with ECT and the other of which was not. There was clear evidence that in this late-onset group the treatment was particularly efficacious. However, this could simply have been the result of age as a predictor of good response. Wesner and Winokur (1989) evaluated the influence of age on the natural history of unipolar depression and treatment with ECT. Patients were separated by dividing them at the index age of 40. Patients treated with ECT were compared with those not treated with ECT. Treated patients age 39 or younger showed significant increases in subsequent episodes and subsequent hospitalization compared with patients of similar age who received no somatic treatment. Thus, the relationship with ECT in the younger patients seemed clear. It was associated with more episodes and hospitalizations. In patients age 40 or older, however, there was no difference in subsequent hospitalizations whether ECT was used or not. These patients, however, were not divided by age of onset; rather they were separated by age at index, and this difference in course as related to ECT may simply have been a matter of age at index admission and treatment rather than age of onset.

We may conclude that there is no overwhelming reason to consider involutional melancholia as a separate illness, though there are some hints in the studies that this should not be totally rejected.

Rather than considering the possibility of a separate illness from the vantage point of the age of onset, which yields a group of patients who have been said to have involutional melancholia, we may approach the problem using the family history. This then gives us a group of patients who can be said to have sporadic depression, the adjective referring to the fact that there is no family history of depression. As part of a large study of familial subtypes of depressive illness, Lowry et al. (1978) published material on the baseline characteristics of FPDD. These findings may be compared with the characteristics of sporadic depressive disease that were published by Behar (1978). The sporadic patients had a later age of onset than the FPDD patients. Of the FPDD patients, 71% had no prior hospitalizations; in the sporadic group, 86% had never been hospitalized before. Because age at index and age of onset are usually correlated in depressive patients, it is difficult to separate out the effect of these variables in this sample. Nevertheless, here are some differences in symptoms between the FPDD patients and the sporadic patients: loss of interest was seen more frequently in FPDD (81% vs. 39%), as was initial insomnia (60% vs. 34%), terminal insomnia (56% vs. 43%), diurnal variation (45% vs. 29%), and fearfulness (50% vs. 28%). The sporadic patients were more likely than the FPDD patients to show concentration difficulties (66% vs. 37%) and agitation (64% vs. 47%). There were some differences in premorbid characterologic features. Sensitivity was more

frequently seen in FPDD (48%) than in sporadic depressive disease
(26%). Shyness was more frequently seen in FPDD (43% vs. 17%), as
was jolliness (33% vs. 16%) and conscientiousness (25% vs. 13%). On
the other hand, being considered good tempered was more frequently found in the sporadic depressive patients (39% vs. 23%).

Perhaps the most interesting finding in these data concerns medical or surgical illness as a precipitating factor. Among the FPDD patients, whether they had an early or late onset, or age at index younger
or older than 40, the presence of medical illness was seen in 11% to
14% of the cases. In the sporadic group, however, the finding was
quite different. Thirty-five percent of the late-index group showed
medical illness, as opposed to only 11% of the early-index group.
Thirty-five percent of the late-onset sporadic patients showed medical
illness, compared with only 12% of the early-onset sporadic patients.
This finding poses a problem. As we have already noted, medical
illness that is related to secondary depression (see Table 12.2) is associated with a sporadic familial background. No doubt any reasonable
study of sporadic illness will have to take into account that a large but
unknown number of sporadic patients essentially have secondary (reactive) depressions to a medical illness that may occur somewhat late
in life. No study so far has separated the depression secondary to
medical illness from those that are not in any study on involutional
melancholia or in any study of sporadic depressive disease. It is a
major source of potential error and needs to be controlled in order to
determine if there is a specific nonreactive late-onset sporadic depression.

Complete recovery with treatment was more frequent in the sporadic group. Forty-nine percent showed a complete recovery and no
relapse, compared with only 27% of the familial group. On the other
hand, the sporadic group was more likely to show chronicity in that
24% never recovered, whereas only 12% of the familial group never
recovered. The sporadic group contained 47% who made a complete
recovery and had no relapse in a short "follow-up." This was true for
only 27% of the FPDD group. Chronicity was seen in 12% of FPDD
patients, but in 23% of the sporadic patients. Chronicity here was
defined as never having recovered. Thus with effective treatment the
sporadic group showed better recovery but also more chronicity.

In order to control for age effects in the above patients, Winokur
(1986) compared 28 female FPDD patients with 53 female sporadic
depressive patients, all over the age of 50. Fearfulness as a premorbid
characteristic was more frequently seen in the familial group than the
sporadic group (61% vs. 28%). Change in sensorium was also more
frequently seen in the familial group (21% vs. 4%). In these two

Table 13.4. Comparison of Familial Pure Depressive Disease and Sporadic Depressive Disease in Female Samples Controlled for Age

Finding	Familial Pure Depressive Disease (%)	Sporadic Depressive Disease (%)
Symptom		
Weight loss	74	56
Terminal insomnia	64	31
Loss of sex drive	56	18
Retardation	36	59
Diurnal mood variation	59	23
Fearfulness	51	28
Personality characteristic		
Conscientious	26	13
Sensitive	49	26
Shy	44	18
Complaining	13	0

Note: All patients were between 30 and 50 years old at index; no significant difference in mean age between familial pure depressive and sporadic depressive samples. $N = 39$ for each sample.

groups, which were essentially matched for age, an even-tempered personality was more frequently seen in the sporadic group than the familial group (49% vs. 11%). All of these differences were significant. None of these differences were found when the FPDD and the sporadic depressive patients were compared if the two groups were younger than 50 at index.

In another sample, sporadic depressive women were less likely to show self-reproach and more likely to be first-admission patients than were patients with FPDD. Both male and female sporadic patients were more likely to be mute on admission and more likely to have had a chronic onset than FPDD patients (Winokur, 1986). However, the effect of age was not controlled in the comparison. The age at index in the sporadic depressive patients was in the late 30s to early 40s and in the FPDD patients was in the early 30s.

Perhaps the best way to evaluate differences between FPDD and sporadic depressive disease is to compare relatively young patients who are unlikely to have significant medical problems. Table 13.4 shows such a comparison (Behar et al., 1980). There were some differences between the two groups, who were well controlled for age at index admission. There was no clear indication which group showed more endogenous symptoms. The FPDD group showed more terminal insomnia, loss of sex drive, and diurnal mood variation, but the sporadic group showed more retardation. As regards personality characteristics, the sporadic group seemed to show less of these than the FPDD group. Though the two groups of patients were different on some symptoms and personality characteristics, the findings did not point to any clear clinical separation of the two groups.

Behar et al. (1981) attempted a classification of familial subtypes using index symptoms, precipitating events, and premorbid personality features. A stepwise discriminant function analysis was selected as the statistical procedure. In a comparison between FPDD and sporadic depressive disease, personality features seemed more discriminating than symptomatic features. The clinical features most strongly associated with FPDD patients were fearfulness, loss of libido, and change in sensorium. Personality abnormalities that might be similar to depressive illness itself were often found among those with FPDD, and they were essentially the ones noted in Table 13.4 (shyness, limited premorbid functioning, and conscientiousness). Sporadic patients were more even-tempered premorbidly. Behar et al. concluded that FPDD patients were somewhat more depressed or limited in function premorbidly. Using the discriminant function analysis, 68% of the sporadic patients were correctly identified. Interestingly, of all three familial subgroups, the sporadic group was the most easily classified.

The concept of a sporadic illness has surfaced from time to time in the psychiatric literature. The concept suggests that there is an illness that occurs de novo in a family. There is no positive family history for the kinds of illnesses that are usually associated with the occurrence of this kind of clinical picture. Winokur (1979a) applied this concept to a group of patients with unipolar depressive disease who had no family history of depression, mania, alcoholism, or antisocial personality. That definition is well and good, but it does not obviate the possibility that some unknown kind of illness, even possibly medical, is familially associated with a sporadic depressive disease. If this were true, it would pose a difficult problem because one would have to separate the reactive depressions to a major medical illness from the associations that are more purely familial or genetic. Because many medical illnesses themselves have a genetic background, this becomes a very large statistical task. Of course, the possibility also exists that a sporadic illness has no genetic background at all and is, in fact, simply due to some kind of exogenous but not necessarily psychologic precipitant.

The concept of sporadic illness has mainly been debated in the context of schizophrenia. Kendler and Hays (1982) examined differences between sporadic schizophrenic patients and familial schizophrenic patients and found a difference in abnormal electroencephalographic findings between the two groups. The sporadic schizophrenic patients had a higher proportion of such findings. This report is reminiscent of the findings in bipolar illness (see Chapter 7), in which abnormal electroencephalographic findings have been reported in bipolar patients who have no family history of affective disorder. Such findings in unipolar sporadic patients have not been reported. Kendler and Hays (1982) pointed out several problems with the concept of sporadic schizophrenia. They noted that factors other than genes could produce a familial schizophrenia, that genetic factors could be important in the etiology of schizophrenia, and that a recessive model for transmission, although generally not accepted in schizophrenia, would predict that some families that have a genetic disease show no overt illness. All of these criticisms could be leveled at the theory of sporadic depression also. A family that was too small to be studied or a family in which the relatives were quite young and not gone through much of the age of risk could be mistakenly considered to have sporadic illness. Penetrance could be involved in that not all patients who have the genetic background might show the disease. Eaves, Kendler, and Schulz (1986) calculated that if one assumed the multifactorial model of disease liability, the sample size of first-degree relatives required to identify etiologic heterogeneity with a familial versus sporadic distinction would be very large. The power of the method requires very large sample sizes of probands and family members, and most studies do not report these. Goldin, DeLisi, and Gershon (1987) also took up the question of the sporadic versus familial distinction. They noted that some families with an autosomal dominant kind of transmission were correctly classified, but that the sporadic families turned out to be the most heterogeneous group of patients. That should fit the findings pointed out above because there should clearly be a certain number of sporadic patients with depression who have reactive depressions. Likewise, Goldin et al. pointed out that the heterogeneity of a group labeled sporadic would depend on the actual proportion of different types of families in the population and the size of the families studied. They, too, came up with the idea that very large samples of patients are required to detect such differences in familial subtypes. However, biologic findings that reflect genetic defects might be detected in smaller studies. Suffice to say, the possibility of a sporadic but nonreactive depression exists but has certainly not been proven. A first step in a comparison between sporadic and familial depressions would be to remove those depressed patients who have a family history of alcoholism and separate the remainder into three groups: those with an early onset and young age at index, those with an early onset and older age at index, and those with a late onset and older age at index. Separating them into male and female would give us six groups, and this would be a reasonable way to look for possible differences in clinical presentation, course, response to treatment, and biologic factors.

There have been some biologic findings that have been reported between FPDD and sporadic depressive disease. In 11 studies FPDD patients were more likely to show nonsuppression than the sporadic patients (63% vs. 41%). There may also be some sleep differences, but these have been variable and have not always been replicated from one study to another. Suffice to say that in some studies, sporadic depressive patients show more Stage 4 sleep and less suppression of REM activity when given amitriptyline (Winokur, 1986).

It is reasonable to consider sporadic depression as a subject for further research. There are suggestions in the literature that there may be a sporadic illness that differs in some symptomatology from FPDD. Such studies, however, sorely need controls because of the possibility that many of the patients who have sporadic depression are, in fact, simply reacting to major medical illness. Also, an appropriate study needs to control for sex, age of onset, and age at index.

As regards the rubric of endogenous depression, it is entirely conceivable that there are many types of endogenous depression related to many different pathophysiologies and different etiologies. There is no need to consider all endogenous depressions as the same illness. Certainly a good benchmark for endogenous depression with which other types might be compared is FPDD.

14 An Exercise in Differential Diagnosis and Classification: Case Studies

Margery Kempe (1985) was a religious woman, born ca. 1373 (died ca. 1440) in Norfolk, England. Hers possibly is the earliest known autobiography of an English person.

At 20 she married a citizen of Lynn and shortly thereafter became pregnant. During her confinement, she had "severe attacks of sickness," and after childbirth she came to believe that she would not live. She had a dread of damnation and was "disturbed and tormented with spirits" for about eight months. During this time, she thought she saw "devils opening their mouths, all alight with burning flames of fire as if they would have swallowed her in." Sometimes these spirits threatened her. The devils called out to her with threats and asked her to abandon her Christian faith and belief and deny her God. During this time, she slandered her husband and her friends as well as herself. The spirits demanded that she kill herself, and this would have caused her to be damned with them in Hell. During this time she bit her own hands so violently that the mark remained with her for the rest of her life. She tore the skin off her chest with her nails and had to be tied up and forcibly restrained day and night so that she could not follow the demands of the spirits.

Ultimately Margery Kempe, after being troubled by these and other temptations, experienced the appearance of the Lord Christ Jesus. He seemed "most beauteous" and appeared in the likeness of a man "clad in a mantle of purple silk." Shortly thereafter she became calm and had a return of reason.

As she improved, she believed that she was "bound to God and would be his servant." Though she bore 13 more children, no mention is made of another postpartum episode.

Margery became very proud and envious of people around her and adopted a very showy form of dress. Her cloaks were "modishly

slashed" and various colors underlay these slashes so that she would
be "stared at and all the more esteemed." She wore "gold pipes" on
her head. She took up brewing and became one of the "greatest
brewers" in the town of Norfolk. This lasted for 3 or 4 years and then
she lost a great deal of money. She had never had any real background
for that business. She asked her husband's pardon at that time because she said her pride and sin were the cause of her being punished.
In spite of the failure of the brewing business, she started a new
enterprise, operating a horse mill. This new business venture also
failed. The reason for this appeared to be interpersonal differences
between Margery Kempe and her employees. She believed that these
adversities were scourges of the Lord and that she needed to forsake
her proud ways and her "covetousness." She did penance and entered
the way of "everlasting life."

Over the ensuing years, she engaged in many religious activities,
even to the extent of going to the Holy Land. Some of her behavior
was histrionic, but it would be difficult to separate this behavior in
such way as to determine whether it was hypomania. She often wept
copiously, "twisted and wrenched her body about and made remark-
able faces and gestures, with vehement sobbings."

It seems clear that Margery Kempe had a major remitting illness
manifested by considerable guilt and depressive feelings that occurred
after childbirth and lasted about eight months. From this, she went to
business ventures that failed and lost money, suggesting a kind of
manic behavior. Although her illness is not possible to diagnose, it
opens up a considerable number of questions that are useful for
classification. Did she have an ordinary postpartum depression? Did
she have bipolar illness with a major depression and some episodes of
hypomania thereafter? Did she have an affective disorder secondary to
her histrionic ways? Nothing describes the need for classification better
than case studies. In some of the cases that follow the kind of treatment
that might be prescribed would depend on the classification. Had there
been effective therapies in the Middle Ages, it would have been equally
necessary to classify Margery Kempe's illness appropriately in order to
use the most appropriate kind of treatment.

Under ordinary circumstances, patients enter the hospital or the
clinic with a depressive or a manic syndrome. Diagnosis follows from
that fact. This chapter presents a series of cases culled from hospital
and clinic records. Like ordinary admissions in a psychiatric setting,
they are not presented in any order. In a sense, then, we have tried to
reproduce the admitting circumstances of a clinical setting. With each
case some of the clinical reasoning that might be necessary for an
appropriate classification is given. Perusal of the medical records in

these cases would allow fitting the patients into manic or depressive syndromes and then making a specific diagnosis. Following the case studies, the importance of classification to the process of differential diagnosis is discussed.

Case Studies

Case A

A 48-year-old married woman is first seen as an outpatient in the spring of 1949 because of nervousness, irritability, and depression of several years' duration. She appears evasive and defensive and feels that she has a problem about which she can do nothing. She complains of loss of interest in her work and believes that she is not up to taking part in activities in or out of the home. She has trouble sleeping and has been taking sleeping medicine for about a year. She does not enjoy herself, in the previous year lost about 20 lb., and has trouble concentrating. Although she dates the illness back 32 years, believing that she has felt this way more or less continuously since then, she does say that she might have been worse in the late summer when she spent about half her time in bed.

She complains of fatigue and sweating and has periods when everything seemed black. She has both initial insomnia and terminal insomnia. She underwent an appendectomy in 1928, a hysterectomy in 1940, and cauterization of the cervix in 1943. She is preoccupied with somatic symptoms.

Hospitalization occurs in the summer of 1949; she is tearful and expresses unhappiness. She is jealous and suspicious of her husband, feeling that he might be unfaithful. She is irritable toward her youngest daughter. In spite of her feelings about her husband, she feels that she cannot bear to be separated from him. The patient is treated with psychotherapy in the hospital for two months and seems to make a good recovery in the hospital. Psychotherapy revolves around her relationships with her mother, her hostility toward her husband and daughter-in-law, and her family life.

At various hospital staff meetings, she is given several diagnoses, including involutional melancholia, manic-depressive illness, depression, and neurasthenia. She is not considered severely depressed and has never been psychotic.

In 1952 she finds it hard to make decisions and concentrate; she withdraws from social contacts and is described as being low in spirits, having a poor appetite, and experiencing early-morning awakening. Again, she does not appear to be very depressed, if depressed at all, on examination. She is readmitted. She has been avoiding people and is disinterested in her household tasks. She notes some vague feelings of depression and perhaps some diurnal variation. She receives seven electroconvulsive treatments, has a good response, and is discharged home. Her diagnosis is involutional psychosis, depression.

She is readmitted in 1955. She is by now a widow and 55 years of age. In the previous summer she developed a depression associated with terminal insomnia, anorexia, 20-lb. weight loss, constipation, crying spells, indecisiveness, and some somatic complaints. She is believed to show a typical involutional depression on this admission and is given another series of electroconvulsive treatments (six in number), with good improvement. It is noted that her previous dependent personality was still present.

A year later (1956) she is readmitted to the hospital. She was treated in between with another course of electroconvulsive therapy but improved for only a short time. Her diagnosis by this admission is involutional psychotic reaction, recurrent. Again, she does not appear to be very deeply depressed though she complains that she feels depressed and is nervous. She complains of anorexia, difficulty in sleeping, and lack of interest. By this time, the physicians in the hospital know her very well, and they believe that because this patient did not respond well to electrotherapy, she should be started on psychotherapy. She is given a sodium amytal interview. The possibility that she lost her goal in life after her children left home and her husband died is discussed in the amytal interview. The physicians believe that she gained some insight into her condition and discharge her as improved. Her diagnosis is involutional psychotic reaction.

This patient's problem existed long before her first psychiatric contact. When seen for the first time in 1949, the social workup is clear. She has been irritable and nervous most of her life. The family cannot put an exact date on the onset of her illness. She was tired all the time and was always fussing. She complained about her troubles, nagged at her son and her husband much of the time, was short tempered, felt that her husband was neglecting her, liked to quarrel, and was often insulting to people. She complained that her housework was too much for her and that she was too tired to do it. Though she picked at her meals, she ate a good bit between meals. She was easily annoyed by small noises. In the chart, the following statement is made: "She delights, in interviews, in reciting her husband's stupidities and incompetencies." The marriage is considered unhappy because of the patient's constant nagging, and she has said that she would divorce her husband if it were not for the children. She was gossipy and had little conversational interests except talking about other people. She was very demanding of the family, never satisfied or pleased with what was done for her, and her feelings were easily hurt. Her sensitivity is described as "making mountains out of molehills." She has had considerable difficulty in sexual adjustment with her husband.

Her family history is positive, but the actual diagnoses of the family members are unknown. Her mother died at the age of 36 during a "nervous breakdown." She suddenly became nervous, was locked up in the city jail, and was due to have an insanity hearing. She jumped out of the window onto the second floor of the courthouse, injured herself, and developed gangrene of her leg. The leg was amputated and she died postoperatively. A somewhat younger sister is similar to the patient in personality, being high strung and irritable. A few years prior to the patient's first hospitalization, the sister had a nervous breakdown and was in the hospital for a period of time. A maternal uncle was known to be "mentally ill."

In general, the patient's life is filled with stormy relationships and unsatisfactory circumstances as far as she is concerned. She is likely to blame other people and the world in general for her difficulties.

In fact, this patient fulfills the criteria for a neurotic depression. Her first admission is relatively late, but she does mention depressive episodes that occurred before the first hospitalization. The physicians debate whether she might have neurasthenia rather than a depression. They note, "She described periods of fatigue when she lost interest in her family for a period of a few months and then would feel all right again." At one point she is diagnosed as manic-depressive, depressed, but "recognizing the psychogenic factors." Her depression can be diagnosed as neurotic because it developed in the context of a stormy life-style, many personal problems, somatic complaints, and difficulties with almost all types of people with whom she had contact. There is no history of alcoholism in the family, and we do not have the kind of information that would document a diagnosis of depression secondary to somatization disorder. Clinically, it is interesting that nobody ever thought of her as being very depressed but nevertheless gave her a diagnosis of involutional depression. Some of the symptoms are rather typically "endogenous," but she is a good case of somebody whose characterologic problems and a stormy life-style predated her depression, and therefore she fits the diagnosis of neurotic depression.

Case B

A 37-year-old man is seen by the psychiatry consultation service upon request from the neurology department. After an accident, he developed a posttraumatic head injury syndrome and complained of depression and suicide ideation. This head injury occurred 14 months prior to the consultation.

There is no history of psychiatric problems until the head injury, during which time he lost consciousness for 20 to 30 minutes and had a skull fracture and a frontal hematoma. Since the injury he has not worked. He states that he has no energy and is "dizzy all the time." His memory is poor, as is his concentration, and he is frightened about driving a car. He is depressed with hopelessness and marked insomnia. Mostly he just sits around. He has entertained mild suicide ideation without a plan. His interest in sexual relations has markedly diminished.

In addition, he has had temper outbursts and yelled a lot at his family and slapped his wife and son in the face. He cries easily. There is no history of alcoholism or drug abuse, and over time symptoms have not improved.

The mental status shows a dysphoric mood, full affect, and suicide ideation. He is mildly tangential and shows normal psychomotor activity. He has some difficulty finding words to express himself.

The patient is diagnosed as having an organic affective disorder and an organic personality disorder secondary to head trauma.

He has been treated before with amitriptyline with no success. Because the patient has a severe temper problem, he is treated with carbamazepine, which is prescribed by the psychiatrist.

A magnetic resonance examination reveals a small area of gliosis in the left frontal lobe.

His response to the carbamazepine is lost in the shrouds of time. There is no note telling us how he did on that drug. However, he is seen off and on for about a year and a half after the psychiatric consultation. He is noted to have memory loss, loss of smell, benign position vertigo, poor concentration, and headaches. He complains of hypersomnolence and states that at times he slept around the clock for two to two-and-a-half days without awakening for any reason. This might occur a couple of times a month. In 1988 (a year and a half after he was seen) no mention is made of depressive affect.

This patient had no psychiatric symptomatology until he had a severe head injury. After that he developed a depressive syndrome. It would seem that this is a good example of an organic affective disorder, depressive type, which was induced by a head injury.

Case C
The index admission of this patient occurs at the age of 29. She is a married woman. Her presenting symptoms at the time of index admission in 1926 are that she is afraid to stay alone, is afraid to do

anything, and believes that she is worthless and might as well be dead. She says that she feels nervous, fidgety, restless, sad, and depressed and is suffering from "paralysis of the will." She expresses a strong fear that she might go crazy. The diagnosis that was originally entertained in the outpatient department prior to her admission was that of psychoneurosis, psychasthenic type.

A mental status examination reveals psychomotor retardation; her memory is unimpaired. There were no hallucinations. She is afraid, however, that she is going to lose her mind. She complains that she is no longer as happy, carefree, and peppy and jolly as she used to be. She believes that people think something is the matter with her mind. After being in the hospital a few days, she worries that she is not going to get well and is quite ruminative. She eats and sleeps well and is cooperative with routine. She is discharged about five weeks after she was admitted. She is noted to show a great deal of improvement compared with her mental condition at admission, when she was depressed, despondent, thought she was a failure, and had no confidence. When discharged, she is elated, talkative, somewhat aggressive, and egotistical, and seems to be "approaching" a manic state. Interestingly, the physicians at that time, in discussing her future, comment, "At the present time, too manic to seriously consider adjustment to her environment." The diagnosis at discharge is manic-depressive, depressed, but it is recognized that she is showing some of the symptoms of mania.

Her past history is very significant. The index admission is in fact her fourth. In 1919 she was admitted to a hospital and was "out of her head entirely." She was very talkative, restless, extremely interested in everything, and constantly on the go. This lasted but a very short time. In 1924 following the death of her father, she says that she felt run down, exhausted, tired, and depressed, and had lost interest. This lasted for a few weeks and she was in the hospital for a month. After that she was talkative, active, and out of the hospital for two years. A few months prior to the index admission, she was hospitalized again. Her symptoms were complaints of despondency, loss of interest, retardation, feeling discouraged, poor appetite, poor sleep, and burning on urination.

Her personal history is not particularly contributory. Her family history is positive. Her father committed suicide after a period of depression. There was some question as to whether he was alcoholic. A paternal uncle is alcoholic, and the mother is considered to be hot tempered and unreasonable.

The course of her illness after index admission is very revealing. In 1930 she has another depression for which she is hospitalized. In

1936 she is admitted because of fatigue, depression, and loss of interest and ambition. She says she is good for nothing and wishes she were dead. She picks up an ice pick to stab herself, but it is taken away from her. She loses weight and worries that she might have cancer. When admitted in 1936 she is unclean and untidy, is disinterested and lacks enthusiasm, and sits alone with a downcast expression. She stays in the hospital for about three weeks but did not improve. She is sent to a state hospital.

In 1940 she is admitted to a hospital with a depression. She is given metrazol shock therapy and, after seven treatments and 19 days of hospitalization, makes sufficient recovery to be discharged. She is admitted to that same hospital two years later, having been transferred from a state hospital. On admission she is cooperative, euphoric, jovial, and overactive. She is given "curare electroshock therapy," improves, and is discharged to be followed as an outpatient. She is readmitted within one week, having become discouraged, anxious, tearful, sleepless, and unable to eat. She is again given a course of electroshock therapy and discharged in an improved state. Eight months later she is given four electroconvulsive therapy treatments for a mild depression.

Her final diagnosis, after having shown illness from 1919 to 1945, is manic-depressive psychosis, cyclic type. She always responded immediately to electroconvulsive therapy but this did not change her susceptibility to subsequent attacks.

This patient is a fairly typical case of manic-depressive illness or bipolar illness. Bipolar illness as a diagnosis always takes precedence over unipolar depression in the classification. She has a very early onset and multiple episodes. She varies between depression and mania, and she is typically ill with both of these syndromes. Her father committed suicide and may or may not have been alcoholic. Of course, in modern times there are very adequate treatments for this kind of syndrome and her prognosis would be better.

Case D

A 27-year-old, married mother of two first presents to an anxiety disorder clinic around 1986. Her complaint is anxiety attacks. At the age of 23, she experienced her first panic attack while away from her home. She recently lost her sister in an automobile accident, and she feels that this has something to do with the onset of the disorder. She says that she had a sudden-onset panic attack with tachycardia, shortness of breath, tremor, and dizziness and lasting several minutes. She presented herself to a local emergency room because she was afraid that she might be having a heart attack. A cardiac and endocrine workup was negative. She was given small doses of amitriptyline and alprazolam with only limited benefit. The attacks became more frequent (two to three per week), and she gave up her job as a hair stylist because of phobic avoidance. She was also phobic about driving on certain streets and found it difficult to tolerate the anticipatory anxiety that she experienced while working in the hair salon.

The family history is quite positive in that her mother and maternal grandmother had similar panic attacks, but they were never treated. A maternal grandfather may have been alcoholic.

After she is evaluated in the anxiety disorders clinics, she is given a three-month trial of low-dose imipramine, which has only a limited effect. She is switched to alprazolam and responds well to a moderate dose for several months. While maintaining a good remission from anxiety symptoms, she develops a full depressive syndrome with low mood, loss of energy, terminal sleep problems, loss of appetite, and irritability. She is given another tricyclic antidepressant with little effect, and both the alprazolam and the tricyclic are stopped. Then the patient is started on phenelzine, 75 mg daily for three months. She has a full remission of both sets of symptoms, anxious and depressive. Although she is quite compliant about taking the phenelzine, she has a return of her panic attacks. There is no return of her affective symptoms, however. Higher doses produce no benefit and the phenelzine is discontinued. Various other tricyclic antidepressants and benzodiazepines are tried with incomplete response. Mild anxiety and depressive symptoms return but are tolerable. After a year, however, she is switched to fluoxetine and remains on that for about a year. She experiences a full remission of all depressive and anxiety symptoms.

This patient has an unequivocal diagnosis of panic disorder with some agoraphobia. She has a good family history for this. She appears to have responded to a variety of treatments. Diagnostically, she has a secondary depression in that the anxiety disorder occurred first. She fits the category of patients who have neurotic depression because patients with secondary depression generally fill the criteria of a long history of difficult problems in living. There is no evidence of personality problems or difficulties in living before the onset of her symptoms, but, by definition, as a person with secondary depression she must be considered to have a neurotic depression. Certainly the concept of neurotic depression as an illness in which considerable neurotic symptomatology coexists with depressive episodes fits her quite well.

Case E

This patient is admitted to the hospital in 1984 at the age of 31. Medical symptoms started approximately four years before admission. They manifested themselves as clumsiness, with frequent falling and stumbling. Later she developed decreased coordination of both upper extremities.

A workup in 1982 revealed abnormal visual evoked responses and abnormal brain stem auditory evoked responses. A lumbar puncture revealed an increased gamma globulin fraction. She was diagnosed as having multiple sclerosis.

In 1983 she had an increase in clumsiness, decreased ability to walk, and trouble reading because of difficulty in focusing. She had increased fecal and urinary incontinence at that time, and she showed abnormal sensory evoked responses. A pontogram was abnormal and compatible with multifocal brain stem pathology. In 1986 a psychiatric consultation is requested because of a note about increased irritability and paranoid ideation. During the psychiatric consultation, the patient and her sister-in-law are interviewed and the chart is reviewed. The patient reports two years of depressive symptoms with recent development of obsessive thoughts about catching germs from farm animals. She is concerned about catching an unknown disease from cattle or hogs. She reports some compulsions about checking items in her purse.

Her depressive symptoms include dysphoria, irritability, initial and terminal insomnia psychomotor retardation, self-deprecatory thoughts, death wishes, and some vague suspiciousness, neither systematized nor flagrantly delusional in character.

The diagnosis is major depressive disorder with obsessive features. A trial of an antidepressant of the tricyclic type is suggested. Because the patient did rather poorly on the mental status examination, an evaluation for dementia is suggested. This is accomplished, and the neuropsychologist notes some evidence of difficulty in thinking, particularly when it comes to nonverbal and sequence-dependent processes. There is mild memory impairment.

She apparently has a good response to the tricyclic antidepressant but becomes depressed again in a year and has another consultation. She is again put on a tricyclic, but the results from this treatment attempt are unknown. The diagnosis is organic affective disorder. There is clear evidence of cerebral involvement over the course of years, and although one can never be certain that the depression is not reactive or endogenous, it is a legitimate possibility that the brain dysfunction is relevant to the onset of the depressive symptoms.

Case F

A 37-year-old single woman is admitted to the hospital in early 1990 for suicidal preoccupation and a failure of previous antidepressant trials.

Her illness is almost impossible to date. She reports lifelong dysphoria but sought psychiatric care only two years before the admission, and in that time she had four psychiatric admissions. A full major depressive syndrome has been present throughout that time. Such symptoms include hypersomnia, anhedonia, decreased concentration, decreased energy, suicide ideation, decreased energy, a feeling of emptiness and hopelessness, and sleep difficulties. She denies any appetite change. Symptoms have persisted for the past two years despite sustained trials of two tricyclic antidepressants, fluoxetine, and a monoamine oxidase inhibitor, and one course of electroconvulsive therapy. She often cut her hands and feet in order to achieve tension relief. This behavior did not occur before two years ago. She is affectively unstable and shows inappropriate anger. Some of these features are typical of a borderline personality disorder (emotional instability reaction), but she does not meet the criteria for such a diagnosis.

She has undergone a vagotomy and has had two laminectomies for herniated discs. She has some somatic complaints but does not meet the criteria for somatization disorder.

Her mental status is that of an alert, cooperative person whose affect is depressed throughout the interview. Her account of symptoms is coherent. She describes pervasive anhedonia. There are no feelings of guilt, but she shows little tendency to blame others. She admits to having ongoing thoughts of suicide.

Her family history is quite positive. Her father suffered alcoholism and she has one sister who engaged in self-mutilation.

This patient is given a staff diagnosis of major depression, unipolar. It is noted that she has some features of "atypical depression," including hypersomnia, hyperphagia, and reactivity. She has a lifelong history of dysphoria. She has a family history of alcoholism and therefore fits the definition of depression-spectrum disease. Depression-spectrum disease is an illness in which the individual has an early onset of depression and a family history of alcoholism with or without a family history of depression. She also has many personal problems, a stormy life-style, and a poor response to treatment without any kind of remission over a long period of time. Thus the patient fills criteria for a neurotic depression with a more specific diagnosis of depression-spectrum disease.

Case G

A 36-year-old married woman is admitted to the hospital in 1988 because of persistent depressive symptoms that have been nonresponsive to either inpatient or outpatient therapy.

Her symptoms at the time of admission include depressive thoughts, anorexia with a 60-lb. weight loss in three months, fatigue, suicide thoughts, insomnia, and mood-congruent auditory and visual hallucinations. Her auditory hallucinations consist of a single voice telling her how bad she is. She has some visual hallucinations of seeing a solitary knife on desk tops and counters. She reports feeling very anxious. She complains of episodes of feeling "high" but these only lasted one to five days.

The patient has had a series of neurologic and somatic complaints. She had an exploratory laparotomy for abdominal pain that was negative for any cause. She complains of "spells" that are characterized by nausea and vomiting and loss of consciousness. Neurologic examinations have been negative. Among the symptoms she has complained of are chronic headaches, feeling sickly, anesthesia, convulsions, spells of unconsciousness, hallucinations, urinary retention, fatigue, fainting spells, dysurea, palpitations, anxiety attacks, chest pains, weight loss, nausea, diarrhea, constipation, abdominal pain, vomiting, menstrual irregularity, sexual indifference, dyspareunia, back pain, nervousness, depressed feelings, inability to work, crying spells, feeling life was hopeless, thinking a lot about dying, wanting to die, and thinking of suicide attempts. In fact, there are 33 symptoms that the patient has complained of, including numerous conversion-type symptoms. In addition to the exploratory laparotomy, she had an appendectomy and a cholecystotomy.

In the nine years prior to admission, she received a wide variety of treatments for depression including electroconvulsive therapy, tricyclic antidepressants, monoamine oxidase inhibitors, lithium, and other drugs. None of these helped. Outpatient records reveal a variety of peculiar side effects and a "whimsical" compliance with medication order. After a course of electroconvulsive therapy, she became markedly worse within a few days of discharge.

Her mental status is that of an alert, cooperative woman who is unable to recall any periods of remission or any benefit from any of the medicines or other treatments that have been given to her in the past nine years. While she reports auditory and visual hallucinations, none of her answers suggest the presence of delusions.

The patient clearly has a somatization disorder. This occurred long before her depressive history, and therefore her diagnosis is that of a secondary depression. This, of course, is considered a neurotic depression.

Her family history is negative for psychiatric illness.

Her past history is turbulent. She reports having been sexually abused by her brother-in-law at the age of 12. Her first hospitalization for a depression occurred at age 28, following approximately six months of some abuse of stimulant drugs. She never finished high school. She is described as having a nervous stomach since childhood. She has considerable anxiety symptoms, including panic attacks. However, the massive nature of her somatic symptomatology makes the diagnosis of somatization disorder with secondary depression rather clear.

Case H

A 68-year-old farmer who was originally admitted to medicine is transferred to psychiatry for treatment of depressive symptoms. This occurs in late 1983. He developed depressive symptoms approximately nine months previously and these have worsened. They include initial and terminal insomnia, anorexia with a 20-lb. weight loss, fatigue, nonpervasive anhedonia, and thoughts of suicide. He also reports crying spells, general loss of interest, and anorexia.

On admission he is well oriented. His mood is low and he appears sad. There are no delusions or hallucinations present. His speech is normal.

The patient states that although he continued to be active as the chairman of the cemetery board in his local community, he does not have strong interest in his other usual activities. He admits to thoughts of suicide but says that his strong religious convictions keep him from accomplishing that. He says that he has been worried about his health during the past couple of years and complains of mild difficulty with recent memory. He was diagnosed in internal medicine as having autoimmune hemolytic anemia and had a splenectomy for this. He also had mitral valve prolapse and pulmonary disease. He is hyperventilating at the time he is seen. He is diagnosed as having major depressive disorder, unipolar and primary. He is treated with nortriptyline. After beginning medication, he has resolution of his sleep difficulties, improved appetite, and decreased dysphoria. He is discharged after only five days in the hospital because the family is quite competent and attentive and believe that they could take care of him. He is seen around two weeks later in the psychiatric clinic, and it is noted that he was congenial and cooperative. His mood is neutral and he denies any suicide ideation.

No positive family history is noted, and the patient is apparently a man who has had considerable success, is a staunch member of his church, and seems to have had little in the way of significant personality problems.

The follow-up on this patient is quite short. Within a month of that visit, he dies of heart failure, probably as a result of multiple pulmonary infarcts.

This is a case of a patient who is severely incapacitated by a variety of medical complaints. Ultimately one that causes significant shortness of breath (pulmonary disease) causes his demise. He was an individual who had no family history of depression. He had no evidence of any psychologic difficulties prior to the time that he became depressed. He had a long period of medical disability. The appropriate diagnosis for this patient is depression secondary to medical illness. This would be a type of reactive depression.

He is a good example of the kind of patient that is seen in a psychiatric hospital and who dies early of natural causes. Most of the excess of natural deaths in psychiatrically ill patients are accounted for by the fact that such patients have both a medical and a psychiatric illness at the same time. It is quite possible that this combination brings patients into the hospital more frequently than patients with either illness alone. In fact, the combination of psychiatric and medical problems was probably very significant in bringing this patient to the psychiatric hospital.

Case I
This patient is admitted at the age of 52 in the early 1950s. She states that she has been depressed and upset for a period of many years and that this has become progressively worse. During the few weeks prior to admission, she cried without provocation; continuously worried; had trouble sleeping, with early-morning awakening; felt a lack of enjoyment and loss of interest; and felt better in the morning.

The fact is that she became ill for the first time long before this. She believes that she had three rather ill-defined episodes of depression, the first starting around the age of 39 when her oldest son was entering the Navy. She worried a lot about him, would wake up easily, had trouble concentrating, had some crying spells, and continued to have difficulties for about a year. Seven years prior to the admission she again became disturbed and again this was related to other family members' going into the Armed Service. She said that she would stay up until 2:00 to 3:00 in the morning and feel very tense. She cried a lot. She was irritable with her husband. She awakened easily but by the time that the family members (her children) were back from the Service she improved considerably. In 1947 she again became seriously upset following the death of her grandson. The patient had spent many nights in attendance and was upset when the baby died. She stated that at that time she almost went out of her mind, screamed, threw things around the house, and was difficult to control. Since that time, her symptoms have increased and she has had episodes of feeling a fullness in her chest associated with anxiety and apprehension. She worries that her husband might be killed in a car wreck. She complains of her memory being poor for the last two or three years. She has some diurnal variation, feeling better in the afternoon. There is a reduction of energy. She has attempted suicide on numerous occasions. She sat on a railroad track waiting for a train, but her husband found her and removed her before the train arrived. She tried to shoot herself on more than one occasion with a shotgun and had decided that she could probably pull the trigger with her toe. Two weeks prior to admission she tried to drink carbolic acid, but her husband knocked the bottle away from her as she had it to her lips. It burned her lip a little bit.

The family history in this patient is quite significant. The father was a severe alcoholic and two older brothers are very heavy drinkers.

Her background is such that she has had considerable trouble over many years. As a child she was frequently angry, and she continues to feel very angry when she is hurt. She often cries. Her sexual adjustment has been poor. She has dyspareunia, and she has never enjoyed intercourse. She has a number of somatic complaints. She is described as being shy and backward at meeting people. She is sensitive and quite easily offended. She has been worrisome and withdrawn and had tended to anticipate trouble over many years.

This patient is called manic-depressive, depressed, when she is admitted in 1950. Certainly she does have a primary major depression. However, this depression is the culmination of a long history of personal problems and the fact that she has a family history of alcoholism makes her diagnosis that of depression-spectrum disease. She is a good example of a person who fills the criteria of neurotic depression.

Case J

A 56-year-old minister is brought to the hospital because of recent threats of and one attempt at suicide. He has been depressed for three years or more but has been particularly depressed for the past month and a half. He is admitted to the hospital in November, 1938.

The onset of his illness was rather vague and the symptoms developed gradually. First, he started to worry over trivial circumstances and then developed retardation and motor activity. This is dated back to about a year and a half before admission. He became very depressed and was very reproachful about himself, and he felt that his actions had contributed to the financial failure of his family. He was relieved of his duties at the parish and placed on a pension. He made a suicide attempt in late October 1938 by swallowing gasoline.

His mental status is striking. He approaches the examining room with his head bowed, shoulders stooped, and a halting gait. His speech is slow and hesitant and replete with self-accusatory ideas. He frequently becomes lachrymose. His orientation and memory are unimpaired.

His past history is contributory. He had an episode of depression at the age of 31. This lasted six months, and he was suicidal at that time also.

He is a conscientious, studious person who likes being alone and is always concerned about life's necessities.

The family history is positive in that his father died at a state hospital (his psychiatric diagnosis was unknown). One of his brothers committed suicide at age 45 when suffering from a nervous breakdown that manifested itself by depression. On the mother's side of the family, the people were considered high-strung and nervous.

The patient is in the hospital for around three months, and during that time he improves. His retardation clears up and he is able to think in an appropriate fashion. The diagnosis of the staff is manic-depressive psychosis, depressed state. They believe that the etiology is "heredity." In follow-up, the patient's wife relates that he is much better in many ways but is still very nervous and easily upset. By September 1939 he is considered quite well. His appetite is good, and he sleeps well. In February 1940 it is noted that he has gained weight and that his mind is "much clearer." He is still nervous and tires easily, however.

This patient shows a fairly clear and unequivocal diagnosis of an endogenous depression and, more particularly, familial pure depressive disease. He had two episodes, about 25 years apart. Both apparently cleared up with no specific treatment. Modern therapy would probably lead to a more rapid resolution of the depression.

Case K
A married 41-year-old farmer is admitted in an overly talkative condition with a certain amount of juvenile facetiousness to his remarks.

In general, the patient has always been expansive in his general attitude and activity, but during the past summer he was overactive in selling seed corn. He was irritable and neglectful and argued a great deal. He was euphoric in mood. He has a tendency to brag and is circumstantial in his speech. He shows considerable punning. He believes people are jealous of him. He has had a series of unrealistic plans, such as leaving the state and changing his business.

He is constantly greeting people about him, waving to people, and continually touching people on the arm or on the back. When restricted in activities, he would become angry and threatening. He is admitted in 1938 in mid-December. He became overtalkative about three months earlier.

His background is such that he is described as an active, sociable, outgoing person. He had been sexually promiscuous and he continually believed he was attractive to the opposite sex.

His family history is somewhat contributory in that the mother is apparently overreligious, and one sister is described as being immoral. All three of his sisters are considered trouble makers and people with whom it is difficult to get along.

The patient is diagnosed as having manic-depressive psychosis, manic type. He remains in the hospital for only a few days and then is transferred to a sanatorium for further recovery. After transfer, he remains at the sanatorium for six months and then a follow-up letter in June 1939 states that he is doing fine and is at home.

This patient is a fairly typical case of bipolar illness. Though he has no family history of bipolar illness, the overreligious behavior of his mother and the immorality of his sister suggest that they may have had some manic symptoms. He is quite outgoing. He is unfaithful in his marriage at a time when this is not as acceptable behavior as it currently appears to be. He is considered outgoing and unstable. He is considered to have good judgment up to the time of his illness, even though he is considered somewhat unstable.

Case L

A 20-year-old married woman is admitted to the University of Iowa Psychiatric Hospital in 1936.

A month before admission she delivered a baby and remained in the hospital for a period of time, somewhat over the expected amount of time because of a temperature elevation. During her obstetrical hospitalization, she seemed to be quite happy and excited, talking continually when her friends were present. When she returned home, she cried occasionally and remarked to her husband that she was not sure she would get well.

After she returned home from her obstetrical hospitalization, she began visiting neighbors in the apartment building to a greater extent than the husband had anticipated. She started to talk about church and wanted to go frequently. She seemed more sensitive. In time she was talking almost continuously, gossiping and criticizing others, which was a distinct change from her usual self. She had periods of crying. She became frightened and screamed and began to talk about religion. She stated that the Devil shouted at her and that a parrot in the house was put there to keep evil spirits away. She thought she was burning up, felt that God was talking to her, and that she could save other people. She was in continuous motion, running about the room. She slept for only short periods of time and continued to talk about God and how he had pointed her in the direction to do things. At night she insisted on keeping a light burning and yelled frequently for help to prevent the Devil from getting at her. She slept poorly and was unable to eat or sleep.

She is admitted to the hospital because of the symptoms. In the hospital, she remarks that God is directing her activities and says that she hallucinated her father's and mother's voices on various occasions. She shows verbigeration and swears violently. It is not possible to tell whether she is correctly oriented because of her overactivity and over-talkativeness. She is lively, sings, and whistles, and in order to examine her it is necessary to hold her down.

She frequently masturbates, spits about her, and is incontinent.

She was ill in the past. When 15 years old, following an appendectomy, she was excited, overactive, and overtalkative for 10 days.

The family history is positive. A paternal grandfather committed suicide, the father is alcoholic, and other brothers are alcoholic.

She is transferred to a state hospital after a month. Her symptoms continue in the state hospital, but she improves over time and nine months later is sent home.

The diagnosis is manic-depressive, manic. This patient is interesting because her illness is reminiscent of that of Margery Kempe. There are similar religious delusions and hallucinations in both cases. Both seemed to be precipitated by childbirth. However, in the case of this patient, a prior episode occurred at the age of 15. In the case of Margery Kempe, the possible manic behavior occurred after recovery from the postpartum psychosis. Also, in this patient's case there is clear evidence of her actions and mind being directed from the outside, which suggests that she has the clinical picture to support a schizoaffective manic diagnosis. As expected, she recovers. It is noteworthy that this recovery occurs in a time when there was no specific treatment for bipolar illness.

Case M

A 30-year-old married farmer is brought to the hospital for feelings of sadness, lack of self-confidence, and diminished energy output. At the age of 22 (1931) he had an episode during which he was sad, hopeless, and depressed that lasted two to three months. In April 1939 he began to feel that running a farm was too much responsibility. He became afraid to begin new tasks and lost self-confidence. He threatened suicide. On numerous occasions, his sleep was poor. His appetite was undisturbed. His speech and thoughts appear retarded. The patient feels he has done wrong and because of it neighbors are leaving the vicinity.

His mental status is such that he is neat and clean but shows marked psychomotor retardation. His voice is dull and monotonous. His mood is deeply depressed, and the content evolves around some real or fancy wrongs that he had perpetrated. He complains frequently of loss of interest, energy, and strength. His memory is fine. His orientation is correct. He shows no evidence of any psychotic symptoms. He is admitted July 4, 1939.

For two weeks he remains very depressed and then begins to recover gradually. The diagnosis is manic-depressive psychosis, depressed.

The family history is very positive. The patient's mother had a depression 15 years before. One maternal aunt committed suicide during a depression, and a maternal cousin had a mental disease of unknown type. The patient's father is somewhat peculiar and describes having heard strange voices telling him how to run his affairs. The quality of the father's unusual experiences is essentially as follows: While out on his farm in 1912 he heard a voice saying, "Robert, you are working too hard." The father states that the next year he hardly did anything but take chiropractic treatments. The cords in his neck did not carry nourishment to his brain and that was the problem. He then states that the voices came to him in the night when he was bed, telling him what to do. These voices have continued since 1912, but his faith does not allow him to worry. Throughout the interview the father quotes scripture quite freely to show his point and seems to have a good sense of humor.

The patient's personality is sociable and ordinarily interested in things. He would stick to a task until it was finished.

He is discharged from the hospital after about six weeks. He improves over time and after about six months he is asymptomatic and enjoys life.

This patient has a unipolar endogenous depression. The familial classification would be familial pure depressive disease because his

mother also had a similar illness. His father's illness, though interesting, is not of the kind that is ordinarily associated with a depression.

Case N
A 31-year-old woman who is unmarried and works as a maid is admitted to the hospital in mid-April 1937 and is discharged 17 days later
against medical advice.

For the four to five months before admission, she was discouraged,
feeling she could never obtain a better job, and made a suicide attempt on April 1 by inhaling illuminating gas.

She is neat and clean. She seems depressed in mood. Retardation is
present, and the patient responds to questions in an evasive manner
by stating, "I don't know." She has had several months of fatigue and
"trouble" with her head. She has had "pains in the back and in the
front," and has not felt like doing very much. She was working as a
housemaid and the future began to look bad to her. She was discouraged and despondent and was fired from her job just before the
suicide attempt. She saw nothing in her future except another housemaid's job. The factors that predated her suicide attempts were difficulties in her work and being fired. Prior to that time she complained
of headaches, and was irritable, very nervous and upset, and very
inefficient.

As contacts with the patient ensue in the hospital, she states that she
left work a couple of weeks previously because she felt tired and her
head hurt. She states that she felt slowed up, lost interest, and did not
enjoy herself. During her stay in the hospital, she spends most of her
days in bed complaining about a headache and a backache. She keeps
talking about the ill treatment that she is receiving in the hospital and
is very irritable. She is vague, and to most questions, even the most
innocent ones, she responds with either silence or "I don't know." She
does say, however, that she wants to leave the hospital as soon as
possible because she feels "severely mistreated" while in the hospital.

Her past history is significant in that four years previously she was
blue and despondent. She had considerable problems getting along
with her sisters, was disinterested, and felt the future was hopeless.
This illness lasted for about six months and then she obtained a job as
a housemaid. In 1933, in addition to being less interested in what was
going on about her, she was somewhat slowed up, slept a great deal,
threatened suicide frequently, and did not talk to people.

Her personality is noted to be different from others. She is more
quiet, more sensitive, more likely to take things to heart, less likely to
mix and meet people, and unwilling to go places. She is always shy and
retiring. Early in life she began biting her fingernails, a trait that

persisted to the present. She had two years of college and took a teaching job but did not enjoy this. She then took a beauty parlor course and had a small shop. She ran the shop four years, but when her family left the town in which the shop was located, she decided to leave also. She was always considered quite dependent on her family. She had been doing rather well in her beauty shop and gave it up rather precipitously. The family could not understand this move on her part. She has held her current job for two years, but before this she did maid's work with several different households for two years.

She has never been interested in the opposite sex and never went out with boys.

She has always felt that her mother and father were the only people who really understood her.

The family history reveals that the patient came from an Irish-English family. Two paternal uncles had tuberculosis but were cured. One maternal uncle is feeble-minded. The father is a day laborer who has a severe problem with alcoholism.

Though the patient is finally diagnosed as having manic-depressive illness, depressed type, there is a large argument as to whether the appropriate diagnosis is neurasthenia.

It would appear that this patient has a primary depression with a long-standing personality problem and a stormy and unsuccessful life. Her father is alcoholic. Thus she fits the concept of depression-spectrum disease and neurotic depressive illness.

Case O
A 27-year-old married woman is admitted to the hospital in 1955. Previously she was seen as an outpatient and received sodium amytal injections; this resulted in improvement, but the improvement lasted only about 24 hours. She is a college graduate, and an extensive work-up showed her to be of superior intelligence (IQ of 117). The psycho-logic test suggested that she could be characterized as having an immature psychopathic personality with some superimposed neurotic features. Finally, she was admitted. Her present illness lasted about a year. She began to feel depressed, slept to excess, ate poorly, and had many crying spells. She began to have difficulty doing her work and started to blame herself over her poor judgment about money. She threatened suicide. When admitted, she is cooperative, but appears somber and unhappy. Her symptoms apparently began after a love affair with a married man. She has difficulty adjusting herself to the ward routine and is finally given a course of six electroconvulsive treatments. She improves considerably. However, within a week she becomes somewhat depressed again and then improves again with

superficial psychotherapy. The diagnosis at the staff meeting varies from depression in a person with an inadequate personality to manic-depressive, depressed, with inadequate personality. The reason that she is considered to have an inadequate personality is that she is vague and shows poor financial judgment, job instability, and inability to form relationships.

Nine years later she is seen again. She appears to be histrionic and says, "I cannot get married because of tension and temper tantrums." At the time of this outpatient visit, she is diagnosed as having features of an inadequate personality and an emotionally unstable personality. Psychiatrists wonder whether she has a thinking disorder and some affective traits of schizophrenia, but there is little documentation for this in the record. It turns out that she is pregnant and that the pregnancy was conceived on her fifth date with a man who was sepa-rated from his alcoholic wife. She remembers becoming too drunk and the man taking her home, but she is unable to recall intercourse. On psychiatric grounds, she has a therapeutic abortion. She is seen again three years later. This time, she is tense, spontaneous, rambling, and histrionic. She is vague and becomes tearful as she talks about her abortion a few years back. At this time her diagnosis is inadequate personality and she is given some sedative medication.

According to her relatives, she is "pronouncedly irresponsible." She ran up bills. She was always given to deception and was secretive. She lied frequently. She was fearful of disapproval. She was rather dependent on her parents. She was always poor in completing tasks and did not fulfill obligations.

The family history is quite positive. The mother was hospitalized for around five years with a diagnosis of undiagnosed psychosis. At other times, she may have had a diagnosis of involutional melancholia. The mother responded positively to electroconvulsive therapy. The patient also has a sister who is unstable emotionally, and a maternal uncle who is alcoholic.

This is a good example of a patient with a stormy life-style and multiple personality problems who develops a depression. There is no first-degree family member who has alcoholism, but her mother had a depression and a brother with alcoholism. Thus, her mother may have had depression-spectrum disease.

One cannot make the diagnosis of depression secondary to a neu-rosis, or well-described antisocial personality, or substance abuse in this patient. Nevertheless, she fills reasonable criteria for a neurotic depression. She is an individual who has had lifelong problems in living and on one occasion became depressed enough to warrant a diagnosis of depression.

Case P

A 40-year-old married woman who is admitted in 1939 to the University of Iowa Psychiatric Hospital. She was referred from the Department of Medicine because she had been moaning and groaning and picking at her bed clothes. While she was on the medical service, she was noted to be fumbling at the window as if trying to jump out. Her illness started around Christmas in 1938 when she began to have "queer ideas." She wrote odd letters to her sister, the minister, and other people, saying that if anything were to happen, her child should be taken care of. She started to worry about finances and sleep poorly at night, and she lost her job. Then she started to have ideas of people talking about her, became more irritable, and finally began to complain of pain in the abdomen, which led her to come to the University of Iowa Hospitals on the medical service. When seen she seemed to very weak and tired. Her facial expression was sad and from time to time she would moan and whimper to herself. She refused to eat anything, saying that she could not swallow, and would not drink for the same reason. At times she would cry and at other times she became very agitated and moaned.

She is admitted to the psychiatric ward on September 3rd and by September 25th her condition has improved and she has gained weight. This has been accomplished by forced feeding and tube feeding. However, her mental state has become worse: whereas she would formerly answer some questions she now answers none. Her personal habits are noted to be filthy. The use of intravenous sodium amytal helps produce an improvement in that, although depressed, she would cooperate and talk.

Her previous personality is described by family members as being marked by chronic nervousness. She was always irritable and a great talker about inconsequential things. She was not sociable, never had many friends, and married her husband for economic advantages only.

Her past history, in fact, is positive. Twenty-two years earlier, in 1917, she had a nervous breakdown, supposedly from overwork. At the time her symptoms were much as they are at the time of the index admission. She was mute, restless, wept, picked at her clothing. This cleared up in about six months, leaving her more high strung than before. Her family history is positive in that her father is an alcoholic.

The impression of the physicians in the hospital is that she has an undiagnosed psychosis with two leading possibilities, schizophrenia and psychosis with organic brain disease. However, by the time she is transferred to a state hospital, the diagnosis has changed to manic-depressive psychosis. The reason that an organic psychosis is con-

sidered is that she was in a debilitated state at time of admission from
the medical service and had some sensorium difficulties. These, however, cleared up in time, leaving her only depressed. There is no
follow-up information in this person's case.

The diagnosis here would vary between a unipolar depression of
an endogenous sort and the possibility that she has some kind of
depression that occurred in the lifelong context of personality problems. Certainly she has a family history of alcoholism (her father),
which qualifies her for a depression-spectrum disease diagnosis, but
her symptoms seem more severe than the usual psychoneurotic depression. Because of these circumstances it would be difficult to place
her in any part of the classification with a great deal of certainty.

Case Q
A 19-year-old single man enters the hospital in 1984 with irritability,
racing thoughts, grandiose ideation, and insomnia. Until the fall of
1983, he had no history of psychiatric treatment or evaluation; but at
that time, he suffered a head injury in a motor vehicle accident. There
was no history of loss of consciousness, and he was hospitalized for
only one night. Over several months he was reported to deteriorate.
He was fired from a construction job because of two fist fights. He
started to drink regularly. Before this time he had rarely used alcohol.
There was a decreased need for sleep. He engaged in excessive spending and accumulated numerous debts. When he enters the psychiatric
clinic, he is noted to be restless, grandiose, flirtatious, and somewhat
euphoric. He is hospitalized.

His family history is negative for affective disorder, but he does
have two paternal uncles with alcoholism.

Over three weeks the symptoms of euphoria, sleeplessness, irritability, grandiosity, and hypersexuality subside in conjunction with
lithium treatment. However, he continues to have poor insight and
poor judgment. Neurologic workup with head computerized to-
mographic scan and electroencephalogram is normal. Neuropsychi-
atric evaluations reveal an average IQ and no focal memory impairment.

He is followed for 24 months. There are no further episodes of
mania but he remains unemployed, disabled functionally secondary
to inability to maintain interpersonal relationships. He is at all times
demanding, irritable, and unreliable. All of these symptoms were
absent before the head trauma. There are no other symptoms more
typical of mania in the follow-up period.

The final diagnosis is induced mania and organic personality disorder.

Case R

A woman is admitted to the hospital in 1949. She is 38 years old and married. Six months before admission, she was seen in the outpatient clinic, complaining of depressions that went back 11 years. In 1937 she became depressed while she was caring for a 4-year-old son who was seriously ill with "intestinal influenza." Since that time, she has not returned to her normal self. Depressed periods seemed to come on with no warning but often occurred after something that upset the patient.

In December 1948 she became ill with what was diagnosed as "influenza" and began to have trouble sleeping. There was terminal as well as initial insomnia. She became depressed and developed the idea that she would never be well again. There was some suicidal thinking. She felt better in the morning than in the afternoon. In February 1949 she was seen as an outpatient and placed on benzedrine and sodium amytal. For a period of four weeks she felt better, and her husband stated that, for the first time in her life, after 19 years of marriage, she experienced an orgasm in intercourse and seemed to enjoy it. In April she came back for another evaluation and was still feeling quite good, but in the middle of June, an 18-year-old daughter to whom the patient was quite attached announced that she was planning to be married in the middle of July. An argument developed and the patient became quite upset. Immediately after this her depressed symptoms became more noticeable; her husband stated that she had been feeling pretty good until the daughter's announcement. Since that time, she felt blue, had frequent crying spells, complained of headaches and neckache, and had marked difficulty in sleeping. She lost interest in work. Her husband, fearing suicide, took her to her parental home almost immediately after the increase in symptoms and visited her almost nightly there. He stated that her symptoms were as severe as they had ever been.

Her personality has always been that of a sensitive person whose feelings were easily hurt. Whenever this happened, the reaction was to become quite upset emotionally. She always visited a lot of doctors, worried a great deal over the health of her children, and was always extremely dependent on her parents and later on her daughter. Up until the patient was put on benzedrine and amytal, she had always been indifferent and cold sexually and never secured any pleasure out of intercourse.

Her family history is positive in that one sister received electroconvulsive treatments for depressed symptoms. The sister was always a jittery and unstable person. Otherwise, the family history is negative for psychiatric illness.

The patient is in the hospital for about a month and a half; during this time, she has eight electroconvulsive treatments with only mild improvement.

The diagnosis is that of manic-depressive psychosis, depressed phase. She shows no psychomotor retardation. Her dependency is noted in a staff conference, as is the fact that her depressions usually came on at a time of personal loss or threatened loss. Interestingly, one of the physicians is asked whether he would use her in a research project on affective disorders, and his response is, "I don't think so. She is not typical."

There is a considerable amount of follow-up. She complains of anxiety and tiredness in March 1950. Her relationship with her husband remains unsatisfactory and she continues to take sodium amytal and benzedrine when she becomes depressed or anxious. This helps her quite a bit. By letter, she relates multiple complaints of severe headaches and feeling so nervous and depressed at times that it causes her to gain weight. In 1951 she is taking somewhat less medication and begins to enjoy socializing, but near the end of 1951 she is once more having trouble getting her work done and feels not as well as before. She returns to the outpatient clinic in 1952 and points out that sometimes she felt quite well and at other times felt quite down emotionally. She complains of chills, being sick at her stomach, and hardly eating anything on one occasion, and reports that sometimes she was so weak she could hardly walk. Her husband is getting tired of her condition because he is having to work and also keep house. She cries a lot of the time, and the husband says this is hard on the family. She continues to have sexual problems and complains that sexual activity made her nauseous and disgusted. She is generally frigid. At one point, one of the physicians notes that she seems to be having anxiety attacks with accompanying depression rather than primarily depressive illness. Her anxiety symptoms include "a fear feeling during which time she had a vague uneasiness and did not want to be left alone." She has urinary frequency. Her appetite is good and she feels energetic. She complains of blurred vision when nervous. This assessment occurs in 1952.

In October 1958 there is a complaint that she is worse. She feels tension in her head that keeps her from doing her work. She has trouble going to sleep and feels jumpy. She has both terminal and initial sleep disturbances. Her energy is poor. She has difficulty breathing and sometimes can hardly speak. The future looks futile. She complains of a dull pain in her vagina. She has frequent crying spells and feels relief afterward.

At this point we lose contact with this patient.

This is a patient with chronic personality problems who becomes depressed off and on. At various times she has clearly met criteria for a major depression. It is conceivable that she has an anxiety disorder with a secondary depression. This diagnosis is certainly entertained. There is no evidence of alcoholism in her family, so she could not have depression-spectrum disease. All in all, however, she fits the category of a neurotic depression, that is, a person who has had personality problems and difficulties in living throughout her entire life. Interestingly, no treatment seems to make a significant difference.

Case S
A 60-year-old man is sent to the psychiatry department by the staff in the neurology department. He has no history of psychiatric disorder. He has been working full time in sales. The reason he was first sent to neurology was because of a right-sided stroke accompanied by a left-sided hemiplegia. Physical therapy was instituted and complicated by low mood, hopelessness, crying spells, and suicidal ideation. He viewed the future as black. The patient is treated with a tricyclic antidepressant and seemed to improve, with the hopelessness and the suicidal ideation clearing. He is transferred from neurology to a nursing home for further physical therapy and lost to psychiatric follow-up. When next seen, two months have elapsed. At the nursing home he was noted to be loud, demanding, overtalkative, hypersexual and disruptive. He is transferred to a psychiatric hospital where he appears to be classically manic. He is euphoric. He talks of being able to return to his sales job despite considerable motor deficits and the need for support to walk. He talks of various theories of how to monopolize various markets. Sleep is poor. The tricyclic is discontinued without improvement. A neuroleptic is used to improve sleep and stop some of the intrusive, disruptive behavior. He does not improve. He becomes suspicious and paranoid. He suffers gross confusion with disorientation to time and date, and he has a poor recall of names. He begins to misinterpret things around him (e.g., he thinks an oxygen tank was a roommate). The neuroleptic is discontinued and the suspected delirium clears. Lithium is started and the patient gradually improves. He is discharged after being in the hospital for six weeks.

The family history is totally negative for psychiatric disorder.

In follow-up he does well on lithium. He continues to improve from the stroke but he dislikes the lithium because of the tremor and loose stools. Finally after six months, the lithium is discontinued and he has no recurrence of affective symptoms over an additional six months of follow-up.

The hospital diagnosis is that of an organic affective syndrome, bipolar type, and a delirium that has resolved. He is a good case of an induced mania as well as an induced depression.

Case T

A 44-year-old married man is brought to the hospital because of depression. He is admitted in 1936, but the present illness goes back to April 1933 when the patient was a government employee in Washington, D.C. During this time, he acted superior to his associates, was overtalkative, and was euphoric in his attitude. In 1935 he began brooding over a financial loss. He was passed over for a significant promotion, and became fearful, hopeless, and despondent. He threatened to jump out of the window on one occasion, and from June 1936 to October 1936 people had to be with him constantly. He is agitated, is unable to sleep, and often paces the floor. He cries significantly.

His past history is such that he was always successful, was considered energetic, hard working, and a good mixer.

His family history is positive. His father had been ill in his 50s. This was characterized by depression and agitation, but the diagnosis was apparently general paresis.

In the hospital he becomes gradually more cooperative and is ultimately transferred to a sanatorium for further recuperation.

The diagnosis in the hospital varies between manic-depressive illness and agitated depression. It is difficult to determine whether the period of overtalkativeness and euphoria in 1933 to 1935 constituted a manic episode. By October 1936, a few weeks after discharge, he is better but is still noted to be depressed. In late November he appears to be calmer and to have lost much of his tenseness. In January 1937 letters reveal that he is feeling better and shows interest and enthusiasm. A year later he is well and managing a business. He remains well so far as the record is concerned.

This patient is difficult to diagnose because it is very hard to determine whether he had a bipolar or unipolar illness. Certainly he was hypomanic, and it appears that this was a fairly long episode of hypomania. Nevertheless, he was functioning and never had to seek treatment during this period of hypomania. The part of his illness that caused difficulty was the depressive episode.

We would have to admit that he is hard to classify, but we should consider either unipolar depression or bipolar illness as the diagnosis.

Affective illness is common, and a chronic inability to function is an uncommon outcome. These two facts suggest that affective illness will be found in a variety of prominent and sometimes famous people. Often biographic or autobiographic materials are available on such people, and these documents would allow one to engage in a classification exercise that could be both stimulating and enlightening. There are many examples of this.

One might cite the case of Elliott Nugent, a playwright and actor, who had what seemed to be a bipolar illness. Such authors as Ernest Hemingway and Virginia Woolf may have shown affective episodes under certain circumstances. It might be possible to classify their depressions within the scheme that is presented in this book. James Joyce probably had a problem with alcoholism and also had depressive periods. Leo Tolstoy drank a lot in his early age and had an unequivocal depression in later life. His friend, the author Vsevolod Garshin, showed manias and severe depression. James Forrestal, a member of a presidential cabinet, committed suicide and showed depressive symptoms. Such poets as Thomas Lovell Beddoes and Sylvia Plath had histories of remitting psychiatric disorders. Abraham Lincoln was said to be depressed, as was one of his most successful generals, William Tecumseh Sherman. The actress Jean Seberg was discovered in Paris on September 8, 1979, by a policeman who found her disintegrating body under blankets in the back of a white Renault. A bottle of mineral water and a container for barbiturates were found near the body. The death was called a suicide, and it was established that she had been dead around 10 days. Horace Frink, a pioneer American psychoanalyst, probably had manic-depressive illness. Finally, Mary Wollstonecraft suffered depressions. She was a writer, feminist, and the mother of Mary Shelley, who herself was the author of *Frankenstein*. It is possible to construct a family history of psychiatric illness in the case of Mary Wollstonecraft. A sister had a serious depression and another daughter, Fanny Imlay, committed suicide at age 22. Construction of a family history is also possible in the case of Hemingway.

In any event, because of the nature of the manias and depressions, there is an extensive amount of material in the literature and biography about people who have suffered from these kinds of illnesses, and such accounts lend themselves to exercises in differential diagnosis and classification.

Differential Diagnosis

In the past decade, we have achieved considerable ability to make reliable diagnoses of affective syndromes. A classification builds on this newfound ability to adding validity to our differential diagnosis. Stephen J. Gould, in an article in the *New York Times* on Sunday, July 30, 1989, noted that "taxonomies . . . embody our fundamental ideas about the causes of natural order." Certainly, a viable and valid classification is necessary for both the clinician and investigator because it is meaningful in terms of separating out groups for research and is the basis for some kind of structure and treatment.

Differential diagnosis is a central issue in clinical psychiatry as well as all of medicine. The principles of classification and differential diagnosis may be the true science of medicine. Much of the laboratory research in medicine belongs to other fields, such as molecular biology, genetics, neurochemistry, and others. However, the aggregation of findings and new knowledge needs to be integrated into an appropriate medical classification, which in turn suggests an algorithm for differential diagnosis.

At this point, psychiatry is to a large extent an observational science rather than experimental one, much like astronomy. From a series of systematic observations, it may be possible to make valid predictions. The psychiatric clinician must act on these observations, knowing something about the course of the illness and the response to treatment. It is not enough to simply know how to make a diagnosis of a major depression or a mania. One must be able to fit these findings into a broader context of specific or autonomous diseases.

The classification of the affective disorders proposed in this book has several points of division. It starts with an affective episode that is related to a dysfunction in the brain or a generalized metabolic dysfunction. It separates patients with the presence of a mania into bipolar and unipolar types of nonorganic affective disorder. In the case of the unipolar type of affective disorder, it divides into reactive, neurotic, and endogenous. The reactive depression is related to major life events that have been clearly associated with the development of an affective episode. Neurotic depression is mainly based on the presence of preexisting personality attributes and difficulties in living. Neurotic depression may be divided into two groups: those patients with depressions that are secondary to neuroses, substance abuse disorders, or personality disorders and those patients whose depression is not secondary to any of these diagnoses but who have a family history of alcoholism. Finally, there is endogenous depression, in which an organic or biologic factor is more clearly involved. There are several types of endogenous depressions: familial pure depressive disease, which is based on the idea that there is a genetic background (and therefore, a biologic background for the endogenous depression); seasonal affective disorder (where there is a clear relationship to environmental circumstances); and finally sporadic depression, which deserves consideration as a possible endogenous depression.

Occasionally threads appear that connect some of the groups.

Postpartum mania appears as a possible autonomous illness under the rubric of bipolar affective disorder but reappears in the discussion of schizoaffective disorder, where it is used to make a case for the possibility of a third psychosis. No doubt, as times goes on, the appropriate placement of postpartum mania will become more apparent.

Another connecting element is the use of a specific family history. Ordinarily in the affective disorders most investigators have been concerned mainly with a family history of an affective illness. However, family histories of other kinds of psychiatric illnesses may be relevant to depression, and we have used this concept to define a type of neurotic illness that has familial alcoholism as its marker. After all, one of the findings that suggests a genetic factor in an illness of unknown etiology is an increased frequency of specific diagnoses or symptoms in relatives when compared with the general population expectancy. This increased frequency might be relevant to the same functional system as is implicated in the illness being studied. Alcoholism, like depression, of course has a strong behavioral element and an increase in alcoholism in relatives of patients with primary depression as opposed to relatives of controls is meaningful because both alcoholism and depression may involve the same functional system. The relationship between such a specific family history of alcoholism and depression may even be more complex because there may be relationships with other psychiatric illnesses. Some studies have shown that patients with anxiety disorders are quite likely to suffer from secondary depression. Other studies have shown that familial alcoholism is high in patients with the anxiety disorders. Thus, alcoholism as a familial marker for neurotic depression ties together the concept of primary neurotic depression (depression-spectrum disease) and a secondary neurotic depression.

Another connecting thread is an unstable personality as opposed to other personality types. Such an unstable personality might be relevant to only certain types of depressions. If the unstable personality were related to a specific family history, the connection would be even stronger. Clustering of possible etiologic factors and premorbid characteristics strengthens the case for an autonomous illness.

Why be concerned with a workable classification of manias and depressions? If one plans to sensibly treat patients, it stands to reason that one should attempt to treat in a specific fashion. One does not treat a fever; one treats a specific infection. Treatment of a heterogeneous group of depressions and manias may be largely ineffective if only some subgroups respond to the particular therapy. In research, one opts for the most specific groups. To include all patients who show a major depression in a research effort seems to beg for failure. The final common pathway of the clinical syndrome that we call depression is probably only skin deep. Many pathophysiologic as well as psychopathologic pathways may lead to the same depressive syndrome. Without an attempt to separate patients into those with homogeneous illnesses, the findings will be unreliable because only some of the subjects who are studied or treated may have the relevant disease.

The separation of these types of affective disorders is based on biologic factors, clinical differences, genetic background, existing problems in life-style, and course of illness. This separation conforms to the disease model. By combining the various aspects of an illness that are useful in establishing validity, there are certainly no fewer than 4 subtypes of affective disorders, and there may be as many as 12; it becomes quite apparent that there may be even more than 12 specific groups. If the possibility of subgroups of induced affective disorders, of reactive depressions, and of neurotic and endogenous depressions is taken into account, it is possible that as we go from the generic to the specific there may be numerous meaningful diagnoses.

References

Abrams R, Taylor M. 1974. Unipolar and bipolar depressive illness, phenomenology, and response to electroconvulsive therapy. *Archives of General Psychiatry* 30:320–321.

Abrams R, Taylor M. 1976. Catatonia: A prospective clinical study. *Archives of General Psychiatry* 33:579–581.

Achté K, Anttinen E. 1963. Suizide bei hirngeschadigten des krieges in Finland. *Forschritte der Neurologie, Psychiatrie* 31:645–667.

Achté K, Hillbom E, Aalberg V. 1967. Post-traumatic psychoses following war brain injuries. In *Reports from the Rehabilitation Institute for Brain-Injured Veterans in Finland* (Vol. 1). Helsinki: Rehabilitation Institute for Brain-Injured Veterans in Finland.

Akiskal H. 1983. Diagnosis and classification of affective disorders: New insights from clinical and laboratory approaches. *Psychiatric Developments* 2:123–160.

Akiskal H. 1984. Characterologic manifestations of affective disorders. Toward a new conceptualization. *Integrative Psychiatry* 83–88, May–June.

Akiskal H, Walker P, Puzantian V, King D, Rosenthal T, Dranon M. 1983. Bipolar outcome in the course of depressive illness. *Journal of Affective Disorders* 5:115–128.

American Psychiatric Association. 1980. *Diagnostic and Statistical Manual of Mental Disorders (Third Edition)*. Washington, D.C.: American Psychiatric Association.

American Psychiatric Association. 1987. *Diagnostic and Statistical Manual of Mental Disorders (Third Edition-Revised)*. Washington, D.C.: American Psychiatric Association.

American Psychiatric Association Task Force on Laboratory Tests in Psychiatry. 1987. The dexamethasone suppression test: An overview of its current status in psychiatry. *American Journal of Psychiatry* 144:1253–1262.

Amsterdam J, Maislin G, Gold P, Winokur A. 1989. The assessment of abnormalities in hormonal responsiveness at multiple levels of the hypothalamic-pituitary-adrenocortical axis in depressive illness. *Psychoneuroendocrinology* 14:43–62.

Andreasen N. 1979. Thought, language and communication disorders II. Diagnostic significance. *Archives of General Psychiatry* 36:1325–1330.

Andreasen N, Powers P. 1974. Overinclusive thinking in mania and schizophrenia. *British Journal of Psychiatry* 125:452–456.

Angst J. 1966. *Zur Atiologie und Nosologie Endogener Depressiver Psychosen.* Berlin: Springer-Verlag.

Angst J. 1986. The course of major depression, atypical bipolar disorder, and bipolar disorder. In Hippius H, Klerman G, Mattussek N (eds.): *New Results in Depression Research* (pp. 26–35). Berlin: Springer-Verlag.

Angst J. 1987. Switch from depression to mania or from mania to depression. *Journal of Psychopharmacology* 1:13–19.

Angst J, Baastrup P, Grof P, Hippius H, Poldenger W, Weis P. 1973. The course of monopolar depression and bipolar psychoses. *Psychiatria Neurologia Neurochirurgia* 76:489–500.

Angst J, Dobler-Mikola A. 1985. The Zurich study. A prospective study of depressive, neurotic, and psychosomatic syndromes. IV. Recurrent and non-recurrent brief depression. *European Archives of Psychiatry and Neurological Sciences* 234:408–416.

Angst J, Frey R, Lohmeyer B, Zerbin-Rüdin E. 1980. Bipolar manic-depressive psychoses: Results of a genetic investigation. *Human Genetics* 55:237–254.

Angst J, Perris C. 1978. Zur nosologie endogener depressionen. *Archiv fur Psychiatrie und Zeitschrift f.d. ges Neurologie* 210:373–386.

Arana G, Baldessarini R, Ornsteen M. 1985. The dexamethasone suppression test for diagnosis and prognosis in psychiatry. *Archives of General Psychiatry* 42:1193–1204.

Asnis G, Sachar E, Halbreich U, Nathan S, Ostrow L, Halpern F. 1981. Cortisol secretion of dexamethasone response in depression. *American Journal of Psychiatry* 138:1218–1221.

Avery D, Lubrano A. 1979. Depression treated with imipramine and ECT. DeCarolis study reconsidered. *American Journal of Psychiatry* 136:559–562.

Avery D, Winokur G. 1977. The efficacy of electroconvulsive therapy and antidepressants in depression. *Biological Psychiatry* 12:507–523.

Ayuso-Gutierrez J, Ramos-Brieva J. 1982. The course of manic depressive illness. *Journal of Affective Disorders* 4:9–14.

Baker M, Dorzab J, Winokur G, Cadoret R. 1971. Depressive disease: Classification and clinical characteristics. *Comprehensive Psychiatry* 12:354–365.

Ban T. 1989. *Code-DD, Composition Diagnostic Evaluation of Depressive Disorders.* Brentwood: JM Productions, Inc.

Baron M, Risch N, Hamburger R, Mandel B, Kushner S, Newman M, Drumer D, Belmaker R. 1987. Genetic linkage between X-chromosome markers and bipolar affective illness. *Nature* 326:289–292.

Basta S. 1988. Amenorrhea/depression in famine. *Lancet* 1:789.

Bebbington P, Katz R, McGuffin P, Tennant C, Hurry J. 1989. The risk of minor depression before age 65: Results from a community survey. *Psychological Medicine* 19:393–400.

Behar D. 1978. Sporadic depressive disease: Symptoms, precipitants, and outcome. In Ayd F (ed.): *Mood Disorders: The World's Major Public Health Problem*. Baltimore: Ayd Medical Communications.

Behar D, Winokur G, VanValkenburg C, Lowry M. 1980. Familial subtypes of depression: A clinical view. *Journal of Clinical Psychiatry* 41:52–56.

Behar D, Winokur G, VanValkenburg C, Lowry M, Lachenbruch P. 1981. Clinical overlap among familial subtypes of unipolar depression. *Neuropsychobiology* 7:179–184.

Beigel A, Murphy D. 1971. Unipolar and bipolar affective illness, differences and clinical characteristics accompanying depression. *Archives of General Psychiatry* 24:215–229.

Bertelsen A, Harvald B, Hauge M. 1977. A Danish twin study of manic-depressive disorders. *British Journal of Psychiatry* 130:330–351.

Bibb R, Guze S. 1972. Hysteria (Briquet's syndrome) in a psychiatric hospital: The significance of secondary depression. *American Journal of Psychiatry* 129:224–228.

Bickford R, Ellison R. 1953. The high incidence of Huntington's chorea in the Duchy of Cornwall. *Journal of Mental Science* 99:291–294.

Black D, Nasrallah A. 1989. Hallucinations and delusions in 1,715 patients with unipolar and bipolar affective disorders. *Psychopathology* 22:28–34.

Black D, Winokur G, Nasrallah A. 1987a. The validity of secondary depression: Clinical features, family history, and response to dexamethasone. *Psychiatrica Fennica* 18:97–102.

Black D, Winokur G, Nasrallah A. 1987b. Treatment and outcome in secondary depression: A naturalistic study of 1087 patients. *Journal of Clinical Psychiatry* 48:438–441.

Black D, Winokur G, Nasrallah A. 1987c. Suicide in subtypes of major affective disorder. *Archives of General Psychiatry* 44:878–880.

Borg V, Weinholdt T. 1982. Bromocriptine in the treatment of the alcohol-withdrawal syndrome. *Acta Psychiatrica Scandinavica* 65:101–111.

Bornstein P, Clayton P, Halikas J, Maurice W, Robins E. 1973. The depression of widowhood after thirteen months. *British Journal of Psychiatry* 122:561–566.

Boyd J, Burke J, Gruenberg E, Holzer C, Rae D, George L, Karno M, Stolzman R, McEvoy L, Nestadt G. 1984. Exclusion criteria of DSM-III. *Archives of General Psychiatry* 41:983–989.

Boyd J, Weissman M. 1981. Epidemiology of affective disorders. *Archives of General Psychiatry* 38:1039–1046.

Bratfos O, Haug J. 1968. The course of manic depressive psychosis. *Acta Psychiatrica Scandinavica* 44:89–112.

Briscoe C, Smith J. 1973. Depression and marital turmoil. *Archives of General Psychiatry* 29:811–817.

Brockington I, Kendall R, Wainwright S. 1980. Depressed patients with schizophrenia or paranoid symptoms. *Psychological Medicine* 10:665–675.

Brockington I, Wainwright S, Kendall R. 1980. Manic patients with schizophrenia or paranoid symptoms. *Psychological Medicine* 10:73–83.

Bronisch T, Hecht H. 1989. Validity of adjustment disorder, comparison with major depression. *Journal of Affective Disorders* 17:229–236.

Bromet E, Schulberg H. 1987. Epidemiologic findings from disaster research. In Hales R, Francis A (eds.): *Psychiatry Update: American Psychiatric Association Annual Review* (pp. 676–689). Washington, D.C.: American Psychiatric Press.

Brown S, Schuckit M. 1988. Changes in depression among abstinent alcoholics. *Journal of Studies on Alcohol* 49:412–417.

Brown G, Sklair F, Harris T, Birley J. 1973. Life events and psychiatric disorders. Part 1: Some methodological issues. *Psychological Medicine* 3:74–87.

Bukberg J, Penman D, Holland J. 1984. Depression in hospitalized cancer patients. *Psychosomatic Medicine* 46:199–212.

Cadoret R, Fowler R, McCabe M, Winokur G. 1974. Evidence for heterogeneity in a group of good prognosis schizophrenics. *Comprehensive Psychiatry* 15:443–450.

Cadoret R, Woolson R, Winokur G. 1977. The relationship of age of onset in unipolar affective disorder to risk of alcoholism and depression in parents. *Journal of Psychiatric Research* 13:137–142.

Carney P, Fitzgerald C, Monaghan C. 1988. Influence of climate on the prevalence of mania. *British Journal of Psychiatry* 152:820–823.

Carney R, Rich M, teVelde A, Saini J, Clark K, Jaffee A. 1987. Major depressive disorder in coronary artery disease. *American Journal of Cardiology* 60:1273–1275.

Carroll B. 1982. The dexamethasone suppression test for melancholia. *British Journal of Psychiatry* 140:292–304.

Carroll B, Feinberg M, Greden J, Tarika J, Albala A, Haskett R, James N, Kronfol Z, Lohr N, Steiner M, deVigre J, Young E. 1981. A specific laboratory test for the diagnosis of melancholia—standardization, validation, and clinical utility. *Archives of General Psychiatry* 38:15–22.

Cassidy W, Flanagan N, Spellman M, Cohen M. 1957. Clinical observations in manic depressive disease. *Journal of the American Medical Association* 164:1535–1546.

Chambers W. 1955. Neurosurgical conditions masquerading as psychiatric diseases. *American Journal of Psychiatry* 112:387–389.

Ciompi L. 1969. Follow-up studies on the evolution of former neurotic and depressive states in old age. *Journal of Geriatric Psychiatry* 3:90–106.

Clayton P. 1982. Schizoaffective disorders. *Journal of Nervous and Mental Disease* 170:646–650.

Clayton P, Desmarais L, Winokur G. 1968. A study of normal bereavement. *American Journal of Psychiatry* 125:168–178.

Clayton P, Halikas J, Maurice W. 1972. The depression of widowhood. *British Journal of Psychiatry* 120:71–77.

Clayton P, Herjanic M, Murphy G, Woodruff R. 1974. Mourning and depression: Their similarities and differences. *Canadian Psychiatric Association Journal* 19:309–312.

Clayton P, Pitts F, Winokur G. 1965. Affective disorder IV. Mania. *Comprehensive Psychiatry* 6:313–322.

Clayton P, Rodin L, Winokur G. 1968. Family history studies: III. Schizoaffective disorder, clinical and genetic factors including a one to two year follow-up. *Comprehensive Psychiatry* 9:31–49.

Cohen S. 1980. Cushing's syndrome. A psychiatric study of 29 patients. *British Journal of Psychiatry* 136:120–124.

Cook B, Shukla S, Hoff A. 1986. EEG abnormalities in bipolar affective disorder. *Journal of Affective Disorders* 11:147–149.

Cook B, Shukla S, Hoff A, Aronson T. 1987. Mania with associated organic factors. *Acta Psychiatrica Scandinavica* 76:674–677.

Copeland J. 1983. Psychotic and neurotic depression: Discriminant function analysis and five year outcome. *Psychological Medicine* 13:373–383.

Coppen A, Noguera R, Bailey J, Burns B, Swani M, Hare E, Gardner R, Maggs R. 1971. Prophylactic lithium in affective disorders, controlled trial. *Lancet* 2:275–279.

Coryell W. 1984. The use of laboratory tests in psychiatric diagnosis: The DST as an example. *Psychiatric Developments* 3:139–159.

Coryell W. 1986. Schizoaffective and schizophreniform disorders. In Winokur G, Clayton P (eds.): *The Medical Basis of Psychiatry* (pp. 102–114). Philadelphia: W.B. Saunders.

Coryell W. 1988. Secondary depression. In Cavenar J (ed.): *Psychiatry*. Philadelphia: J.B. Lippincott.

Coryell W, Endicott J, Reich T, Andreasen N, Keller M. 1984. A family study of bipolar II disorder. *British Journal of Psychiatry* 145:49–54.

Coryell W, Gaffney G, Burkhardt P. 1982. DSM-III melancholia and the primary-secondary distinction: A comparison of concurrent validity by means of the dexamethasone suppression test. *American Journal of Psychiatry* 139:120–122.

Coryell W, Gaffney G, Burkhardt P. Winokur G. 1982. Hypothalamic-pituitary-adrenal axis activity: The importance of delusions and familial subtyping. In Usdin E, Handin I (eds.): *Biological Markers in Psychiatry and Neurology* (pp. 261–267). New York: Pergamon Press.

Coryell W, Grove W, vanEerdewegh M, Keller M, Endicott J. 1987. Outcome in RDC schizoaffective depression: The importance of diagnostic subtyping. *Journal of Affective Disorders* 12:47–56.

Coryell W, Keller M, Endicott J, Andreasen N, Clayton P, Hirschfeld R. 1989. Bipolar II illness: Course and outcome over a five year period. *Psychological Medicine* 19:129–141.

Coryell W, Keller M, Lavori P, Endicott J. Affective syndromes, psychotic features and prognosis. I. Depression. Manuscript submitted for publication.

Coryell W, Keller M, Lavori P, Endicott J. Affective syndromes, psychotic features and prognosis. II. Mania. Manuscript submitted for publication.

Coryell W, Smith R, Cook B, Moucharafieh S, Dunner F, House D. 1983. Serial dexamethasone suppression test results during antidepressant therapy: Relationship to diagnosis and clinical change. *Psychiatry Research* 10:165–174.

Coryell W, Tsuang M. 1982. Primary unipolar depression and the prognostic importance of delusions. *Archives of General Psychiatry* 39:1181–1184.

Coryell W, Tsuang M. 1985. Major depression with mood-congruent or mood incongruent psychotic features: Outcome after 40 years. *American Journal of Psychiatry* 142:479–482.

Coryell W, Tsuang M, McDaniel J. 1982. Psychotic features in major depression. *Journal of Affective Disorders* 4:227–236.

Coryell W, Turner R. 1985. Outcome with desipramine therapy in subtypes of non-psychotic major depression. *Journal of Affective Disorders* 9:149–154.

Coryell W, Zimmerman M. 1984. Outcome following ECT for primary unipolar depression: A test of newly proposed response predictions. *American Journal of Psychiatry* 141:862–865.

Coryell W, Zimmerman M. 1987. Progress in the classification of functional psychosis. *American Journal of Psychiatry* 144:1471–1473.

Coryell W, Zimmerman M. 1988. Diagnosis and outcome in schizoaffective depression: A replication. *Journal of Affective Disorders* 15:21–27.

Coryell W, Zimmerman M, Pfohl B. 1985. Short term prognosis in primary and secondary major depression. *Journal of Affective Disorders* 9:265–270.

Das M, Berrios G. 1984. Dexamethasone suppression test in acute grief reaction. *Acta Psychiatrica Scandinavica* 70:278–281.

Davidson J, Strickland R, Turnbull C, Belyea M, Miller R. 1984. The Newcastle Endogenous Depression Diagnostic Index: Validity and reliability. *Acta Psychiatrica Scandinavica* 69:220–230.

Davidson J, Woodbury M, Pelton S, Krishnan R. 1988. A study of depressive typologies using grade of membership analysis. *Psychological Medicine* 18:179–189.

del Zompo M, Bocchetta A. Goldin L, Corsini G. 1984. Linkage between X-chromosome markers and manic depressive illness. *Acta Psychiatrica Scandinavica* 70:282–287.

Derogatis L, Morrow G, Fetting J, Penman D, Piastetsky S, Schmale A, Henrichs M, Carnicke C. 1984. The prevalence of psychiatric disorders among cancer patients. *Journal of the American Medical Association* 249:751–757.

Detera-Wadleigh S, Berrettini W, Goldin L, Boorman D, Anderson S, Gershon E. 1987. Close linkage of C-Harvey-*ras*-1 and the insulin gene to affective disorder is ruled out in three North American pedigrees. *Nature* 325:806–808.

Detre T, Himmelhoch J, Swartzburg M, Anderson C, Bych, R, Kupfer D. 1972. Hypersomnia and manic-depressive disease. *American Journal of Psychiatry* 128:1303–1305.

Dewhurst K. 1969. The neurosyphilitic psychoses today: A survey of 91 cases. *British Journal of Psychiatry* 115:31–38.

Dunner D, Gershon E, Goodwin F. 1976. Heritable factors in the severity of affective disorders. *Biological Psychiatry* 11:31–42.

Eaves L, Kendler K, Schulz C. 1986. The familial sporadic classification: Its power for the resolution of genetic and environmental etiologic factors. *Journal of Psychiatric Research* 20:115–130.

Egeland J, Gerhard D, Pauls D, Sussex J, Kidd K, Allen C, Hostetter A, Horseman D. 1987. Bipolar affective disorders linked to DNA markers on chromosome II. *Nature* 325:783–787.

Endicott J, Nee J, Andreasen N, Clayton P, Keller M, Coryell W. 1985. Bipolar II. Combine or keep separate? *Journal of Affective Disorders* 8:17–28.

Feighner J, Robins E, Guze S, Woodruff R, Winokur G, Munoz R. 1972. Diagnostic criteria for use in psychiatric research. *Archives of General Psychiatry* 26:57–63.

Feinberg M, Carroll B. 1982. Separation of subtypes of depression using discriminant analysis. Part 1: Separation of unipolar endogenous depression from non-endogenous depression. *British Journal of Psychiatry* 140:284–391.

Fish F. 1962. *Schizophrenia*. Baltimore: Williams & Wilkins.

Fish F. 1964. The cycloid psychoses. *Comprehensive Psychiatry* 5:155–169.

Folstein S, Abbott M, Chase G, Jensen B, Folstein M. 1983. The association of affective disorder with Huntington's disease in a case series in families. *Psychological Medicine* 13:537–542.

Frangos E, Althanassenas G, Tsitourides S, Psilolignos P, Robos A, Katsanou N, Bulgaris C. 1980. Seasonality of episodes of recurrent affective psychoses. *Journal of Affective Disorders* 2:239–247.

Fukuda K, Etoh T, Iwadate T, Ishii A. 1983. The course and prognosis of manic depressive psychosis: A quantitative analysis of episodes and intervals. *Tokohu Journal of Experimental Medicine* 139:299–307.

Garvey M, Schaffer C, Tuason V. 1984. Comparison of pharmacological treatment response between situational and non-situational depressions. *British Journal of Psychiatry* 145:363–365.

Gershon E, Hamovit J, Guroff J, Dibble E, Leckman J, Sceery W, Targum S, Nurnberger J, Goldin L, Bunney W. 1982. A family study of schizoaffective, bipolar I, bipolar II, unipolar, and normal control probands. *Archives of General Psychiatry* 39:1157–1167.

Gershon E, Targum S, Matthysse S, Bunney W. 1979. Color blindness not closely linked to bipolar illness: Report of a new pedigree series. *Archives of General Psychiatry* 36:1423–1430.

Giles D, Biggs M, Roffwarg H, Orsulak P, Rush A. 1987a. Secondary depression: A comparison among subtypes. *Journal of Affective Disorders* 12:251–258.

Giles D, Kupfer D, Roffwarg H, Rush A, Biggs M, Etzel B. 1989. Polysomnographic parameters in first degree relatives of unipolar probands. *Psychiatry Research* 27:127–136.

Giles D, Roffwarg H, Schlesser M, Rush A. 1986. Which endogenous depressive symptoms relate to REM latency reduction? *Biological Psychiatry* 21:473–482.

Giles D, Rush J. 1982. Relationship of dysfunctional attitudes and dexamethasone response in endogenous and non-endogenous depression. *Biological Psychiatry* 17:1303–1314.

Giles D, Schlesser M, Rush A, Orsulak P, Fulton C, Roffwarg H. 1987b. Polysomnographic findings and dexamethasone nonsuppression in unipolar depression: A replication and extension. *Biological Psychiatry* 22:872–882.

Gill M, McKeon P, Humphries P. 1988. Linkage analysis of manic depression in an Irish family using H-*ras*-1 and INS DNA markers. *Journal of Medical Genetics* 25:634–637.

Glassman A, Roose S. 1981. Delusional depression: A distinct clinical entity? *Archives of General Psychiatry* 38:424–427.

Goldin L, DeLisi L, Gershon E. 1987. Unravelling the relationship between genetic and environmental risk factors in psychiatric disorders. *British Journal of Psychiatry* 151:302–305.

Goodwin D, Schulsinger F, Knop J, Mednick S, Guze S. 1977a. Alcoholism and depression in adopted out daughters of alcoholics. *Archives of General Psychiatry* 34:751–755.

Goodwin D. Schulsinger F, Knopf J, Mednick S, Guze S. 1977b. Psychopathology in adopted and non-adopted daughters of alcoholics. *Archives of General Psychiatry* 34:1005–1009.

Grossman L, Harrow M, Fudala J, Melzer H. 1984. The longitudinal course of schizoaffective disorders. *Journal of Nervous and Mental Disease* 172:140–149.

Grove W, Andreasen N, Clayton P, Winokur G, Coryell W. 1987a. Primary and secondary affective disorders: Baseline characteristics of unipolar patients. *Journal of Affective Disorders* 13:249–257.

Grove W, Andreasen N, Winokur G, Clayton P, Endicott J, Coryell W. 1987b. Primary and secondary affective disorders: Unipolar patients compared on familial aggregation. *Comprehensive Psychiatry* 28:113–126.

Guze S. 1977. The future of psychiatry: Medicine or social science (editorial). *Journal of Nervous and Mental Disease* 165:225–230.

Guze S, Cloninger C, Martin R, Clayton P. 1983. A follow-up and family study of schizophrenia. *Archives of General Psychiatry* 40:1273–1276.

Guze S, Woodruff R, Clayton P. 1971. 'Secondary' affective disorder: A study of 95 cases. *Psychological Medicine* 1:426–428.

Hamilton M. 1967. Development of a rating scale for primary depressive illness. *British Journal of Social and Clinical Psychology* 6:278–296.

Hamilton M, White J. 1959. Clinical symptoms in depressive states. *Journal of Mental Science* 105:985–998.

Harris E, Noyes R, Crowe R, Chaudry D. 1983. Family study of agoraphobia: Report of a pilot study. *Archives of General Psychiatry* 40:1061–1064.

Harris H, 1973. *Biographical Memoirs of Fellows of The Royal Society* 19:521–561.

Hawton K, Fagg J, Simkin S. 1988. Female unemployment and attempted suicide. *British Journal of Psychiatry* 152:632–637.

Helgason T. 1961. Frequency of depressive states within geographically deliminated population groups. *Acta Psychiatrica Scandinavica* 37(Suppl. 162):81–90.

Helgason T. 1964. Epidemiology of mental disorders in Iceland. *Acta Psychiatrica Scandinavica* 40(Suppl. 173).

Henriksen B, Juul-Jensen P, Lund M. 1970. The mortality of epileptics. In Brackenridge R, Pittman (eds.): *Life Assurance Medicine: Proceedings of the 10th International Conference of Life Assurance Medicine.* London.

Hill E, Wilson A, Elston R, Winokur G. 1988. Evidence for possible linkage between genetic markers and affective disorders. *Biological Psychiatry* 74:903–917.

Himmelhoch J, Detre T, Kupfer D, Swartzburg M, Byck R. 1972. Treatment of previously intractable depressions with tranylcypromine and lithium. *Journal of Nervous and Mental Disease* 155:216–220.

Himmelhoch J, Fuchs C, Symons B. 1982. A double blind study of tranylcypromine treatment of major anergic depression. *Journal of Nervous and Mental Disease* 170:628–634.

Himmelhoch J, Thase M, Mallinger A, Fuchs C. 1986. Tranylcypromine versus imipramine in manic depression. In *Abstracts of the 1986 New Research Program of the American Psychiatric Association* (p. 78). Washington, D.C.: American Psychiatric Association.

Hirschfeld R. 1981. Situational depression: Validity of the concept. *British Journal of Psychiatry* 139:297–395.

Hirschfeld R, Klerman G, Andreasen N, Clayton P, Keller M. 1985. Situational major depressive disorder. *Archives of General Psychiatry* 42:1109–1114.

Hirschfeld R, Klerman G, Keller M, Andreasen N, Clayton P. 1986. Personality of recovered patients with bipolar affective disorder. *Journal of Affective Disorders* 11:81–89.

Hodgkinson S, Sherrington R, Gurling H, Marchbanks R, Reeders S, Mallet J, McInnis M, Petursson H, Brynjolfsson J. 1987. Molecular genetic evidence for heterogeneity in manic-depression 325:805–806.

Hoff A, Shukla S, Cook B, Aronson T, Ollo C, Pass H. 1988. Cognitive function in manics with associated neurologic factors. *Journal of Affective Disorders* 14:251–255.

Hong B, Smith M, Robson A, Wetzel R. 1987. Depressive symptomatology and treatment in patients with end-stage renal disease. *Psychological Medicine* 17:185–190.

Hopkinson G, Ley P. 1969. A genetic study of affective disorder. *British Journal of Psychiatry* 115:917–922.

Huber S, Paulson G, Shuttleworth E. 1988. Depression in Parkinson's disease. *Neuropsychiatry, Neuropsychology and Behavioral Neurology* 1:47–51.

Hudson J, Hudson M, Griffing G, Melby J, Pope H. 1987. Phenomenology and family history of affective disorder in Cushing's disease. *American Journal of Psychiatry* 144:951–952.

Hunter R, Blackwood W, Bull J. 1968. Three cases of frontal meningiomas presenting psychiatrically. *British Medical Journal* 3:9–16.

Huston P, Locher L. 1948. Involutional psychosis: Course when untreated and when treated with electric shock. *Archives of Neurology and Psychiatry* 59:385–394.

James N, Carroll B, Haines R. 1977. Genetic markers in affective disorders: ABO and HLA. Presented at the Sixth World Congress of Psychiatry, Honolulu.

Jann M, Garretts J, Ereschefsky L, Saklad S. 1984. Alternative drug therapies for mania: A literature review. *Drug Intelligence and Clinical Pharmacy* 18:577–589.

Jellinek F. 1962. Alcoholism: Phases of alcohol addiction. *Quarterly Journal of Studies on Alcohol* 23:673–684.

Jenkins R. 1933. Etiology of mongolism. *American Journal of Diseases of Children* 45:506–519.

Johnson G. 1978. HLA antigens and manic depressive disorders. *Biological Psychiatry* 13:409–412.

Kadrmas A, Winokur G, Crowe R. 1979. Postpartum mania. *British Journal of Psychiatry* 135:551–554.

Kallman F. 1954. Genetic principles in manic depressive psychosis. In Zubin J, Hoch P (eds.): *Depression*. New York: Grune & Stratton.

Kasper S, Beckman H. 1983. Dexamethasone suppression test in a pleuridiagnostic approach: Its relationship to psychopathological and clinical variables. *Acta Psychiatrica Scandinavica* 68:31–37.

Kathol R. 1985. Persistent elevation of urinary free cortisol and loss of circannual periodicity in recovered depressive patients. *Journal of Affective Disorders* 8:137–145.

Kay D, Garside R, Beamish P, Roy J. 1969a. Endogenous and neurotic syndromes of depression: A factor analytic study of 104 cases, clinical features. *British Journal of Psychiatry* 115:377–388.

Kay D, Garside R, Roy J, Beamish P. 1969b. "Endogenous" and "neurotic" syndromes of depression: A 5–7 year follow-up of 104 cases. *British Journal of Psychiatry* 115:389–399.

Keeler M, Taylor I, Miller W. 1979. Are all recently detoxified alcoholics depressed? *American Journal of Psychiatry* 136:586–588.

Kelly W, Checkley S, Bender D. 1980. Cushing's syndrome, tryptophane and depression. *British Journal of Psychiatry* 136:125–132.

Kelsoe J, Ginns E, Egeland J, Gerhard D, Goldstein A, Bale S, Pauls D, Long R, Kidd K, Conte G, Housman D, Paul S. 1989. Re-evaluation of the linkage relationship between chromosome 11p loci and the gene for bipolar affective disorder in the Old Order Amish. *Nature* 343:238–243.

Kempe M. 1985. *The Book of Margery Kempe* (Windeatt BA, trans.). Middlesex, England: Penguin.

Kendall R. 1968. *The Classification of Depressive Illnesses*. London: Oxford University Press.

Kendall R. 1976. The classification of depression: A review of contemporary confusion. *British Journal of Psychiatry* 129:15–28.

Kendall R. 1982. The choice of diagnostic criteria for biological research. *Archives of General Psychiatry* 39:1334–1339.

Kendler K, Hays P. 1982. Familial and sporadic schizophrenia: A symptomatic, prognostic and EEG comparison. *American Journal of Psychiatry* 139:1557–1562.

Kiloh L, Andrews G, Nielsen M: 1988. Long-term outcome of depressive illness. *British Journal of Psychiatry* 153:752–757.

Kiloh L, Garside R. 1963. The independence of neurotic depression and endogenous depression. *British Journal of Psychiatry* 109:451–463.

Kirkegaard C, Carroll B. 1980. Dissociation of TSH and adrenocortical disturbances in endogenous depression. *Psychiatry Research* 3:253–264.

Kraepelin E. 1921. *Manic-Depressive Insanity and Paranoia.* Edinburgh: E. & S. Livingston.

Krauthammer C, Klerman G. 1978. Secondary mania: Manic syndrome associated with antecedent physical illness or drugs. *Archives of General Psychiatry* 35:1333–1339.

Kroessler D. 1985. Relative efficacy rates for therapies of delusional depression. *Convulsive Therapy* 1:173–182.

Kupfer D. 1976. REM latency: A psychobiologic marker for primary depressive disease. *Biological Psychiatry* 11:159–174.

Kupfer D, Carpenter L, Frank E. 1988. Possible role of antidepressants in precipitating mania and hypomania in recurrent depression. *American Journal of Psychiatry* 145:804–808.

Kupfer D, Ulrich R, Coble P, Jarrett D, Grochocinski V, Doman J, Matthews G, Borbely A. 1985. Electroencephalographic sleep of younger depressives. *Archives of General Psychiatry* 42:806–810.

Landolt A. 1957. Follow-up studies on circular manic-depressive reactions occurring in the young. *Bulletin of the New York Academy of Medicine* 33:65–73.

Larson C. 1940. Intracranial tumors in mental hospital patients. *American Journal of Psychiatry* 97:49–58.

Lazare A, Klerman G. 1968. Hysteria and depression. The frequency and significance of hysterical personality features in hospitalized depressed women. *American Journal of Psychiatry* 124 (suppl.):48–56.

Lee A, Murray R. 1988. The long-term outcome of Maudsley depressions. *British Journal of Psychiatry* 153:741–751.

Leff J, Fischer M, Bertelsen A. 1976. A cross-national epidemiological study of mania. *British Journal of Psychiatry* 129:428–442.

Leonhard K. 1957. *Aufteilung der Endogenen Psychosen.* Berlin: Akademie Verlag.

Lesser I, Rubin R, Rifkin A, Swinson R, Ballenger J, Burrows G, Dupont R, Noyes R, Pecknold J. 1989. Secondary depression in panic disorder and agoraphobia. II. Dimensions of depressive symptomatology and their response to treatment. *Journal of Affective Disorders* 16:49–58.

Lewis A. 1934. Melancholia: A clinical survey of depressive states. *Journal of Mental Science* 80:277–378.

Lewis A. 1938. States of depression: Their clinical and aetiological differentiation. *British Medical Journal* 2:875–878.

Lewis D, Kathol R, Sherman B, Winokur G, Schlesser M. 1983. Differentiation of depressive subtypes by insulin insensitivity in the recovered phase. *Archives of General Psychiatry* 40:167–170.

Lewis D, McChesney C. 1985. Tritiated imipramine binding distinguishes among subtypes of depression. *Archives of General Psychiatry* 42:485–488.

Lewis D, Winokur G. 1983. The familial classification of primary unipolar depression: Biological validation of distinct subtypes. *Comprehensive Psychiatry* 24:455–501.

Lewis J, Winokur G. 1982. The induction of mania: A natural history study with controls. *Archives of General Psychiatry* 39:303–306.

Lipsey J, Spencer W, Rabins P, Robinson R. 1986. Phenomenological comparison of post-stroke depression and functional depression. *American Journal of Psychiatry* 143:527–529.

Lishman W. 1983. *Organic Psychiatry—The Psychological Consequences of Cerebral Disorder.* Oxford: Alden Press.

Lowry M, VanValkenburg C, Winokur G, Cadoret R. 1978. Baseline characteristics of pure depressive disease. *Neuropsychobiology* 4:333–343.

Lunden W. 1977. *The Suicide Cycle.* Montezuma, Iowa: Sutherland Printing.

Lusznat R, Murphy D, Nunn C. 1988. Carbamazepine vs lithium in the treatment and prophylaxis of mania. *British Journal of Psychiatry* 153:198–204.

Marten S, Cadoret R, Winokur G, Ora E. 1972. Unipolar depression: A family history study. *Biological Psychiatry* 4:203–213.

Mayeux R. 1988. Depression and Parkinson's disease. In *CME Syllabus and Proceedings Summary of the American Psychiatric Association 141st Annual Meeting.* Washington, D.C.: American Psychiatric Association.

McElroy S, Keck P, Pope H. 1987. Sodium valproate: Its use in primary psychiatric disorder. *Journal of Clinical Psychopharmacology* 7:16–24.

McFarlane A. 1986. Post-traumatic morbidity of a disaster: A study of cases presenting for psychiatric treatment. *Journal of Nervous and Mental Disease* 174:1–22.

McFarlane A. 1989. The aetiology of posttraumatic morbidity: Predisposing precipitating and perpetuating factors. *British Journal of Psychiatry* 15:221–228.

Mendels J. 1968. Depression: The distinction between syndrome and symptoms. *British Journal of Psychiatry* 114:1549–1554.

Mendlewicz J, Baron M. 1981. Morbidity risks in subtypes of unipolar depressive illness: Differences between early and late onset forms. *British Journal of Psychiatry* 139:463–466.

Mendlewicz J, Linkowski P, Willmotte J. 1980. Linkage between glucose-6-phosphate-dehydrogenase deficiency and manic-depressive psychosis. *British Journal of Psychiatry* 137:337–342.

Mendlewicz J, Rainer J. 1977. Adoption study supporting genetic transmission in manic-depressive illness. *Nature* 268:327–329.

Mendlewicz J, Simon P, Sevy S, Charon F, Brocas H, Legros S, Vassart G. 1987. Polymorphic DNA marker on X-chromosome and manic depression. *Lancet* 1:1230–1232.

Mitsuda H. 1962. The concept of atypical psychoses from the aspect of clinical genetics. *Folia Psychiatrica et Neurological Japonica* 16:214–221.

Moffic H, Paykel E. 1975. Depression in medical inpatients. *British Journal of Psychiatry* 126:346–353.

Monnelly E, Woodruff R, Robins L. 1974. Manic depressive illness and social achievement in a public hospital sample. *Acta Psychiatrica Scandinavica* 50:318–325.

Morrison J, Clancy J, Crowe R, Winokur G. 1972. The Iowa 500. I. Diagnostic validity in mania, depression and schizophrenia. *Archives of General Psychiatry* 27:457–461.

Murphy G. 1986. Suicide and attempted suicide. In Winokur G, Clayton P (eds.): *The Medical Basis of Psychiatry* (pp. 562–579). Philadelphia: W.B. Saunders.

Nelson J, Charney D. 1987. The symptoms of major depressive illness. *American Journal of Psychiatry* 138:1–13.

Nelson J, Charney D, Quinlan D. 1980. Characteristics of autonomous depression. *Journal of Nervous and Mental Disease* 168:637–643.

Nielsen J, Nielsen J. 1977. A census study of mental illness in Samso. *Psychological Medicine* 7:491–503.

Noyes R, Dempsey M, Blum A, Cavanaugh G. 1974. Lithium treatment of depression. *Comprehensive Psychiatry* 15:187–193.

Noyes R, Kathol R. 1986. Depression and cancer. *Psychiatric Developments* 2:77–100.

Nyström S. 1979. Depressions: Factors related to 10 year prognosis. *Acta Psychiatrica Scandinavica* 60:225–238.

Olsen T. 1961. Follow-up study of manic depressive patients whose first attack occurred before age of 19. *Acta Psychiatrica Scandinavica* 45 (Suppl. 162).

Oppler W. 1950. Manic psychosis in a case of parasagittal meningioma. *Archives of General Psychiatry* 64:417.

Parker G, Walter S. 1982. Season variation in depressive disorders and suicidal deaths in New South Wales. *British Journal of Psychiatry* 140:626–632.

Paykel E. 1971. Classification of depressed patients: A cluster analysis derived grouping. *British Journal of Psychiatry* 118:275–288.

Paykel E. 1979. Causal relationships between clinical depression and life events. In Barrett J (ed.): *Stress and Mental Disorder* (pp. 71–86). New York: Raven Press.

Paykel E. 1982. Life events and early environment. In Paykel E (ed.): *Handbook of Affective Disorders* (pp. 146–161). London: Livingstone.

Paykel E, Klerman G, Prusoff B. 1974. Prognosis of depression and the endogenous-neurotic distinction. *Psychological Medicine* 4:57–64.

Pecknold J, Chang D, Fleury D, Koszychi R, Quirion N, Suranyi-Cadotte B. 1987. Platelet imipramine binding in patients with panic disorder and major familial depression. *Journal of Psychiatric Research* 21:319–326.

Pederson A, Poort R, Schou H. 1947. Periodical depression as an independent nosological entity. *Acta Psychiatrica et Neurologica* 23:285–319.

Penrose L. 1938. *A Clinical and Genetic Study of 1,280 Cases of Mental Defect* (Medical Research Council Special Report Service No. 229). London: Her Majesty's Stationery Office.

Perris C. 1966. A study of bipolar (manic depressive) and unipolar recurrent depressive psychoses. *Acta Psychiatrica Scandinavica* 42 (Suppl. 194):1–189.

Perris C. 1988. The concept of cycloid psychotic disorder. *Psychiatric Developments* 1:37–56.

Perris H, von Knorring L, Perris C. 1982. Genetic vulnerability for depression and life events. *Neuropsychobiology* 8:241–247.

Pfohl B, Stangl D, Zimmerman M. 1984. The implications of DSM-III personality disorders for patients with major depression. *Journal of Affective Disorders* 7:309–318.

Pfohl B, Vasquez N, Nasrallah H. 1981. The mathematical case against unipolar mania. *Journal of Psychiatric Research* 16:259–265.

Pfohl B, Vasquez N, Nasrallah H. 1982. Unipolar versus bipolar mania: A review of 247 patients. *British Journal of Psychiatry* 141:453–458.

Pichot J, Jensen P. 1989. Seasonal affective disorder: SAD or fad? *Jefferson Journal of Psychiatry* 7:41–50.

Pichot P, Pull C. 1981. Is there an involutional melancholia? *Comprehensive Psychiatry* 22:2–10.

Pollock H. 1931. Recurrence of attacks in manic depressive psychosis. *American Journal of Psychiatry* 22:567–574.

Pottenger M, McKernon J, Patrie L, Weissman M, Ruben H, Newberry P. 1978. The frequency and persistence of depressive symptoms in the alcohol abuser. *Journal of Nervous and Mental Disease* 166:562–570.

Potter W, Rudorfer M, Goodwin F. 1987. Biological findings in bipolar disorders. In Hales R, Frances A (eds.): *Psychiatry Update: American Psychiatric Association Annual Review* (pp. 32–60). Washington, D.C.: American Psychiatric Press.

Price J. 1968. The genetics of depressive behavior. In Coppen A, Walk A (eds.): *Recent Developments in Affective Disorders* (pp. 37–54). Ashford, England: Headly Brothers.

Price, L, Nelson J. 1986. Alcoholism and affective disorder. *American Journal of Psychiatry* 143:1067–1068.

Price L, Nelson J, Charney D, Quinlan D. 1984a. Family history in delusional depression. *Journal of Affective Disorders* 6:109–114.

Price L, Nelson J, Charney D, Quinlan D. 1984b. The clinical utility of family history for the diagnosis of melancholia. *Journal of Nervous and Mental Disease* 172:5–11.

Prien R, Kupfer D, Mansky P, Small J, Tuason V, Voss C, Johnson W. 1984. Drug therapy in the prevention of recurrences in unipolar and bipolar affective disorders. *Archives of General Psychiatry* 42:1096–1104.

Procci W. 1976. Schizoaffective psychosis: Fact or fiction? *Archives of General Psychiatry* 33:1167–1177.

Rao A, Nammalvar N. 1977. The course and outcome in depressive illness. *British Journal of Psychiatry* 130:392–396.

Reich T, Clayton P, Winokur G. 1969. Family history studies. V. The genetics of mania. *American Journal of Psychiatry* 125:1358–1369.

Reich T, Winokur G. 1970. Postpartum psychoses in patients with manic depressive disease. *Journal of Nervous and Mental Disease* 151:60–68.

Rihmer Z, Tariska P, Csisz R. 1982. Manic-depressive illness and EEG anomalies. *Ideggy y szati Szemle* 35:299–303.

Rinieris P, Stefanis C, Lykouras E, Varson E. 1979. Affective disorders and ABO blood types. *Acta Psychiatrica Scandinavica* 60:272–278.

Risch N, Baron M. 1982. X-linkage and genetic heterogeneity in bipolar-related major affective illness: Reanalysis of linkage data. *Annals of Human Genetics* 46:153–166.

Robins E, Guze S. 1970. Establishment of diagnostic validity in psychiatric illness: Its application to schizophrenia. *American Journal of Psychiatry* 126:983–987.

Robins L, Helzer J, Weissman M, Orvaschel H, Gruenberg E, Burke J, Regier D. 1984. Lifetime prevalence of specific psychiatric disorders in three sites. *Archives of General Psychiatry* 41:949–958.

Robinson R, Kubos K, Starr L, Rao K, Price T. 1983. Mood changes in stroke patients: Relationship to lesion location. *Comprehensive Psychiatry* 24:555–566.

Rose J. 1963. Reactive and endogenous depressions—response to ECT. *British Journal of Psychiatry* 109:213–217.

Rosenthal N, Davenport Y, Cowdry R, Webster M, Goodwin F. 1980. Monoamine metabolites in cerebrospinal fluid of depressive subgroups. *Psychiatry Research* 2:113–119.

Rosenthal N, Wehr T. 1987. Seasonal affective disorder. *Psychiatric Annals* 17:670–674.

Rosenthal S, Gudeman J. 1967. The self-pitying constellation of depression. *British Journal of Psychiatry* 113:485–489.

Rowe C, Daggett D. 1954. Prepsychotic personality traits in manic depressive disease. *Journal of Nervous and Mental Disease* 119:412–420.

Rush A, Erman M, Giles D, Schlesser M, Carpenter G, Vasavada N, Roffwarg H. 1986. Polysomnographic findings in recent drug free and clinically remitted patients. *Archives of General Psychiatry* 43:878–885.

Rush A, Giles D, Parker C, Roffwarg H. 1980. Sleep EEG findings and dexamethasone suppression in depression. In *Society of Biological Psychiatry: Scientific Proceedings of the Thirty-Fifth Annual Convention* (Abstract 7, p. 39). Society of Biological Psychiatry.

Saran B. 1969. Lithium. *Lancet* 2:1208–1209.

Schildkraut J. 1970. *Neuropsychopharmacology in the Affective Disorders*. Boston: Little, Brown.

Schlesser M, Winokur G, Sherman B. 1980. Hypothalamic-pituitary-adrenal axis activity in depressive illness. *Archives of General Psychiatry* 37:737–743.

Schou H. 1927. La depression psychique. *Acta Psychiatrica et Neurologica* 2:345–353.

Sedler M. 1983. Falret's discovery: The origin of the concept of bipolar affective illness. *American Journal of Psychiatry* 140:1127–1133.

Shagass C. 1981. Neurophysiological evidence for different types of depression. *Journal of Behavioral Therapy and Experimental Psychiatry* 12:99–111.

Shuckit M, Pitts F, Reich T, King L, Winokur G. 1969. Alcoholism I. Two types of alcoholism in women. *Archives of General Psychiatry* 20:301–306.

Shapiro R, Boch E, Rafaelsen O, Ryder L, Svejgaard A. 1976. Histocompatability antigens and manic depressive disorders. *Archives of General Psychiatry* 33:823–825.

Shore J, Tatum E, Vollmer W. 1986. Evaluation of mental effects of disaster: Mt. St. Helen's eruption. *American Journal of Public Health* 76 (Suppl.):76–83.

Sinyor D, Jacques P, Kaloupek D, Becker R, Goldenberg M, Coopersmith H. 1986. Post-stroke depression and lesion location. An attempted replication. *Brain* 109:537–546.

Slater E. 1938. Zur erbpathologie des manisch-depressiven irreseins, die eltern und kinder von manisch-depressiven. *Zeitschrift Ges. Neurological and Psychiatry* 163:1–147.

Smith L, North C. 1988. Familial subtypes of depression: A longitudinal perspective. *Journal of Affective Disorders* 14:145–154.

Spicer C, Hare E, Slater E. 1973. Neurotic and psychotic forms of depressive illness: Evidence from age-incidence in a national sample. *British Journal of Psychiatry* 123:535–541.

Spitzer R, Endicott J, Robins E. 1978. *Research Diagnostic Criteria* (3rd ed.). New York: Biometrics Research, New York State Department of Mental Hygiene.

Stanley M, Visgilio J, Gershon S. 1982. Tritiated imipramine binding sites are decreased in the frontal cortex of suicides. *Science* 216:1337.

Starkstein S, Boston J, Robinson R. 1988. Mechanisms of mania after brain injury. *Journal of Nervous and Mental Disease* 176:87–100.

Starkstein S, Robinson R, Price T. 1988. Comparison of patients with and without poststroke major depression matched for size and location of lesion. *Archives of General Psychiatry* 45:247–252.

Stenstedt A. 1952. A study in manic depressive psychosis. *Acta Psychiatrica Neurologica Scandinavica* 79 (Suppl.): 1–111.

Stenstedt A. 1959. Involutional melancholia: An aetiological, clinical and social study in endogenous depression in later life, with special reference to genetic factors. *Acta Psychiatrica Scandinavica* Suppl. 127.

Stern K, Dancey T. 1942. Glioma of the diencephalon in a manic patient. *American Journal of Psychiatry* 98:716–719.

Stewart M, Drake F, Winokur G. Depression among medically ill patients. *Diseases of the Nervous System* 26:479–484.

Tanna V, Wilson A, Winokur G, Elston R. 1989. Linkage analysis of pure depressive disease. *Journal of Psychiatric Research* 23:99–107.

Tanna V, Winokur G. 1968. A study of association and linkage of ABO blood types and primary affective disorder. *British Journal of Psychiatry* 114:1175–1181.

Taylor M, Abrams R. 1980. Familial and non-familial mania. *Journal of Affective Disorders* 2:111–118.

Thase M, Kupfer D, Ulrich R. 1986. Electroencephalographic sleep in psychotic depression. *Archives of General Psychiatry* 43:886–893.

Thompson W, Orvaschel H, Prusoff B, Kidd K. 1982. An evaluation of the family history method for ascertaining psychiatric disorders. *Archives of General Psychiatry* 39:53–57.

Trzebiatowska-Trzeciak O. 1977. Genetical analysis of unipolar and bipolar endogenous affective psychoses. *British Journal of Psychiatry* 131:478–485.

Tsuang M. 1979. 'Schizoaffective disorder.' *Archives of General Psychiatry* 36:633–634.

Tsuang M, Faraone S, Fleming J. 1985. Familial transmission of major affective disorders: Is there evidence supporting the distinction between unipolar and bipolar disorders? *British Journal of Psychiatry* 146:268–271.

Tsuang M, Winokur G, Crowe R. 1984. Psychiatric disorders among relatives of surgical controls. *Journal of Clinical Psychiatry* 45:420–422.

Tsuang M, Woolson R. 1977. Mortality in patients with schizophrenia, mania, depression, and surgical conditions. *British Journal of Psychiatry* 130:162–166.

Tsuang M, Woolson R, Flemming J. 1979. Long-term outcome of major psychoses. *Archives of General Psychiatry* 36:1295–1301.

Tsuang M, Woolson R, Winokur G, Crowe R. 1981. Stability of psychiatric diagnosis. *Archives of General Psychiatry* 38:535–539.

Van Valkenburg C, Lilienfeld B, Akiskal H. 1987. The impact of familial personality disorder and alcoholism on the clinical features of depression. *Psychiatrie und Psychobiologie II* 3:195–201.

Van Valkenburg C, Lowry M, Winokur G, Cadoret R. 1977. Depression spectrum disease versus pure depressive disease. *Journal of Nervous and Mental Diseases* 165:341–347.

Von Knorring A-L, Cloninger C, Bohman M, Sigvardsson S. 1983. An adoption study of depressive disorders and substance abuse. *Archives of General Psychiatry* 40:943–950.

Von Zerssen D. 1977. Premorbid personality and affective psychoses. In Burrows G (ed.): *Handbook of Studies on Depression.* Amsterdam: Excerpta Medica.

Wägner A, Alberg-Wistedt A, Åaberg, M, Ekquist B, Mårtensson B, Montero D. 1985. Lower ^{3}H-imipramine binding in platelets from untreated depressed patients compared to healthy controls. *Psychiatry Research* 16:131–139.

Wasserman I. 1984. The influence of economic business cycles on U.S. suicide rates. *Suicide and Life-Threatening Behavior* 14:143–156.

Watts C. 1952. The mild endogenous depression. *British Medical Journal* 1:4–8.

Webster's New Collegiate Dictionary. 1980. Springfield: G & C Merriam Co.

Wehr T, Jacobsen F, Sach D, Arendt J, Tamarkin L, Rosenthal N. 1986. Phototherapy of seasonal affective disorders—time of day and suppression of melatonin are not critical for antidepressant effects. *Archives of General Psychiatry* 43:870–875.

Wehr T, Sack D, Rosenthal N, Goodwin F. 1987. Sleep and biological rhythms in bipolar illness. In Hales R, Frances A (eds.): *Psychiatry Update: American Psychiatric Association Annual Review* (pp. 61–80). Washington, D.C.: American Psychiatric Press.

Weissman M, Pottenger M, Leber H, Williams D, Thompson W. 1977. Symptom patterns in primary and secondary depression. *Archives of General Psychiatry* 34:854–862.

Wells K, Golding J, Burnam M. 1988. Psychiatric disorder in a sample of the general population with and without chronic medical conditions. *American Journal of Psychiatry* 145:976–981.

Wender P, Kety S, Rosenthal D, Schulsinger F, Ortmann J, Lunde I. 1986. Psychiatric disorders in the biological and adoptive families of adopted individuals with affective disorders. *Archives of General Psychiatry* 43:923–929.

Wertham F. 1929. A group of benign chronic psychoses: Prolonged manic excitements. *American Journal of Psychiatry* 9:17–18.

Wesner R, Winokur G. 1989. The influence of age on the natural history of unipolar depression when treated with electroconvulsive therapy. *European Archives of Psychiatry and Neurological Sciences* 238:149–154.

Wilson A, Tanna V, Winokur G, Elston R, Hill E. 1989. Linkage analysis of depression spectrum disease. *Biological Psychiatry* 26:163–175.

Winokur G. 1970. Genetic findings and methodological considerations in manic-depressive disease. *British Journal of Psychiatry* 117:267–274.

Winokur G. 1972a. Family history studies. VIII. Secondary depression is alive and well, and . . . . *Diseases of the Nervous System* 33:94–99.

Winokur G. 1972b. Types of depressive illness. *British Journal of Psychiatry* 120:265–266.

Winokur G. 1973. Depression in the menopause. *American Journal of Psychiatry* 130:92–93.

Winokur G. 1974a. Genetic and clinical factors associated with course in depression. *Pharmakopsychiatry* 7:122–126.

Winokur G. 1974b. The division of depressive illness into depression spectrum disease and pure depressive disease. *International Pharmacopsychiatry* 9:5–13.

Winokur G. 1975. The Iowa 500: Heterogeneity and course in manic-depressive illness (bipolar). *Comprehensive Psychiatry* 16:125–131.

Winokur G. 1979a. Familial (genetic) subtypes of pure depressive disease. *American Journal of Psychiatry* 136:911–913.

Winokur G. 1979b. A family history (genetic) study of pure depressive disease. In Mendlewicz J, Shopsin B (eds.): *Genetic Aspects of Affective Illness* (pp. 27–33). New York: SP Medical and Scientific Books.

Winokur G. 1979c. Unipolar depression. Is it divisible into autonomous subtypes? *Archives of General Psychiatry* 36:47–52.

Winokur G. 1982. The development and validity of familial subtypes in primary unipolar depression. *Pharmacopsychiatry* 15:142–146.

Winokur G. 1984. Psychosis in bipolar and unipolar affective illness with special reference to schizoaffective disorder. *British Journal of Psychiatry* 145:236–241.

Winokur G. 1985a. Comparative studies of familial psychopathology in affective disorders. In Sakai T, Tsuboi T (eds.): *Genetic Aspects of Human Behavior* (pp. 87–96). Tokyo: Igaku-Shoin.

Winokur G. 1985b. The validity of neurotic-reactive depression. *Archives of General Psychiatry* 42:1116–1121.

Winokur G. 1986. Familial classification of depressive illnesses. In Hippius H, Klerman G, Matussek N (eds.): *New Results in Depression Research*. Berlin: Springer-Verlag.

Winokur G. 1987. Family (genetic) studies in neurotic depression. *Journal of Psychiatric Research* 21:357–363.

Winokur G. 1988. Anxiety disorders: Relationships to other psychiatric illnesses. *Psychiatric Clinics of North America* 287–293.

Winokur G, Behar D, VanValkenburg C, Lowry M. 1978. Is a familial definition of depression both feasible and valid? *Journal of Nervous and Mental Disease* 166:764–768.

Winokur G, Black D, Nasrallah A. 1987a. DST nonsuppressor status: Relationship to specific aspects of the depressive syndrome. *Biological Psychiatry* 22:360–368.

Winokur G, Black D, Nasrallah A. 1987b. Neurotic depression: A diagnosis based on pre-existing characteristics. *European Archives of Psychiatry and Neurological Sciences* 236:343–348.

Winokur G, Black D, Nasrallah A. 1988. Depressions secondary to other psychiatric disorders and medical illnesses. *American Journal of Psychiatry* 145:233–237.

Winokur G, Black D, Nasrallah A. In press. The schizoaffective continuum: Non-psychotic, mood congruent and mood incongruent.

Winokur G, Cadoret R. 1975. The irrelevance of the menopause to depressive disease. In Sachar E (eds.): *Topics in Psychoendocrinology*. New York: Grune & Stratton.

Winokur G, Cadoret R, Dorzab J, Baker M. 1971. Depressive disease: A genetic study. *Archives of General Psychiatry* 24:135–144.

Winokur G, Clayton P. 1967. Family history studies I. Two types of affective disorders separated according to genetic and clinical factors. In Wortis J (ed.): *Recent Advances in Biological Psychiatry* (pp. 25–30). New York: Plenum Press.

Winokur G, Clayton P, Reich T. 1969. *Manic Depressive Illness*. St. Louis: C. V. Mosby.

Winokur G, Crowe R. 1983. Bipolar illness: The sex-polarity effect in affectively ill family members. *Archives of General Psychiatry* 40:54–55.

Winokur G, Crowe R, Kadrmas A. 1981. Bipolar illness: The question of heterogeneity. Presented at the Third World Congress of Biological Psychiatry, Stockholm.

Winokur G, Dennert J, Angst J. 1986. Independent familial transmission of psychotic symptomatology in the affective disorders or does delusional depression breed true? *Psychiatrica Fennica* 17:9–16.

Winokur G, Kadrmas A. 1989. A polyepisodic course in bipolar illness: Possible clinical relationships. *Comprehensive Psychiatry* 30:121–127.

Winokur G, Kadrmas A, Crowe R. 1986. Schizoaffective mania: Family history and clinical characteristics. In Marneros A, Tsuang M (eds.): *Schizoaffective Psychoses* (pp. 115–122). Berlin: Springer-Verlag.

Winokur G, Morrison J. 1973. The Iowa 500: Follow-up of 225 depressives. *British Journal of Psychiatry* 123:543–548.

Winokur G, Morrison J, Clancy J, Crowe R. 1972. The Iowa 500: A blind family history comparison of mania, depression and schizophrenia. *Archives of General Psychiatry* 27:462–464.

Winokur G, Morrison J, Clancy J, Crowe R. 1973. The Iowa 500: Familial and clinical findings favor two kinds of depressive illness. *Comprehensive Psychiatry* 14:99–107.

Winokur G, Pfohl B, Sherman B. 1985. The relationship of historically defined subtypes of depression to ACTH and cortisol levels in depression: Preliminary study. *Biological Psychiatry* 20:751–757.

Winokur G, Pitts F. 1964. Affective disorder: I. Is reactive depression an entity? *Journal of Nervous and Mental Disease* 138:541–547.

Winokur G, Reich T, Rimmer J, Pitts F. 1970. Alcoholism III. Diagnosis and familial psychiatric illness in 259 alcoholic probands. *Archives of General Psychiatry* 23:104–111.

Winokur G, Rimmer J, Reich T. 1971. Alcoholism IV. Is there more than one type of alcoholism? *British Journal of Psychiatry* 118:525–531.

Winokur G, Ruangtrakool S. 1966. Genetic versus non-genetic affective disorder. *American Journal of Psychiatry* 123:703–705.

Winokur G, Scharfetter C, Angst J. 1985a. A family study of psychotic symptomatology in schizophrenia, schizoaffective disorder, unipolar depression and bipolar disorder. *European Archives of Psychiatry and Neurological Sciences* 234:295–298.

Winokur G, Scharfetter C, Angst J. 1985b. Stability of psychotic symptomatology (delusions, hallucinations), affective syndromes, and schizophrenic symptoms (thought disorder, incongruent affect) over episodes in remitting psychoses. *European Archives of Psychiatry and Neurological Sciences* 234:303–307.

Winokur G, Tanna V. 1969. Possible role of X-linked dominant factor in manic depressive disease. *Diseases of the Nervous System* 30:89–94.

Winokur G, Tsuang M. 1975. Elation versus irritability in mania. *Comprehensive Psychiatry* 16:435–436.

Winokur G, Tsuang M, Crowe R. 1982. The Iowa 500: Affective disorder in relatives of manic and depressed patients. *American Journal of Psychiatry* 139:209–212.

Winokur G, Wesner R. 1987. From unipolar depression to bipolar illness: 29 who changed. *Acta Psychiatrica Scandinavica* 76:59–63.

Woodruff R, Guze S, Clayton P. 1971. Unipolar and bipolar primary affective disorder. *British Journal of Psychiatry* 119:33–38.

Woodruff R, Murphy G, Herjanic M. 1967. The natural history of affective disorders. I. Symptoms of 72 patients at the time of index hospital admission. *Journal of Psychiatric Research* 5:255–263.

Woodruff R, Robins L, Winokur G, Reich T. 1971. Manic depressive illness and social achievement. *Acta Psychiatrica Scandinavica* 47:237–249.

Yerevanian B, Akiskal H. 1979. 'Neurotic,' characterological and dysthymic depressions. *Psychiatric Clinics of North America* 2:595–617.

Zhenyi X, Mingdao Z, Heqin Y. 1980. Affective psychosis, a follow-up, retrospective classification and heredofamilial study. *Chinese Medical Journal* 93:365–368.

Zimmerman M, Black D, Coryell W. 1989. Diagnostic criteria for melancholia. *Archives of General Psychiatry* 46:361–368.

Zimmerman M, Coryell W, Pfohl B. 1985. Importance of diagnostic thresholds in familial classification. *Archives of General Psychiatry* 42:300–304.

Zimmerman M, Coryell W, Pfohl B. 1986. Validity of familial subtypes of primary unipolar depression. *Archives of General Psychiatry* 43:1090–1096.

Zimmerman M, Coryell W, Pfohl B, Stangl D. 1985. Four definitions of endogenous depression and the dexamethasone suppression test. *Journal of Affective Disorders* 8:37–45.

Zimmerman M, Coryell W, Pfohl B, Stangl D. 1988. Prognostic validity of the familial subtypes of depression. *European Archives of Psychiatry and Neurological Sciences* 237:166–170.

Zimmerman M, Coryell W, Stangl D, Pfohl B. 1987. Validity of an operational definition for neurotic unipolar major depression. *Journal of Affective Disorders* 12:29–40.

Zorumski C, Rutherford J, Burke W, Reich T. 1986. ECT in primary and secondary depression. *Journal of Clinical Psychiatry* 47:298–300.

Index

Acute mania, symptoms of, 14–15
Adoption studies: and bipolar illness, 83; for depression-spectrum disease, 139–40; and unipolar depression, 188
Adrenal hyperplasia, 63
Affective disorders: classification, 236–38; life events causing, 167–68; tests, 51–53
Affective disorders, primary, 30
Age of onset: in bipolar illness, 87; in bipolar vs. unipolar disorder, 36–38; in depression-spectrum vs. familial pure depressive disease, 145–46; and depressive symptoms, 6; for diagnostic validity, 24; in familial affective depression, 49; and familial risk, 134; in neurotic vs. endogenous depression, 125; in unipolar affective disorder, 137
Agrophobia, 166
Alcohol consumption: in bipolar illness, 75; in mania, 14
Alcoholism: and depression-spectrum disease 132–33, 141–43; and early- vs. late-onset depression, 138; and endogenous depression, 45–46; familial, 134–35; and neurotic depression, 123–24, 128–29; parental, 22; in primary vs. secondary depression, 159–61; risks for depression, 137; and secondary depression, 27, 157–58
Alcohol withdrawal syndrome, 65–66
Amish study, 86

Anger, in bipolar vs. unipolar disorder, 31
Antidepressant drugs: in bipolar illness, 91; for bipolar vs. unipolar disorder, 40–41; in depression-spectrum disease, 148–50; in schizoaffective disorder, 112
Antisocial personality: in depression, 6; and depression-spectrum disease, 132; and early- vs. late-onset depression, 138; in primary vs. secondary depression, 159, 161; and secondary depression, 27
Anxiety: in depression, 5; in familial pure depressive disease, 144
Anxiety disorder: in primary vs. secondary depression, 159, 161; rate of, 155–56; and secondary depression, 27
Anxious depression, 48
Atypical psychosis: and family history, 105; as schizoaffective disorder, 101
Autonomous depression, 120, 180–81

Benign stupor, 101
Bereavement: and medication consumption, 177; vs. primary depression, 170; as a reactive depression, 26–27, 168–71
Biological variables: in depression-spectrum vs. familial pure depressive disease, 196–97; in endogenous depression, 188–93; in sporadic depressive disease vs. familial pure

Biological variables (*cont.*)
  depressive disease, 206. *See also*
  Dexamethasone suppression test;
  Rapid eye movement latency test
Bipolar illness: age of onset, 87; alcohol
  intake, 75; case study, 212–14;
  classification, 26; drug treatment,
  40–41, 91; electroencephalographic
  studies, 95–96; external variables, 77;
  and heredity, 29, 79–87;
  hospitalization rates, 33; morbidity
  risks, 198–99; mortality rate, 93;
  organic, 71–72; prognosis for early
  onset, 91–92; psychotic symptoms,
  12; risks, 76; and schizoaffective
  mania, 108–9; and suicide, 105;
  symptoms, 74–75; tests, 93–94;
  treatment, 94–95
Bipolar vs. unipolar disorder:
  characteristics, 36–39; chronic illness
  in, 30; course of illness, 88–90; drug
  treatment, 40–41; family history, 41;
  frequency, 178; medical model, 30,
  42; multifactorial model, 41–42;
  psychotic symptoms, 116; symptoms,
  31
Bipolar II vs. bipolar I illness, 97–98
Birth trauma, and bipolar disorder, 71
Blood type, and bipolar illness, 84
Brain disorder, and personality, 27
Brain imaging for schizophrenia, 56
Brain lesions: and depression, 64; and
  mania, 70; and organic bipolar
  disorder, 71
Break-point model, 22
Bromocriptine, 66

Cancer, and depression, 171–72
Character spectrum disorder: and
  depression-spectrum disorder, 138; in
  neurotic depression, 131
Chronic characterologic depression,
  130–31
Chronic illness, in bipolar disorder, 30
Circular insanity, 10
Classification: limitations, 28; methods,
  21–22; overview, 25–28
Color blindness, 85
Conflictual depression, 131
Cushing's syndrome, 63–64

Cycloid psychosis: and family history,
  105; as schizoaffective disorder, 101
Cyclothymia, 26
Cyclothymic personality: in bipolar
  illness, 78; in bipolar vs. unipolar
  disorder, 36

Delirious melancholia, 8
Delusional depression, 181
Delusions: in bipolar vs. unipolar
  disorder, 31; in depression, 5–6, 9; in
  familial pure depressive disease, 145;
  in neurotic depression, 123, 129;
  nihilistic, 8; in schizophrenia, 12;
  treatment, 193
Depression: age of hospitalization, 6;
  and alcoholism, 137; bipolar outcome,
  90–91; and cancer, 171–72;
  classification, 20, 44–49; compared
  with unhappiness, 8; definition, 3;
  and heredity, 29; and mania, 15–16,
  43; pain in, 8; prevalence of, 35;
  psychotic symptoms, 8; rate of, 155–
  56; risk, 180; screening criteria, 3;
  severity, 9; sex differences, 4–6;
  symptoms, 4–6; tests, 51–53; time of
  onset, 167–68
Depression, secondary. *See* Secondary
  depression
Depression-spectrum disease: age of
  onset in, 145–46; and alcoholism,
  141–43; biological variables, 195–97;
  case study, 217, 226–27;
  characteristics, 132–33; diagnostic
  criteria, 144–45; and early-onset
  unipolar illness, 137; and endogenous
  depression, 144; family history, 55;
  frequency, 145; genetic basis, 139–41;
  as major syndrome, 130; as neurotic
  depression, 27, 55, 118–19, 121;
  treatment, 148–50
Depression-spectrum disease vs. familial
  pure depressive disease: biological
  variables, 196–97; characteristics, 139,
  142–43; course of illness, 146–47
Depressive episodes, prevalence of, 155
Desipramine, 165
Dexamethasone suppression test (DST):
  for affective disorders, 51–53; for
  bereavement, 169; and

electroconvulsive therapy, 149–50; for endogenous depression, 189–90; for neurotic depression, 126; for primary depression, 164; in psychotic vs. nonpsychotic patients, 114; and rapid eye movement latency, 193; for schizoaffective disorder, 108; for unipolar and bipolar illness, 93. *See also* Biological variables

Diagnostic and Statistical Manual of Mental Disorders (3d. ed., rev.) *(DSM-III-R):* for classification, 20; for comparison of depressions, 164; for depression-spectrum vs. familial pure depressive disease, 145; for diagnostic criteria, 8; for endogenous depression, 50–51; for hysteria, 153–54; melancholia definition, 184; for neurotic depression, 120; on organic affective syndrome, 61

Diagnostic validity, 22–25

Disasters and reactive depression, 175–76

Diseases, definition, 3

Diurnal variation: in bipolar vs. unipolar disorder, 31; in familial pure depressive disease, 144; in melancholia simplex, 7

Divorce, 174

Double-form insanity, 10

Down's syndrome, 23–24

Drug abuse, 27

Drugs and induced mania, 71

DST. *See* Dexamethasone suppression test

Dysthymic disorder: classification, 20–21; dexamethasone suppression test for, 52

Echolalia, 15

Echopraxia, 15

Education and bipolar illness, 77–78

Electroconvulsive therapy: for bipolar illness, 89–90, 94–95; for depression, 48, 112; for depression-spectrum disease, 148–50; for endogenous depression, 45; for involutional depression, 200–201; for neurotic depression, 119; for neurotic vs. endogenous depression, 126; for

nonmelancholic personality, 124; for reactive depression, 174–75; for schizoaffective disorder, 112

Electroencephalographic tests: for bipolar illness, 95–96; for depression diagnosis, 53–54

Encephalitis, 71

Endogenous depression: as autonomous depression, 120; biological studies, 188–93; chronicity, 185, 187; comparison among depressions, 144; definition, 178; and delusions, 193; electroconvulsive therapy for, 45; family history, 186–88; grade of membership model, 183; morbidity risks, 198–99; psychosis in, 123; recovery, 47; severity of symptoms, 44–48; sleep variables, 192–93; symptoms, 179–80; tests, 193

Endogenous unipolar depression: case study, 225; classification, 27, 50

Endogenous vs. neurotic depression. *See* Neurotic vs. endogenous depression

Epidemiologic Catchment Area study, 76

Epidemiology for diagnostic validity, 23

Epilepsy, and induced mania, 71

Episode length: in bipolar vs. unipolar disorder, 37; in primary vs. secondary depression, 163

Etiology, classification by, 21–22, 25

Familial affective disorder: age of onset, 49, 135; in bipolar illness, 80

Familial depression and endogenous depression, 27

Familial diagnoses, algorithm for, 133

Familial pure depressive disease: age of onset, 145–46; biological variables, 206; case study, 221–22; characteristics, 194–95; and endogenous depression, 139, 144; frequency, 145; and sporadic depression, 201–4

Familial pure depressive disease vs. depression-spectrum disease. *See* Depression-spectrum disease vs. familial pure depressive disease

Family history: and bipolar illness, 26, 31–35, 72; and bipolar II illness, 98;

Family history (*cont.*)
for classification, 44; depression-spectrum disease, 55; for diagnostic validity, 25; and early- vs. late-onset unipolar depression, 138; and electroencephalographic studies, 95–96; and major affective disorder, 35; and mania, 30, 34–35; for melancholic vs. nonmelancholic depression, 124; and neurotic depression, 123; and primary affective disorder, 30; in primary vs. secondary depression, 159–60, 162; and psychotic symptoms, 106; and schizoaffective disorder, 104, 108–9; and sporadic depressive disease, 197–98
Family history method, 79–81
Family relationships, and neurotic depression, 128
Famous people with affective illness, 235
Fantastic melancholia, 7–8
Feighner criteria: for classification, 20; for diagnosis, 8–9; for mania, 16
Fever and induced mania, 71
5-hydroxyindole acetic acid (5-HIAA), 63

Genetic factors: in bipolar illness, 82–87; in depression-spectrum disease, 139–41
Genetic Linkage Study, 140–41
Glioma of the diencephalon, 70
Global Adjustment Scale, 127
Global Assessment Scale, 163
Grade of membership model, 182–83
Guilt: in bipolar vs. unipolar disorder, 31; in depression, 5; in melancholia gravis, 7; psychotic symptoms, 7

Hallucinations: for assessing depression severity, 9; in bipolar vs. unipolar disorder, 31; in depression, 6; as Schneiderian first-rank symptoms, 12
Hamilton Depression Rating Scale: and depression-spectrum disease, 149; and familial pure depressive disease, 195; and induced depressions, 62–63
Head injury: and organic bipolar disorder, 71; and suicide, 67

Hemodialysis, and induced mania, 71
Heredity, and depression, 29
Hormones, in depression, 190–91
Hospitalization: for bipolar disorder, 33; for bipolar vs. unipolar disorder, 38–40; for mania, 13; for neurotic depression, 129; for neurotic vs. endogenous depression, 126, 130; for neurotic vs. psychotic depression, 130; rates of, 159
Hostile depression, 49
Huntington's chorea, 67–68
Hypochondria: in familial pure depressive disease, 144; in fantastic melancholia, 8
Hypomania: in bipolar vs. unipolar disorder, 36; symptoms, 15
Hysteria: diagnosis, 153–54; and neurotic depression, 128–29; in primary vs. secondary depression, 158

Iceland, and bipolar illness: genetic study, 86–87; incidence, 75–76
Imipramine: binding in platelets, 193; for bipolar vs. unipolar disorder, 40; for reactive depression, 174–75; for recurring depression, 91. *See also* Biological variables
Induced affective disorders: bromocriptine for, 66; case study, 211–12, 216, 233–34; causes, 61; classification, 25–26; comparative study model, 69; diseases causing, 63–64; and 5-hydroxyindole acetic acid (5-HIAA), 63; and Huntington's chorea, 67; levodopa-carbidopa for, 62; suicide from, 67
Induced mania: and brain diseases, 69–70; case study, 230; diseases causing, 71
Influenza and induced mania, 71
Involutional melancholia: classification, 49; early vs. late onset, 199–200; symptoms, 198
Ireland, and bipolar illness, 87
Irritability: and bipolar illness, 72; in hypomania, 15

Kempe, Margery, case study, 207–8
Klein Endogenomorphic Scale, 120

Levodopa-carbidopa, 62
Lithium: for bipolar illness, 89, 94; for
bipolar vs. unipolar disorder, 40; for
induced mania, 70; plasma ratio, 94;
for schizoaffective mania, 114
Lymphocyte antigens, 84–85

Mania: acute, symptoms of, 14–15;
definition, 10; and depression-
spectrum disease, 132; drug
treatment, 95; and family history, 30,
80–81; hospitalization, 13; induced
(*see* Induced mania); and personality,
36; postpartum, 97, 107–9;
prevalence, 35; and psychotic
depression, 179; psychotic vs.
nonpsychotic symptoms, 114–16; and
schizoaffective disorder, 101–2; and
schizophrenia, 104; seasonal variation,
77; symptoms, 11–16
Maniaco-melancholicus, 10
Manic-depressive disease. *See* Bipolar
illness
Manic episode, duration of, 75
Marital status: for bipolar vs. unipolar
disorder, 38; for depression-spectrum
vs. familial pure depressive disease,
142–43
Max Planck Institute of Psychiatry, 174
Medical model: for bipolar vs. unipolar
disorder, 30, 42; for classification, 22
Medication consumption, 177
Melancholia: delirious, 8; fantastic, 7–8;
gravis, 7; involutional (*see* Involutional
melancholia); paranoid, 7; simplex,
6–7
Melancholic depression: and bipolar
illness, 78; course of illness, 183; and
dexamethasone response, 150; and
nonmelancholic depression, 124;
psychosis in, 123. *See also* Endogenous
depression
Melatonin theory, 191–92
Memory problems, 126
Meningioma: and induced depression,
64; and induced mania, 70
Menopause, 200
Michigan Diagnostic Index, 120
Molecular genetic method, 86–87
Mood-incongruent, 113, 114
Multifactorial model, 41–42

Neoplasms and induced mania, 71
Neurochemicals, in depression, 165
Neuroendocrine studies, 191
Neuroleptics, for schizoaffective
disorder, 112
Neurologic abnormalities, 71
Neurotic depression: affective disorders
as, 152; case studies, 209–11, 220–21,
226–28, 231–33; as chronic disorder,
119; classification, 27, 50; comparison
with reactive depression, 167; and
depression-spectrum disease, 143;
diagnosis, 46, 121–31; familial
definition, 118; and personality, 120–
21; terminology, 54
Neurotic vs. endogenous depression:
comparison, 124–26; course of illness,
154–55; diagnosis, 47; hospitalization
rates, 48; Newcastle Endogenous
Depression Diagnostic Index for, 51
Newcastle Endogenous Depression
Diagnostic Index: on endogenous vs.
neurotic depression, 51; for neurotic
depression, 120
Nonnuclear schizophrenia, 101
Nonprocess schizophrenia, 101
Norepinephrin in plasma, 94

Obsessional disorder, 152
Organic affective syndrome. *See*
Induced affective disorders

Panic disorder: case study, 214–15; and
neurotic depression, 128–29; rate,
156; and secondary depression, 166
Paranoid melancholia, 7
Paresis: epidemiology, 23; and induced
mania, 69–70
Parkinson's syndrome: etiology, 19; and
induced depression, 62–63
Pellagra, 23
Personality: and alcoholism, 142; in
bipolar vs. unipolar disorder, 36; in
neurotic depression, 123, 126–27,
152–53
Personality, antisocial. *See* Antisocial
personality
Personality, premorbid: in bipolar
illness, 78–79; for diagnostic validity,
24–25

Phobias: in depression, 5, 6; and
  neurotic depression, 128
Phototherapy, 191–92
Primary affective disorder, 30
Primary depression: and bereavement,
  169, 170; and neurotic depression,
  128; Protan-deutan glucose 6
  phosphate dehydrogenase (G6PD), 86
Primary vs. secondary affective
  disorder: age of onset, 154; course of
  illness, 161–63; demographic
  variables in, 157; and family history,
  160; recovery, 163; symptoms, 151–
  52, 156–60; tests, 164–65; treatment,
  165
Psychogenic psychosis, 101
Psychosis, in endogenous depression,
  123
Psychotic depression: characteristics, 48;
  and mania, 179; rapid eye movement
  latency test, 53–54
Psychotic symptoms: for assessing
  depression, 9; in bipolar illness, 12;
  comparison among depression types,
  113; and family history, 106;
  frequency in depression, 8

Rapid eye movement (REM) latency test:
  for affective disorders, 51, 53–54; for
  bipolar illness, 94; for neurotic
  depression, 131; for primary vs.
  secondary depression, 164; for
  schizoaffective disorder, 108. *See also*
  Biological variables
Reactive depression: and bereavement,
  168–71; case study, 219–20; causes,
  171; comparison with neurotic
  depression, 167; definition, 26; and
  life events, 44–48; symptoms, 192–93
Recurrence of illness: bipolar vs.
  unipolar disorder, 37–38; primary vs.
  secondary depression, 163; secondary
  to medical illness, 173; treatment,
  174–75
Remitting schizophrenia, 101
Research Diagnostic Criteria: for
  depression-spectrum vs. familial pure
  depressive disease, 145; for diagnosis,
  8; for endogenous depression, 50; for
  neurotic depression, 120; for
  schizoaffective disorders, 103, 110–12

Responsive depression, 120
Rheumatoid arthritis and depression, 64

Schizoaffective disorder: course of
  illness, 109–12; drug treatment, 112;
  and family history, 100–101;
  psychotic symptoms, 112–14; and
  schizophrenia, 105–6, 114, 117; tests,
  108; types, 102–3, 108
Schizoaffective mania: in bipolar illness,
  108–9; case study, 223–24; outcome,
  111–12
Schizophrenia: brain imaging for, 56;
  and bipolar illness, 26, 92; and mania,
  11–12, 14–16, 104; and secondary
  depression, 27, 104–5
Schizophrenia, sporadic, vs. sporadic
  depression: comparison, 205;
  subtypes, 101; symptoms, 39
Schneiderian first-rank symptoms: in
  schizoaffective disorder, 109; in
  schizophrenia, 11–12
Screening criteria, 3
Seasonal affective disorder, 191–92
Seasonal variation in bipolar illness, 77
Secondary depression: and associated
  conditions, 154; case study, 218–19;
  causes, 156–57, 163–65;
  dexamethasone suppression test for,
  164; medical disorders in, 155; as
  neurotic depression, 27, 55–56, 118–
  19, 121, 128; and nonaffective illness,
  130; and panic disorder, 166; and
  personality, 143; in psychiatric vs.
  medical illness, 172–73; rate of, 153;
  in schizoaffective disorder, 103–5
Secondary mania. *See* Induced mania
Secondary vs. primary affective
  disorder. *See* Primary vs. secondary
  affective disorder
Seizure disorders, 71
Sex changes in mania, 14
Sex differences: in bipolar illness, 82; in
  depression-spectrum disease, 132; in
  depressive episode during mania, 15–
  16; in schizoaffective disorder, 113; in
  unipolar depression, 136
Sex problems, in depression-spectrum
  disease, 142–43
Situational depression: as neurotic

depression, 130–31; as reactive
depression, 177
Sleep changes: in depression, 9; in
mania, 13–14
Sleep problems: in bipolar vs. unipolar
disorder, 31; in neurotic depression,
129
Society of Biological Psychiatry, 29
Socioeconomic status in bipolar illness,
77
Sociopathy, familial, 134
Somatic complaints: in bipolar vs.
unipolar disorder, 31; in depression,
5; in neurotic vs. endogenous
depression, 154
Somatization disorder: case study, 218–
19; and neurotic depression, 152–53,
158
Sporadic depressive illness: biological
variables, 206; as endogenous
unipolar depression, 27; and familial
pure depressive disease, 201–5; and
family history, 55, 197–98; frequency
of, 145; and secondary depression,
202; and sporadic schizophrenia, 205;
as unipolar depression, 133
St. Louis criteria. *See* Feighner criteria
Stroke and induced depression, 64–65
Substance abuse: drug abuse, 27; family
history, 128; and neurotic depression,
152. *See also* Alcoholism
Suicide and family history, 105
Suicide attempts: in depression, 5; in
depression-spectrum disease, 144;
from induced depression, 67; in
neurotic depression, 129; in neurotic
vs. endogenous depression, 126; in
primary vs. secondary depression, 163

Suicide thoughts: in depression, 4, 5, 9;
in neurotic vs. endogenous
depression, 126
Symbolism, in schizophrenia, 12
Syndrome, definition of, 3
Syphilis: epidemiology, 23; and induced
depression, 64; and induced mania,
69–70

Tests, laboratory, for bipolar illness, 93–
94. *See also* Dexamethasone
suppression test; Rapid eye movement
latency test
Treatment response: for bipolar vs.
unipolar disorder, 41; for diagnostic
validity, 25
Tritiated imipramine binding sites, 165
Twin studies: and bipolar illness, 82–83;
for bipolar vs. unipolar disorder, 32

Unhappiness and depression, 8
Unipolar depression: change to bipolar,
39; classification, 26–27; course of
illness, 184–85; drug treatment, 40–
41; early vs. late onset, 138; and
involutional melancholia, 198;
prevalence, 36; sex differences, 136
Unipolar depression, endogenous. *See*
Endogenous unipolar depression
Unipolar vs. bipolar disorder. *See*
Bipolar vs. unipolar disorder

Women, depressed, and familial
alcoholism, 142
Work history, and bipolar vs. unipolar
disorder, 38

Designed by Glen Burris
Set in Baskerville and Helvetica by The Composing Room of Michigan, Inc.
Printed on 60-lb. Glatfelter Hi-Brite Offset and bound in Holliston Roxite cloth
by The Maple Press Company